IMAGES
of America

COATESVILLE

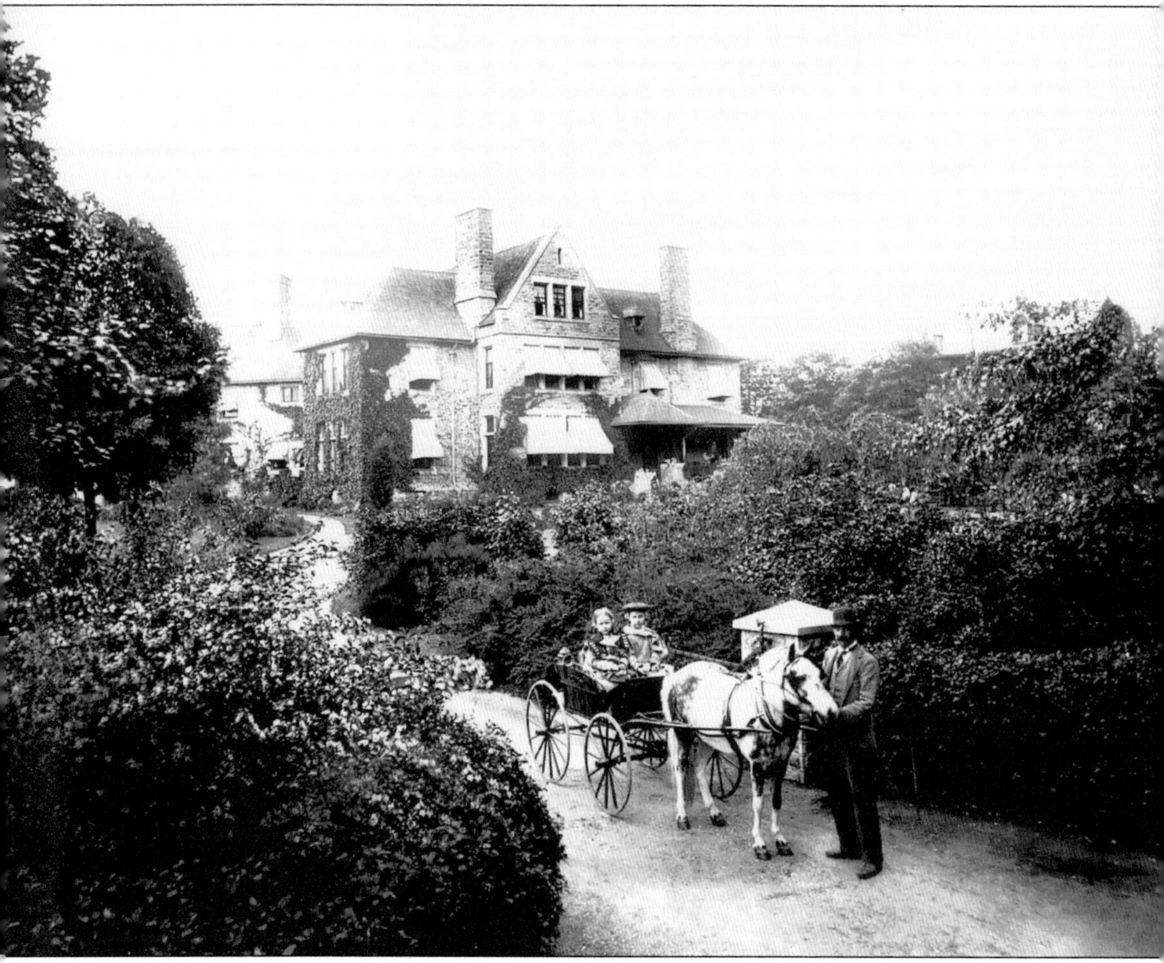

Graystone was constructed in 1889 by A.F. Huston, son of Dr. Charles Huston. Many rare trees and shrubs were planted on the grounds. Coatesville purchased the property in 1938 for its city hall. The carriage house of Graystone was transformed into the town's police station. The property has passed to the Graystone Society and is now being developed as a historic museum.

IMAGES
of America

COATESVILLE

Bruce Edward Mowday

ARCADIA
PUBLISHING

ISBN 978-0-7385-1198-6

Published by Arcadia Publishing
Charleston, South Carolina

Printed in the United States of America

Library of Congress Catalog Card Number: 2003101693

For all general information contact Arcadia Publishing at:
Telephone 843-853-2070
Fax 843-853-0044
E-mail sales@arcadiapublishing.com
For customer service and orders:
Toll-Free 1-888-313-2665

Visit us on the Internet at www.arcadiapublishing.com

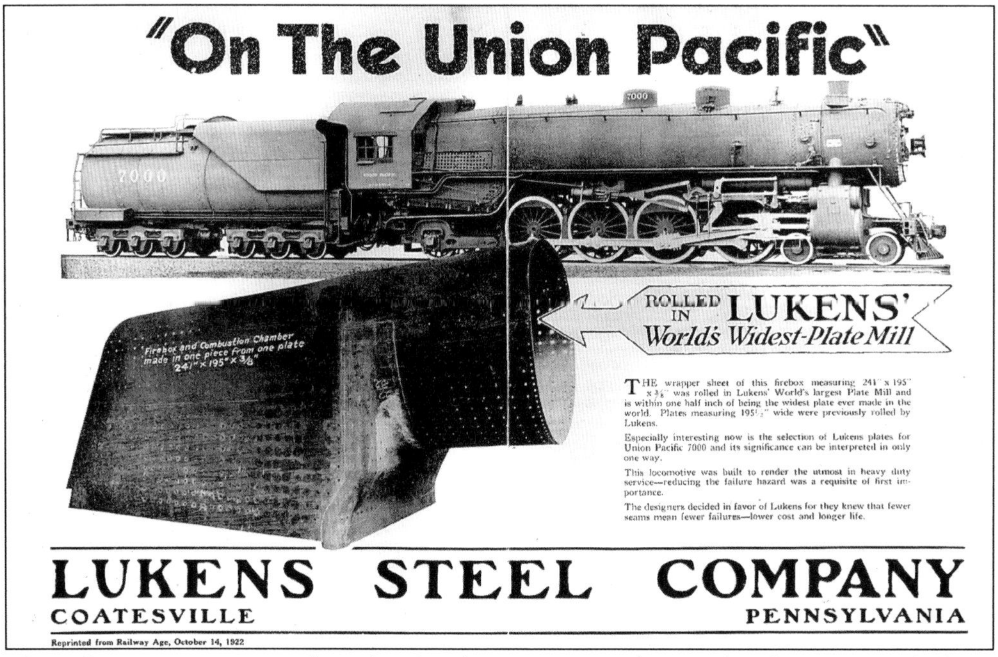

This advertisement appeared in the October 14, 1922 edition of *Railway Age* and shows locomotive No. 7000. The advertisement is for Lukens Steel Company wide plates.

Contents

ACKNOWLEDGMENTS

My participation in this photographic history of the Coatesville community began with a discussion with Scott G. Huston, executive director of the Stewart Huston Charitable Trust. Scott has a deep interest in all things historical, especially the city of Coatesville and the Lukens Steel Company. His participation and cooperation in this project were key to my agreeing to undertake direction of this much-needed volume on the photographic history of this historic community.

Representatives of Arcadia Publishing contacted Scott about doing a book on Coatesville and the Lukens Steel Company. Scott, a descendant of the founders of the Lukens Steel Company, enlisted the help of renowned Chester County historian Paul Rodebaugh and Eugene L. DiOrio, executive director of the Graystone Society and a recognized expert on Coatesville's history.

Sadly, the week before our first meeting on this project, Paul Rodebaugh died. Paul was interested in history throughout his life and lectured and taught courses on many subjects involving the area's history. He also owned probably the finest and most extensive collection of books on Chester County and its residents. He was an author himself and aided in the publication of two books for Arcadia. Everyone who knew Paul misses him.

Scott and Gene have devoted countless hours to this project and spearheaded the effort of gathering the images contained in this book. They also used their expertise to identify the people and locations in the photographs. Without their help, this book would not have been published.

Photographer Samuel J. Radziviliuk, who worked for many years for the Lukens Steel Company, provided great assistance. He expertly made copies of original negatives and went through the company's archives to identify key images. One group of photographs—the Frank P. Pennegar Collection, which belongs to the Coatesville Historical Commission—has been taken care of by the Chester County Historical Society. Pam Powell, Chester County Historical Society photographic archivist, assisted us in selecting and retrieving photographs from the Pennegar collection for this book. The Graystone Society photographs, including the Ellis E. Stern Collection, are also a big part of this book.

Gathering information on the history of Coatesville for the text was a team effort as well. Coatesville Area Public Library director Michael Geary opened up all of the files of the library for research. Alexandra Curran, as part of an internship at West Chester University, was immensely helpful in gathering information and checking facts for this text. Much of the information on Coatesville's history came from the files of the Coatesville Area Public Library, the Chester County Library, and the Chester County Historical Society. Wayne C. Woodward's *Coatesville Revisited* was also used for background material. Woodward, a former reporter for the *Coatesville Record*, is a town historian.

Many individuals offered assistance and encouragement for this project, and they all deserve to be acknowledged. That group includes those at Arcadia, in particular editor Jennifer Villeneuve, who assisted in the publication of this book. Arcadia does a great service in keeping our country's history alive by publishing history books on the communities of America.

—Bruce Edward Mowday
March 2003

INTRODUCTION

In many ways, the development of Coatesville mirrors that of many other communities in the eastern portion of the United States. Before our nation was founded, Native Americans roamed the area that now includes present-day Coatesville. When Europeans settled in the rich lands of the region, the area that is now Coatesville was contained within Chester County, the first of William Penn's original three counties. As Lancaster became a key market city that supplied Philadelphia, Coatesville became a place for travelers to stop between the two cities. Indeed, the first toll road in this country was the Lancaster Turnpike, and one of the tollgates was within the borders of present-day Coatesville, the only city in Chester County. The Lancaster–Philadelphia turnpike was authorized in 1792 and was completed in 1795.

With the scenic Brandywine River running through the town and offering energy to run its industry, Coatesville fast became a manufacturing community. Several iron and steel companies, along with other mills, thrived at various times along the Brandywine, but the Lukens Steel Company was the one that prospered and was the main industry during the years when Coatesville was the center of industry for Chester County. One of the first women in the United States to run a major company, Rebecca Pennock Lukens, was in charge of Lukens. Through hard work and business acumen, she earned the nickname "Woman of Steel."

One of the first settlers of the area was Pierre Bizallion, a French fur trader who settled here in the early 1700s and eventually acquired 500 acres near what is now the Veterans Administration Hospital. Bizallion, because of his knowledge and his relationship with the local Native Americans, is said to have acted as an interpreter for William Penn.

William Fleming of Scotland was another key settler. He purchased a 207-acre tract of land and settled near what is now Harmony Street, between Fifth and Sixth Avenues. His son Peter Fleming built a sawmill along the Brandywine. Moses Coates, for whom the town is named, was Coatesville's first postmaster. He purchased the Fleming house in 1787. It was later acquired by Jesse Kersey and Isaac Pennock, founders of the Brandywine Iron Works and Nail Factory, predecessor to the Lukens Steel Company. Pennock's son-in-law and daughter, Dr. Charles Lukens and Rebecca Pennock Lukens, also lived in the house.

Before being named Coatesville, the town was known as Bridge-Town, because of two bridges that were used to cross the Brandywine River and a strip of land known as Goose Island. Coatesville was not incorporated as a borough until 1867, after the Civil War. As rail service catered to the needs of the growing business community and growing populace, the town began to thrive. Coatesville became a city in 1915. As the Lukens Steel Company continued to prosper and grow, so did Coatesville and its neighboring municipalities. Other industries—including the Viaduct Iron Works; the Brandywine Rolling Mills, operated by the Worth brothers; and the Valley Iron Works, run by W.W. Kurtz and Sons—contributed to the town's growth. Coatesville was known in some circles as "the Pittsburgh of the East."

With the dawn of the 20th century, the community exploded as its population approached 6,000. A hospital was constructed, and the school system was expanded. The religious community prospered as the educational and spiritual needs of the community were met. At least five hotels operated during the town's heyday. In 1932, Coatesville had 22 churches. The town has always taken pride in its sports teams and musical organizations. Lukens had its own band, and the high school's Meistersingers group made appearances throughout the country. Buffalo Bill was even attracted to the community, as he made Coatesville the winter home for his Wild West Show for years.

The eyes of the nation were focused on Coatesville in 1911 with the lynching of Zachariah Walker, an African American who was charged with murdering a white mill policeman, Edgar Rice. A mob took Walker from his bed at Coatesville Hospital and burned him at the stake. The last lynching in Pennsylvania has left a stain on the history of the city. The community has healed over the years, as its members have joined together to help each other during crippling snowstorms, to fight a typhoid epidemic, and to rally to support the nation during World War I and World War II.

With the end of World War II, the steel industry went into decline and with it the once prosperous city of Coatesville. Lukens was sold. Employment at the mill dropped from more than 5,000 workers to fewer than 2,000, and the city today is looking at ways to reinvent itself. Major changes and improvements are being made, and Coatesville looks to the future and to being once again a center of commerce.

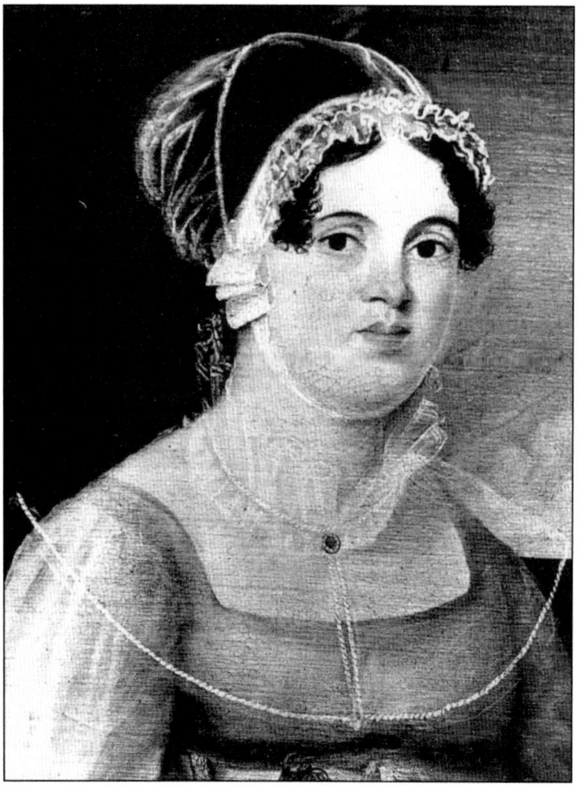

Coatesville's most famous citizen is Rebecca Pennock Lukens. After the death of her husband, Dr. Charles Lukens, Rebecca Lukens oversaw the running of the Brandywine Iron Works, later to become the Lukens Steel Company. She became one of the nation's first female executives. Her tenure at the iron company took place during the mid-1800s. Lukens became known throughout the world for making special steel products.

One

The Early Days

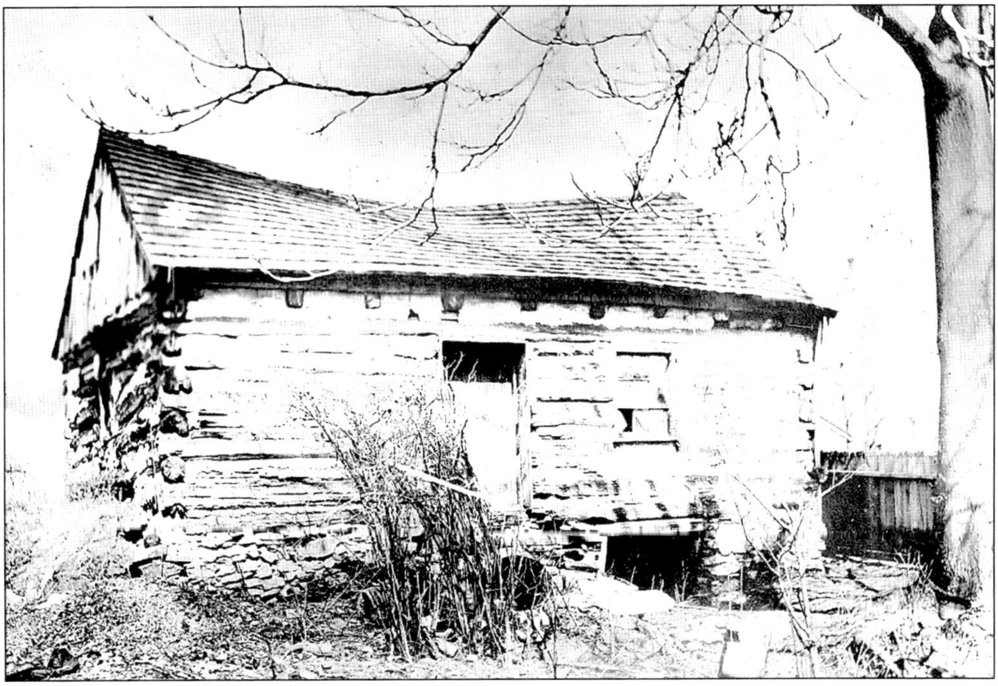

The first house in Coatesville was a log cabin built by William Fleming as a temporary home. It was located on the north side of Kersey Street, between Third and Fourth Avenues, as depicted in this photograph taken in 1899. Fleming, who was from Creenolk, Scotland, purchased 207 acres in 1714. He had eight children. One of his sons, Peter Fleming, later built a sawmill along the Brandywine River.

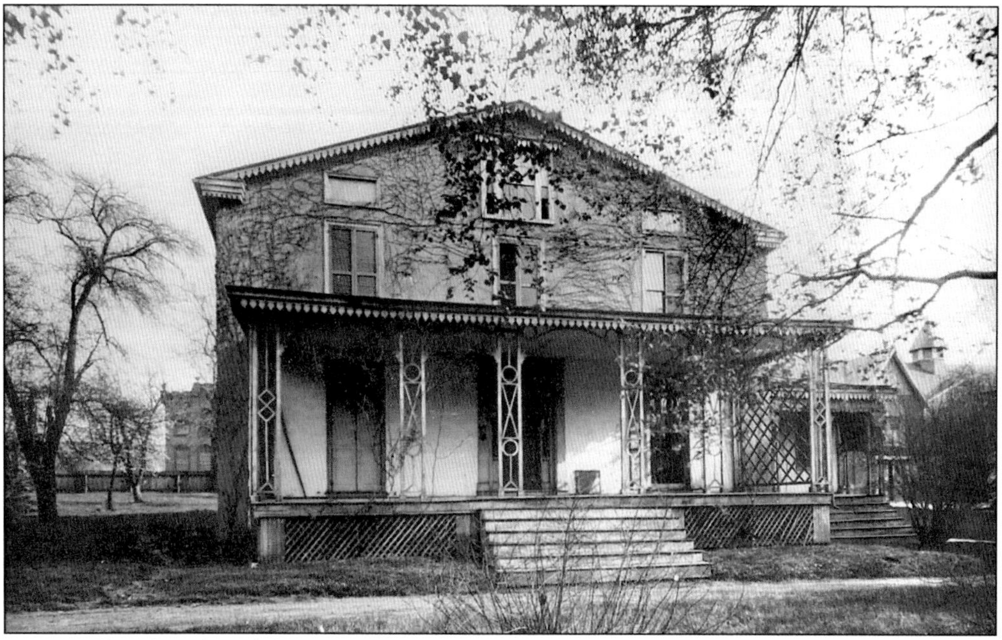

Coatesville's founding fathers constructed large homes during the 19th century. The house pictured above was built by Dr. Jesse Coates, son of Moses Coates. Coatesville was named after Moses Coates, who was the first postmaster. The Homestead, as it was called, was built *c.* 1835 on Main Street. It was destroyed in 1934. The dwelling pictured below was built in 1890 by William Gibbons. Gibbons was a president of the board of health in Coatesville and also the first vice president of the town's Young Men's Christian Association (YMCA).

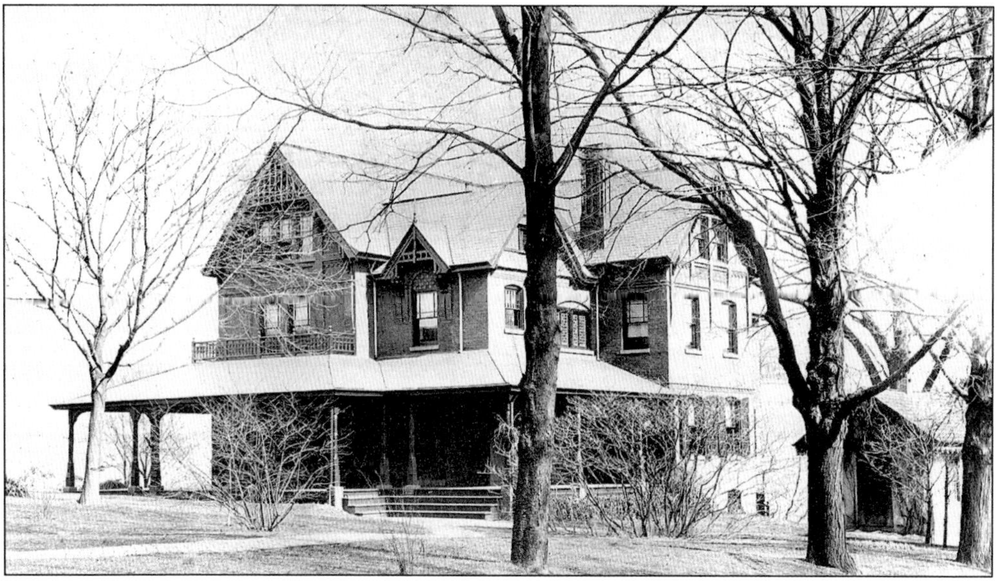

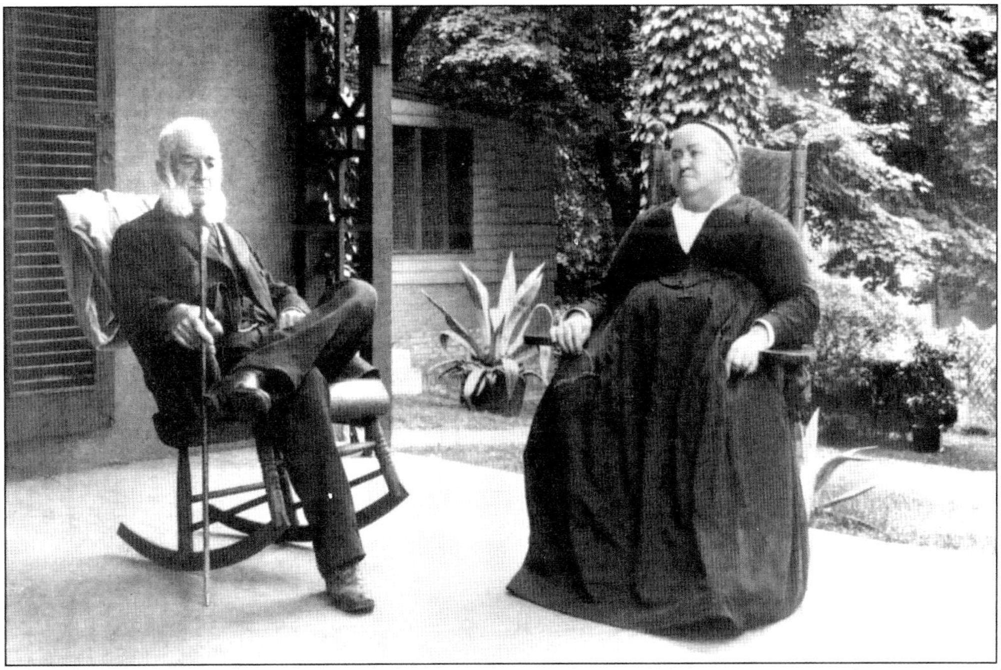

Coatesville's leading citizen of all time is Rebecca Pennock Lukens, known as "the Woman of Steel" for her leadership role in the Brandywine Iron Works during the mid-1800s. She had a house constructed for her daughter Isabella Lukens. Isabella is shown here on the porch of Terracina with her husband, Dr. Charles Huston, who designed the home. Dr. Huston was president of Lukens from 1856 to 1897. Terracina is also shown in the photograph below.

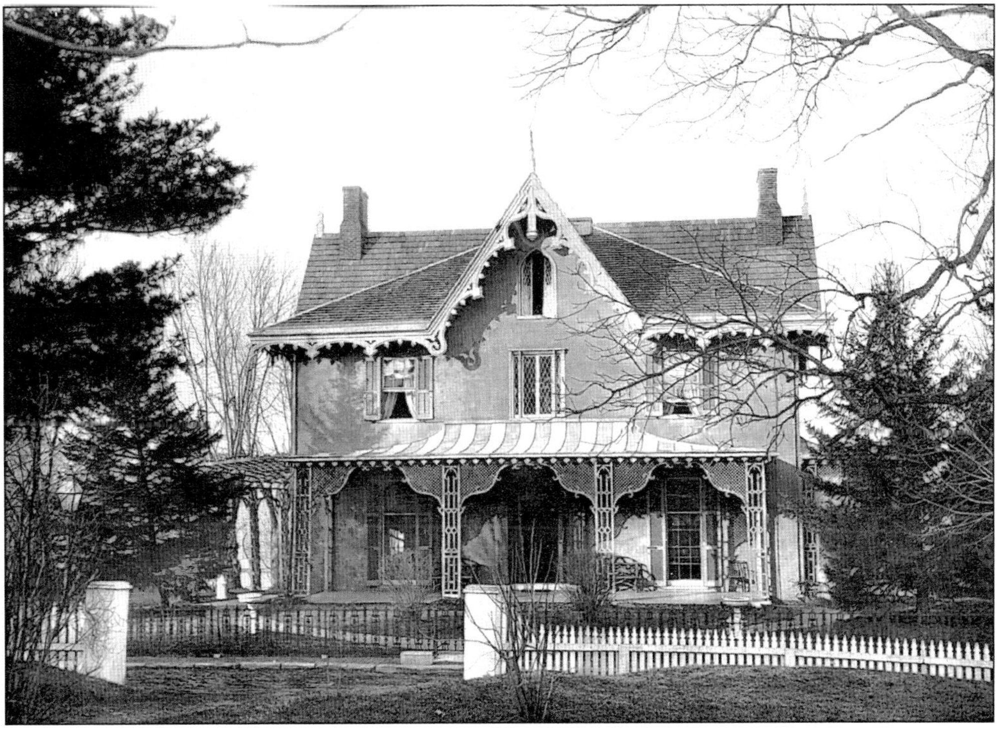

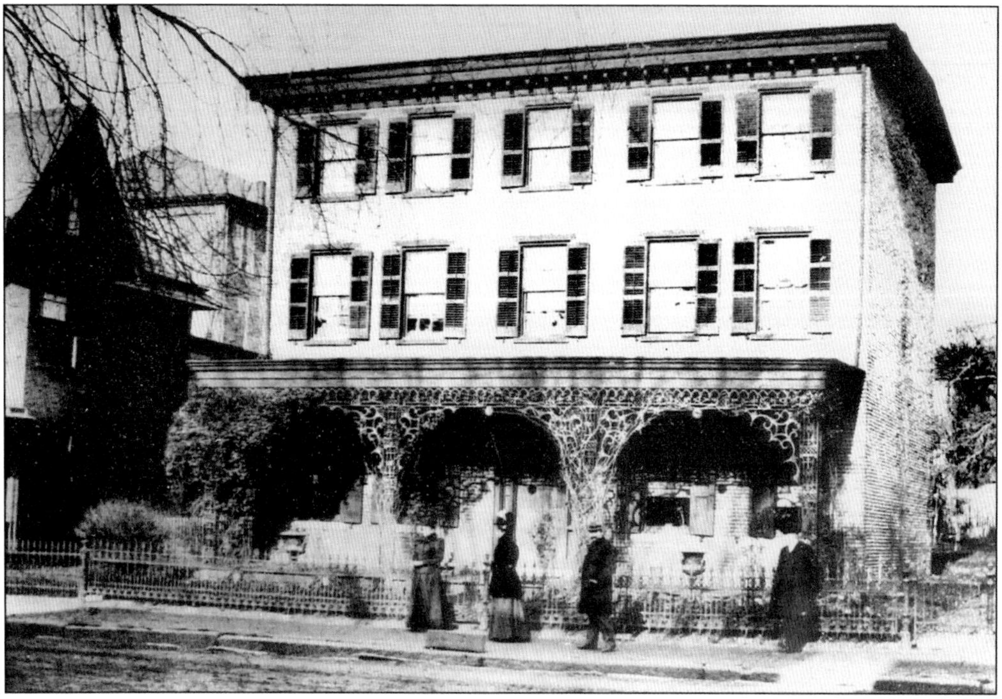

The four people shown above are standing in front of the residence of the Pennock sisters, daughters of Charles Pennock, in Coatesville. Isaac Pennock was one of the founders, along with Jesse Kersey, of the Brandywine Iron Works. The photograph below shows the house built in 1808 by Moses Coates. The house was located on the northeast corner of Third Avenue above the Pennsylvania Railroad station. It was torn down in 1911.

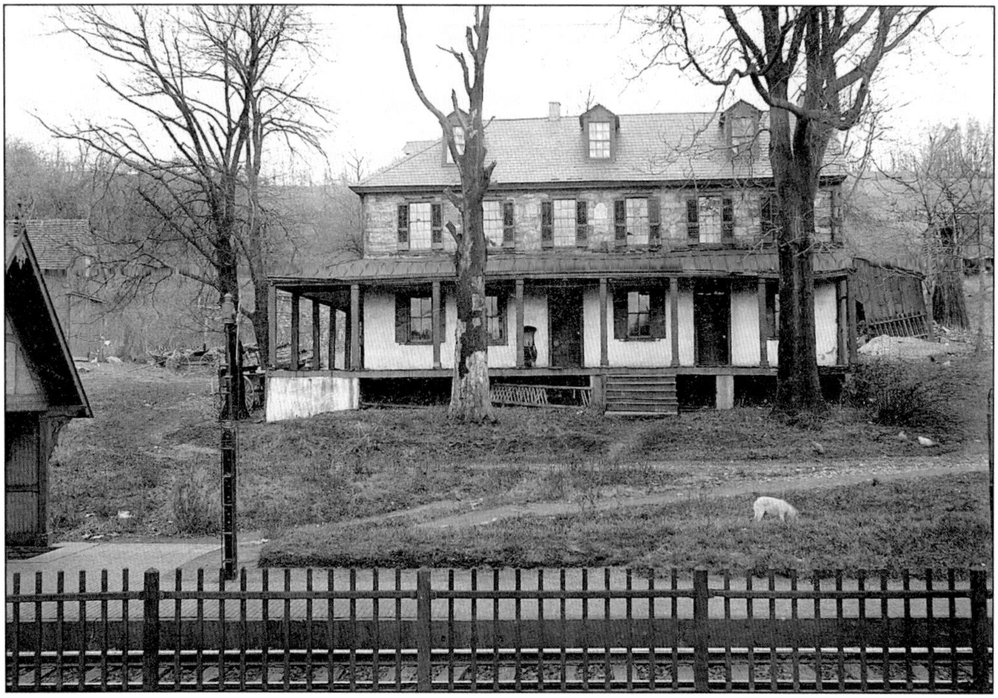

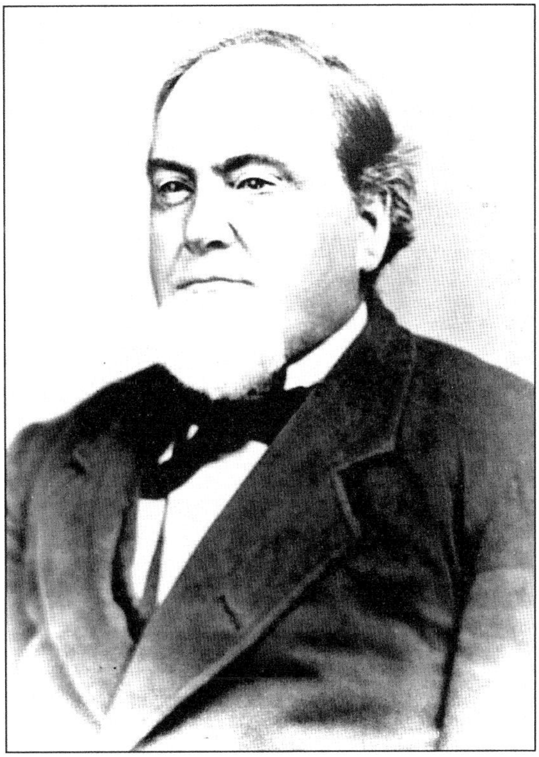

The first burgess of Coatesville was William B. Morrison, shown to the right. He served from 1867, the year Coatesville was incorporated, until 1874. He also served as the sheriff of Chester County from 1875 until 1880. Morrison was a cavalry officer during the Civil War. George W. Price, pictured below, succeeded Morrison as the second burgess of Coatesville and served for two years, 1874 and 1875.

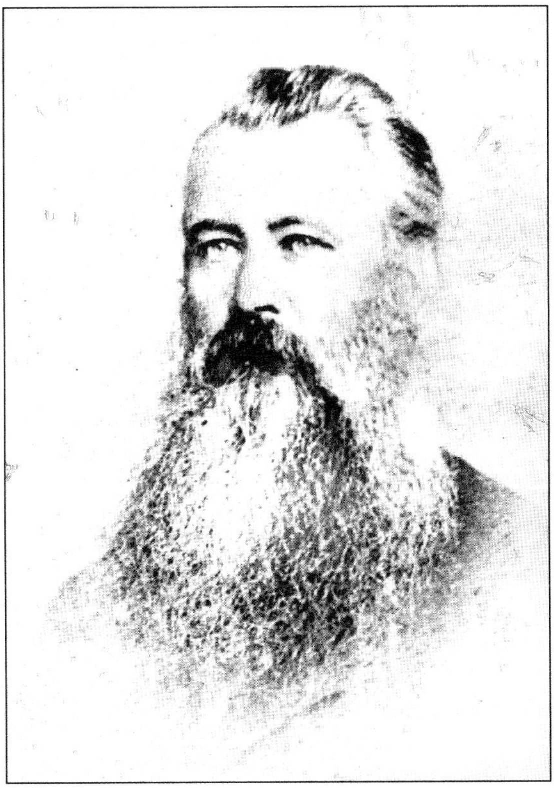

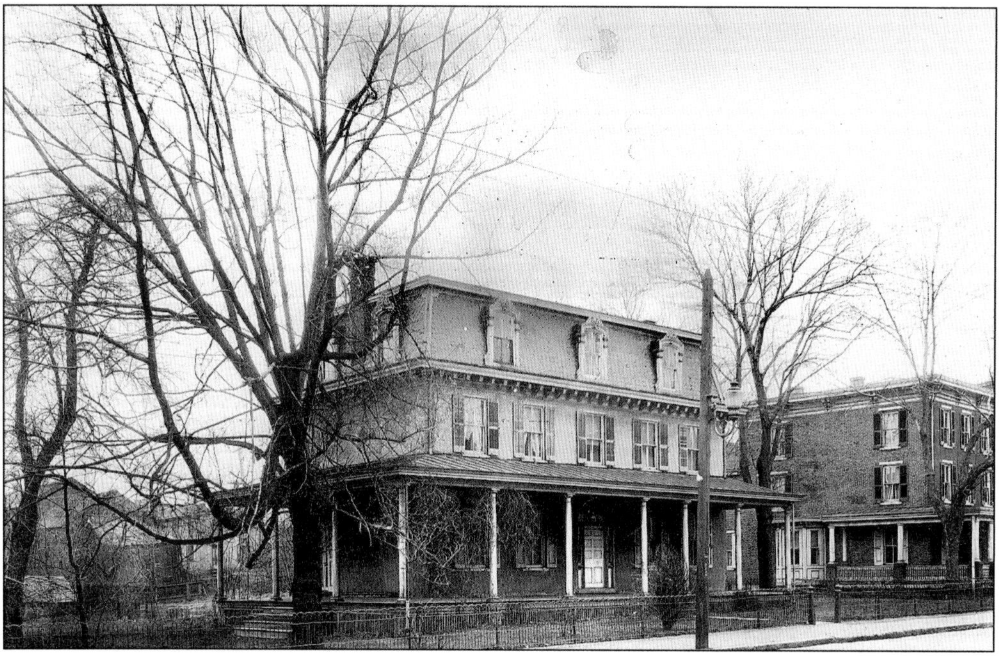

Two longtime landmarks of Coatesville are pictured in the above photograph. The Perkins house, to the left, was razed in 1949 to make way for a supermarket. To the right is the former John Speakman home. The photograph below depicts the Graystone mansion, the most architecturally significant residence of Coatesville. It was the home of Abram F. Huston, who succeeded his father, Dr. Charles Huston, as president of the Lukens Iron and Steel Company in 1897.

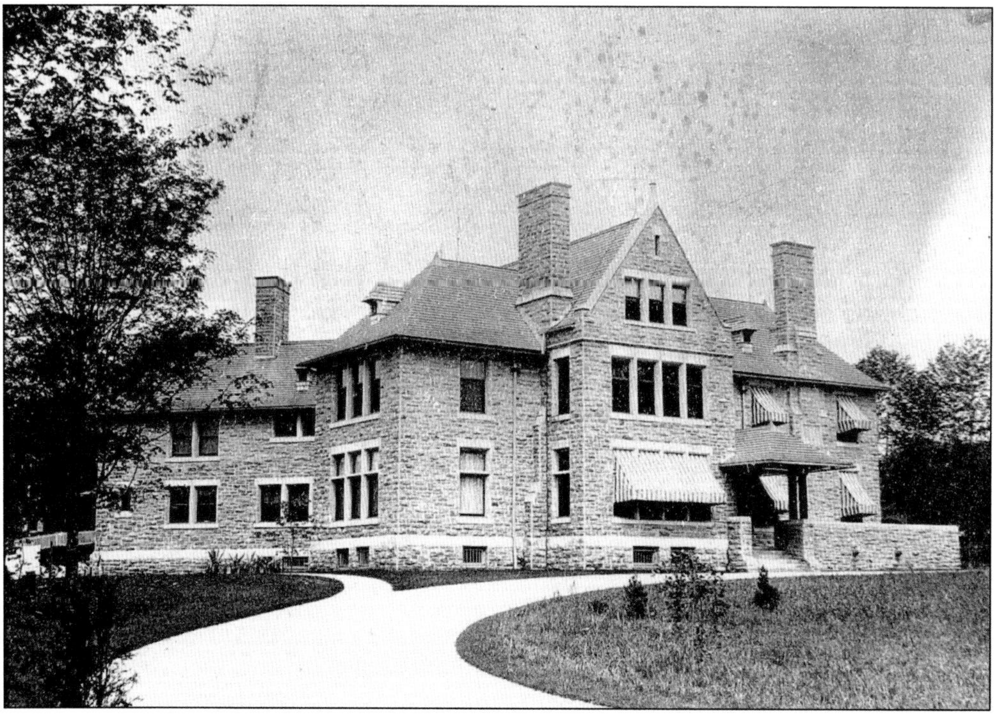

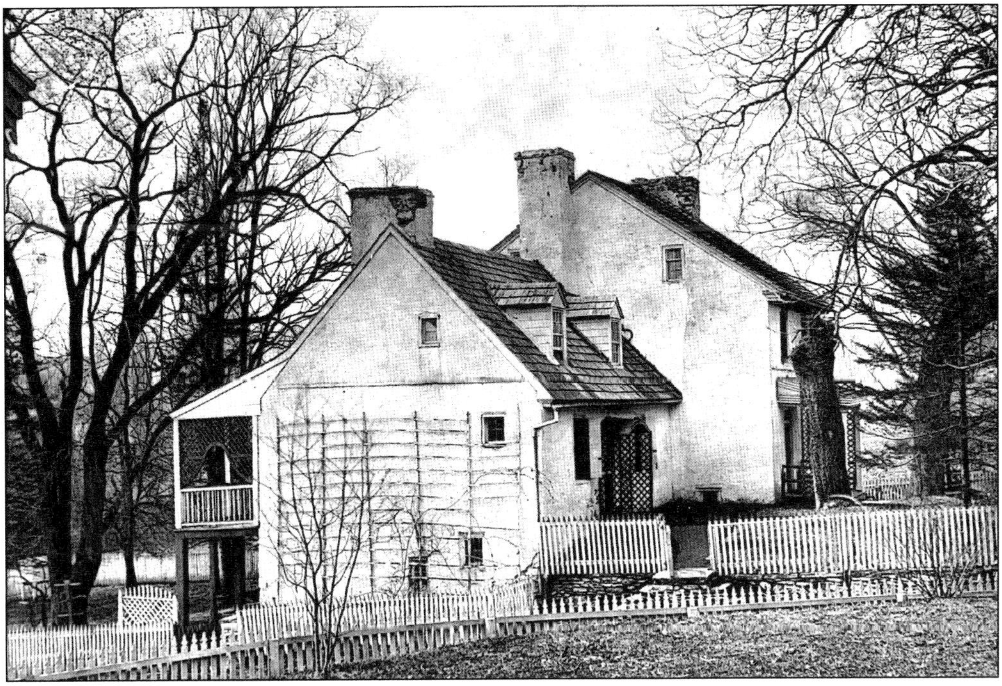

The Brandywine mansion, shown above, was the home of Moses Coates until Isaac Pennock acquired it in 1810. Shown below is an early rendition of the Lukens Rolling Mills, with the railroad seen on the hills north of the business site. The history of Lukens begins in 1810. A charter for the Lukens Iron and Steel Company was made in 1890.

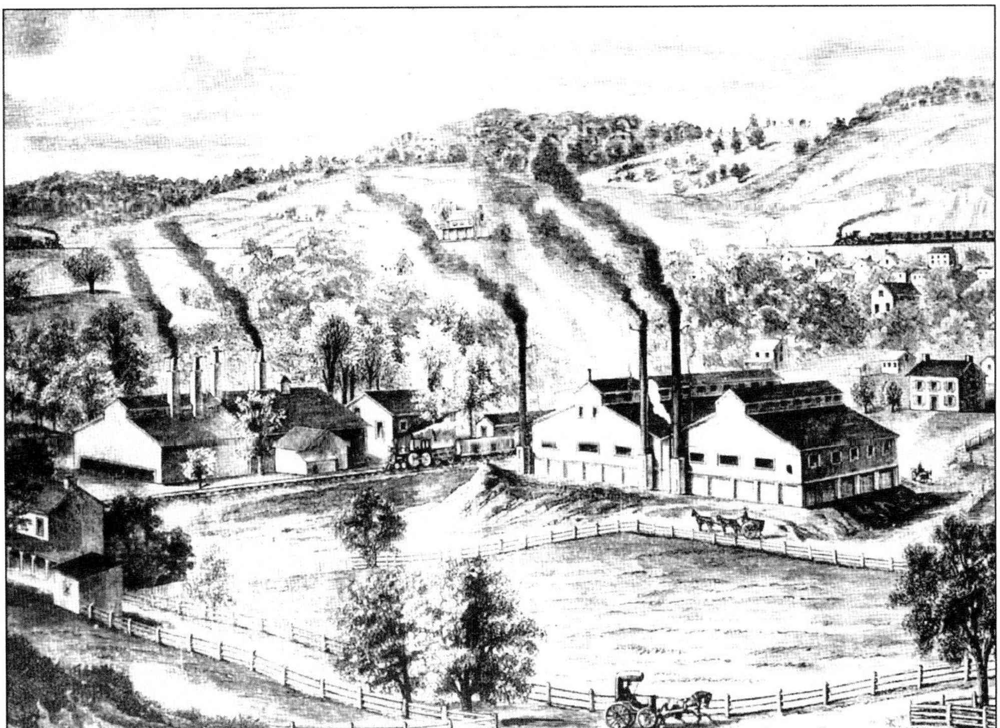

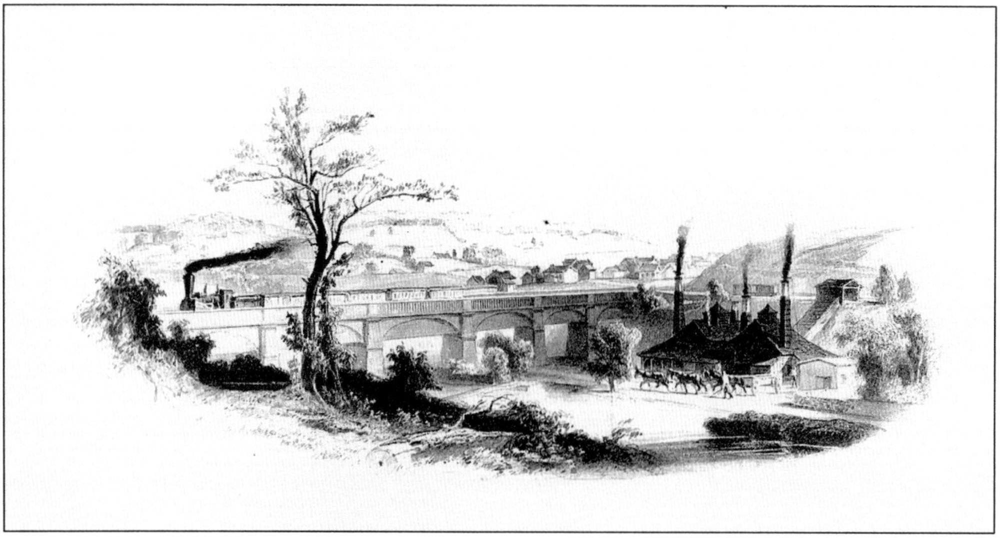

The West Branch of the Brandywine River was vital to the development of the mills that helped establish Coatesville. Pictured above is a drawing of a mill and the high bridge built for the railroads. When the Philadelphia and Columbia Railroad was constructed in 1834, a station was built west of the Brandywine and was called Midway. The rendering below depicts one of the early Lukens mills.

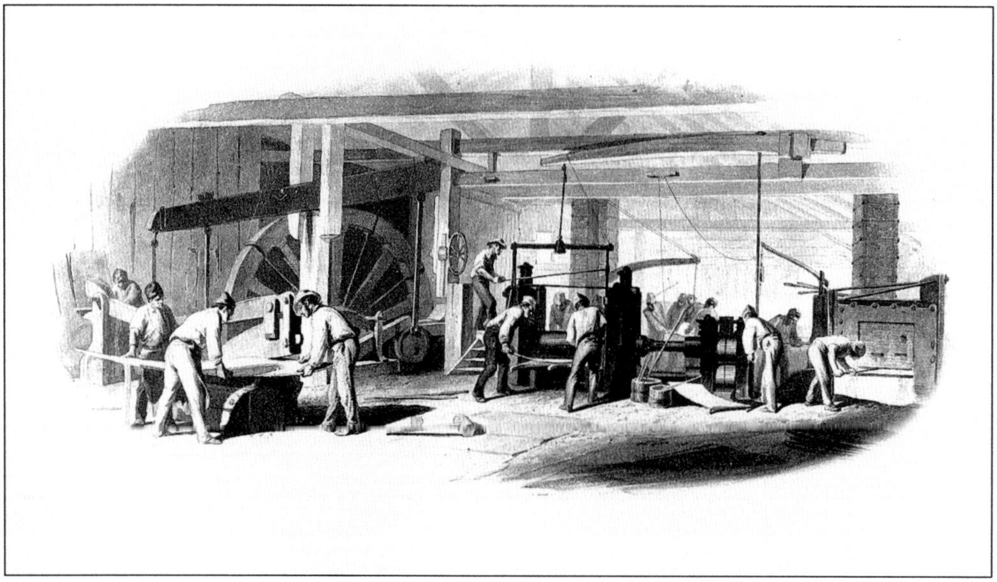

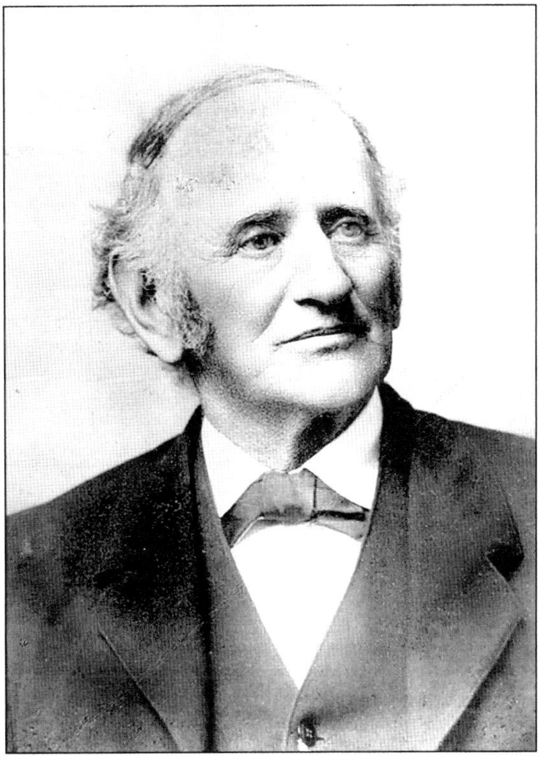

Many prominent Coatesville citizens have served in Chester County government positions over the years, including Joseph Doan, to the right, and Thomas H. Windle, below. Both were early burgesses of Coatesville. Doan, the 5th burgess, became a Chester County commissioner in 1867. Windle, the 11th burgess, was sworn in as Chester County clerk of courts in 1863.

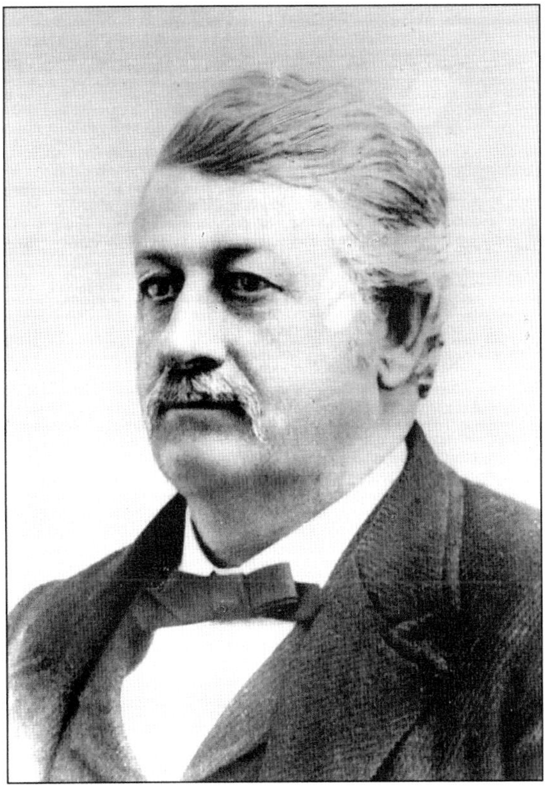

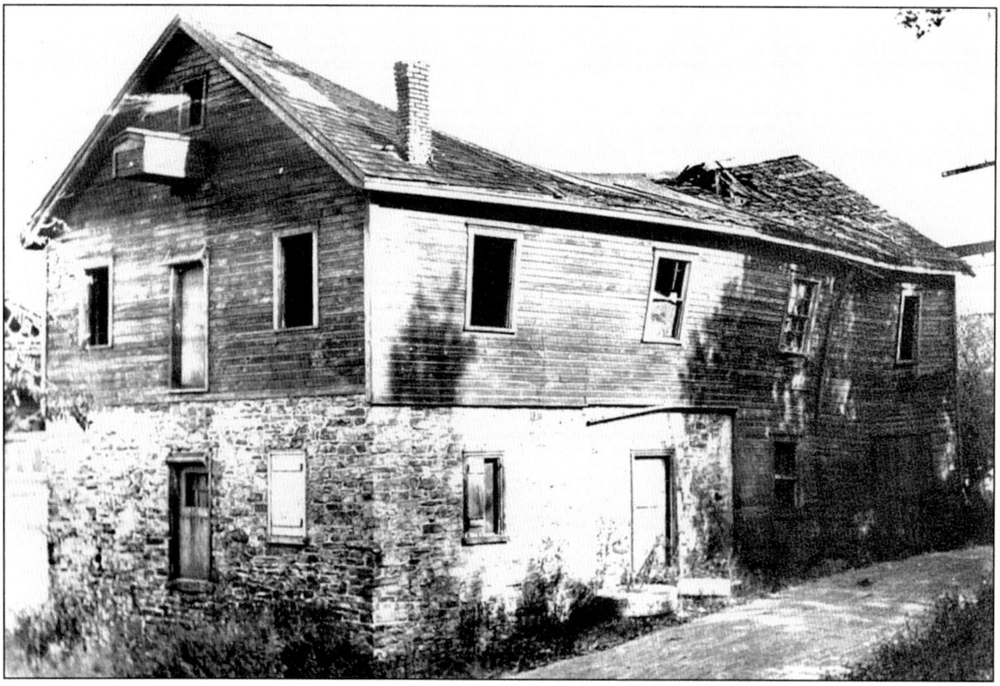

In addition to the Lukens Steel Company, a number of different types of mills operated and thrived near the Brandywine River in Coatesville over the years. The Ezekel Rambo Grist Mill is shown above in 1917, just before it was razed. The Pratt's Cider Mill is pictured below.

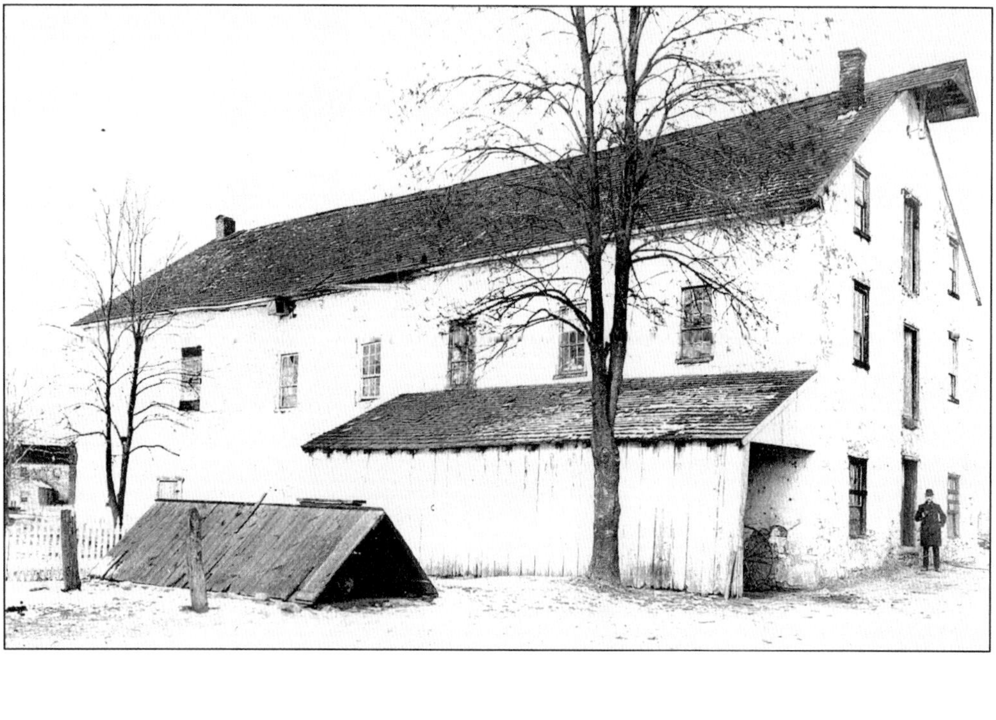

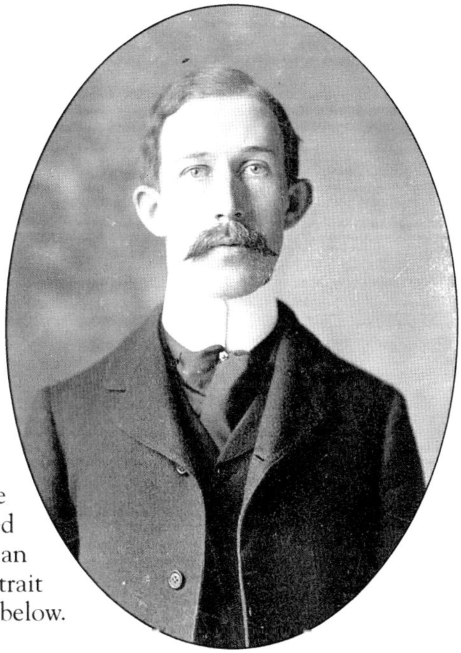

As the mills provided jobs for the residents of the area, a business and a residential district developed east of the Brandywine River. Benjamin Young was an early Coatesville druggist. He is shown in the portrait to the right and in the center of the photograph below. He ran his own pharmacy on Main Street.

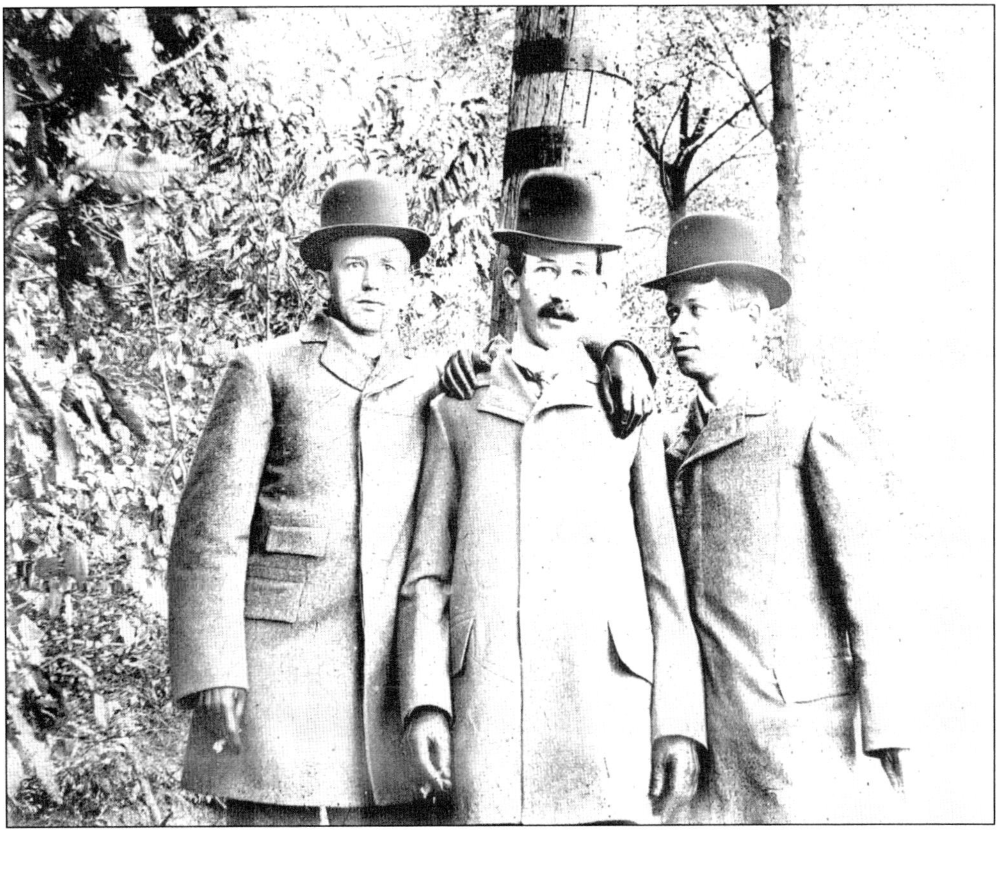

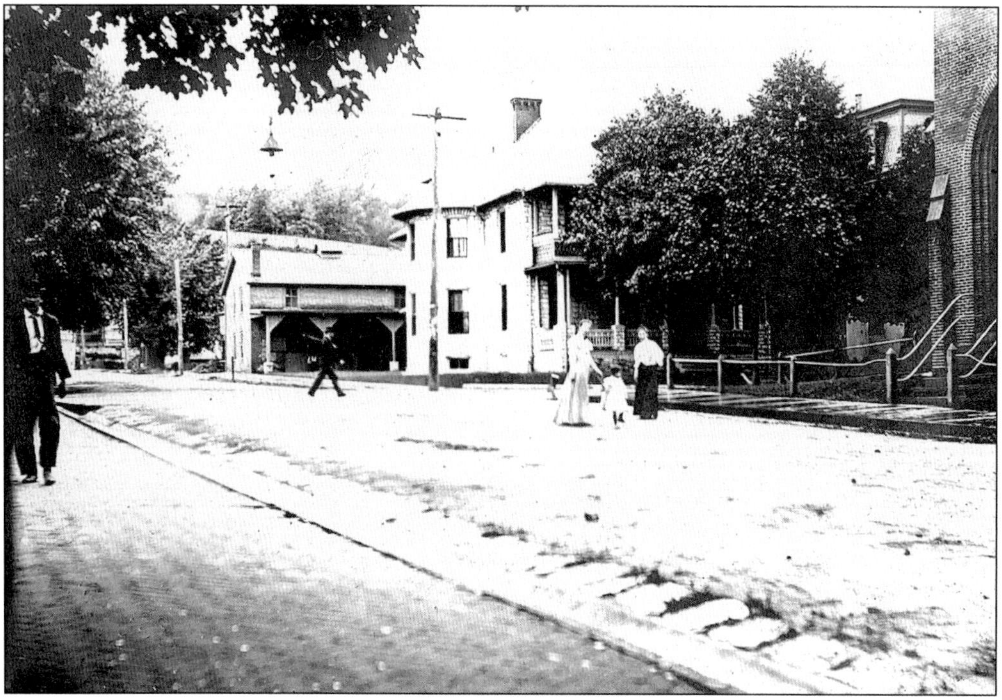

All types of traffic, foot and horse-drawn carriage, were to be seen on the streets of Coatesville during its early history. The adults and children in the above photograph are walking in the vicinity of North Third Avenue and Chestnut Street, while the man in the photograph below is at an unidentified Coatesville location.

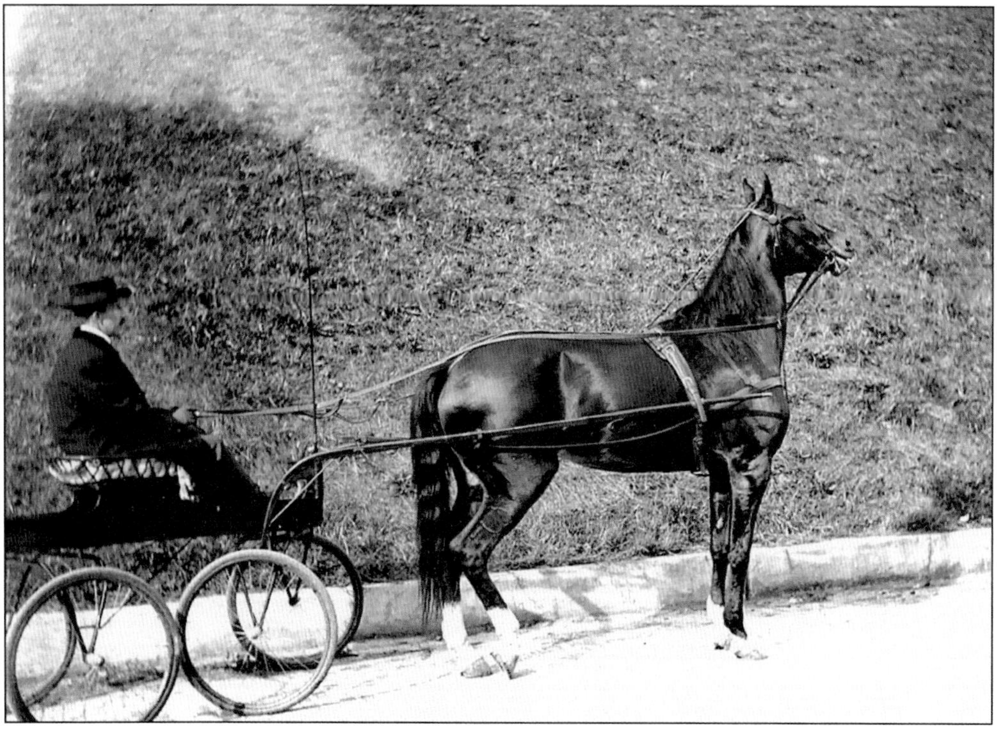

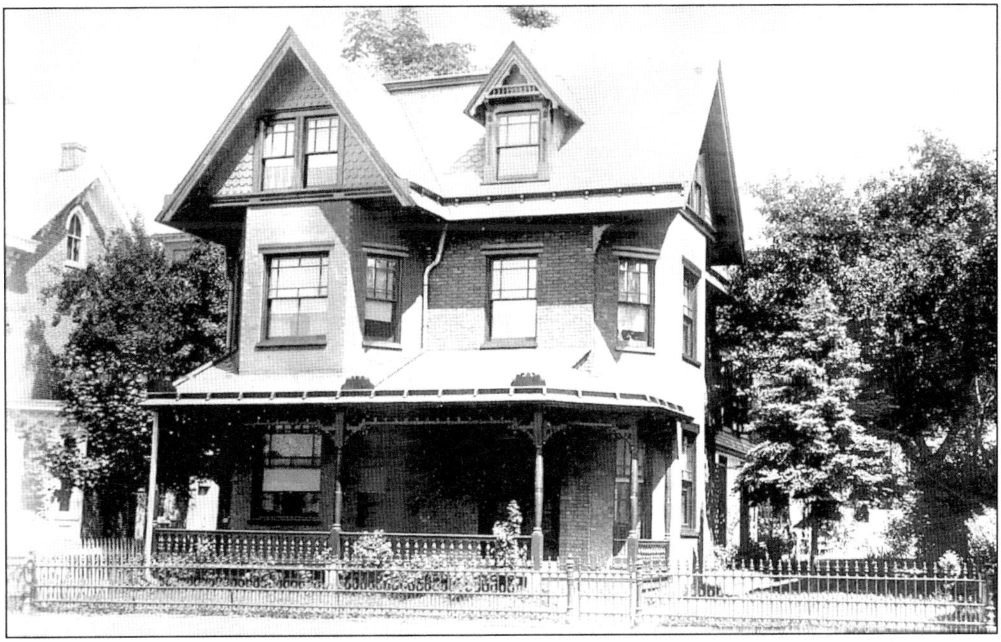

Many of the prosperous citizens of Coatesville had fine homes in the borough. W.A.P. Thompson's residence was known as the "Kenedy" and underwent a remodeling in 1886. The home shown below belonged to W.P. Worth. Built in 1906 at the southeast corner of Third Avenue and Main Street, it was razed in the 1940s. Worth and his brother J. Sharpless Worth were partners in the Worth Brothers Company.

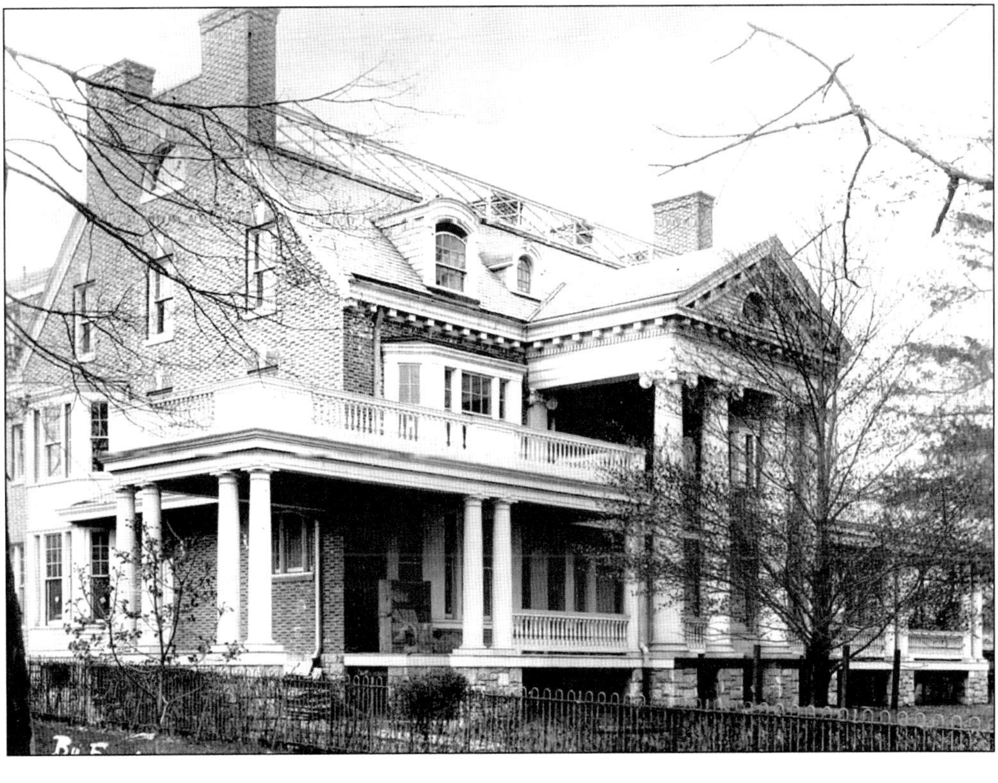

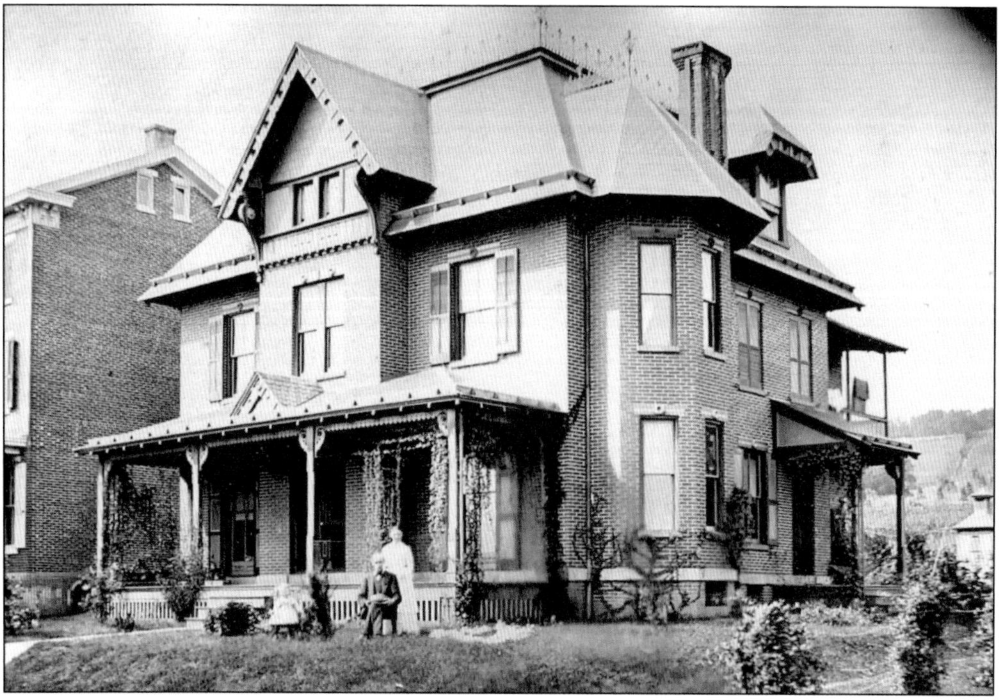

W.W. Mast was a prominent Coatesville merchant and dry-goods store owner. His house, shown here, was constructed between Third and Fourth Avenues on Chestnut Street. The above photograph, showing Mast and his wife near the porch of their home, was taken in 1883. The photograph below was taken during a Valentine's Day snowstorm in 1899.

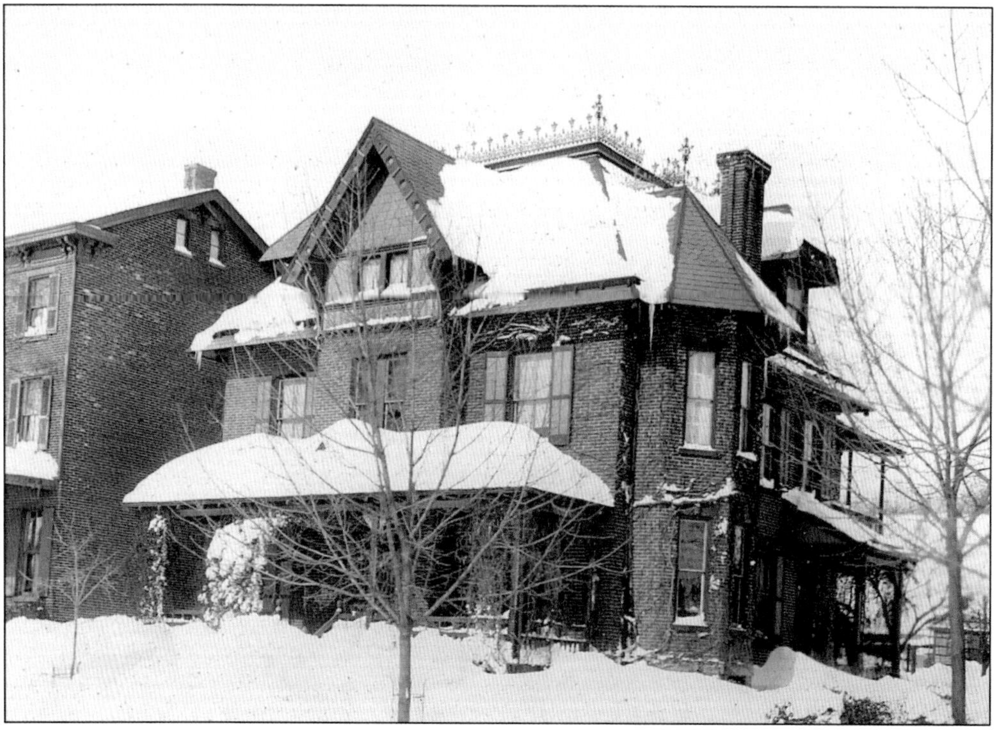

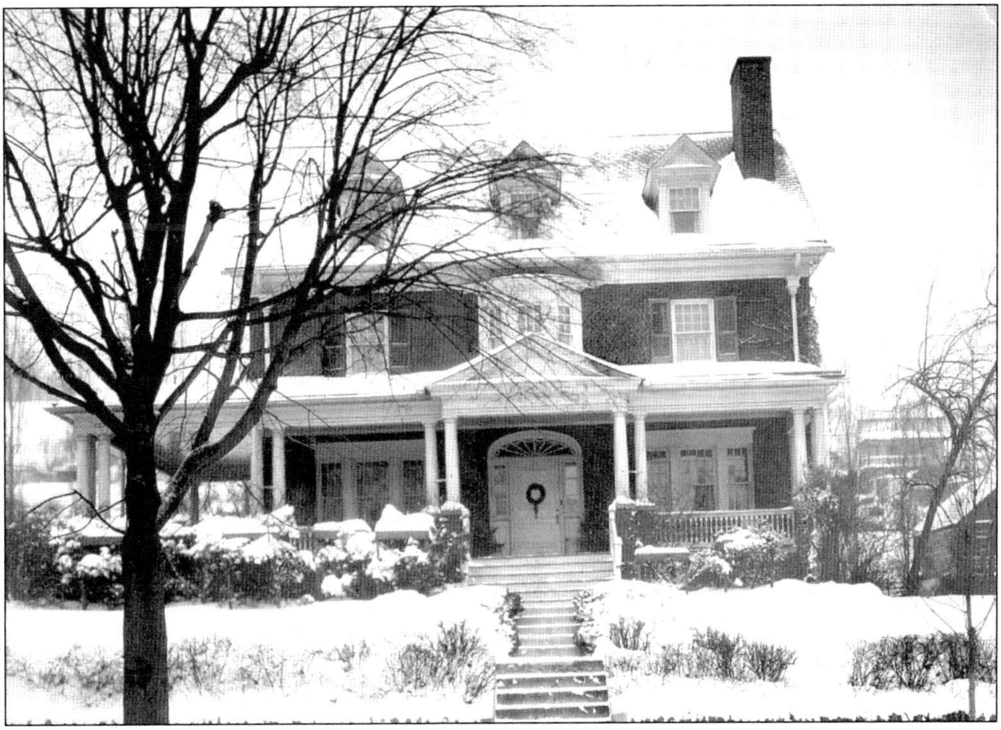

Another snowstorm covered the home of the Ridgeways, shown above. Coatesville citizens have a reputation for helping each other in times of need, including offering transportation during storms to those in need of medical attention. Coatesville has also had a number of volunteer fire companies. Below is a photograph of Wesley Riday riding on a sprinkler wagon at Chestnut Street between Third and Fourth Avenues.

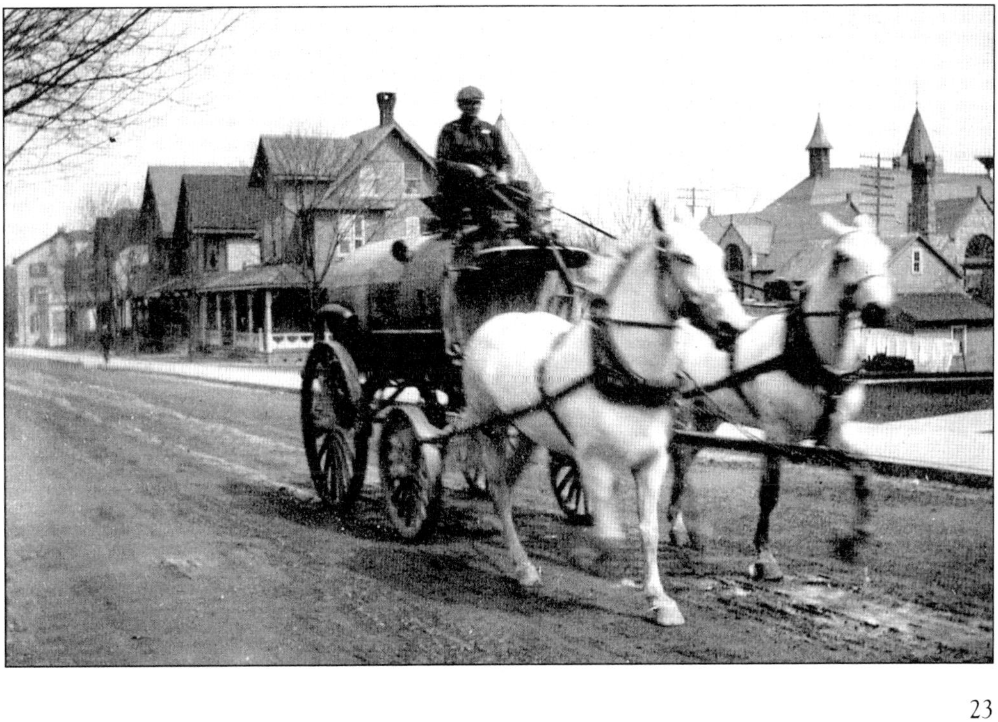

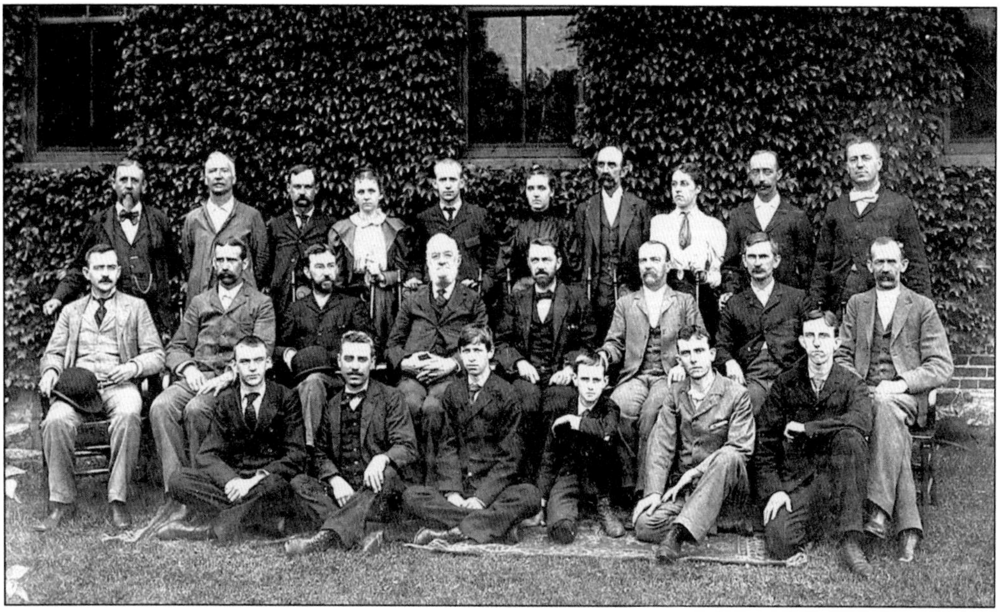

Above is a group photograph of Lukens Steel Company officials. Seated in the center of the middle row is Dr. Charles Huston, flanked by his sons A.F. Huston, to the left, and C.L. Huston. Shown below is a group of leading women. They are, from left to right, as follows: (front row) Anna Davis, Mrs. Benjamin Young, and Elizabeth Baker; (middle row) Mrs. Charles Innes, Mrs. Charles Humpton, and Mrs. Frank Soule; (back row) unidentified, Mrs. Fred Speakman, unidentified, and Mrs. John S. Pennock.

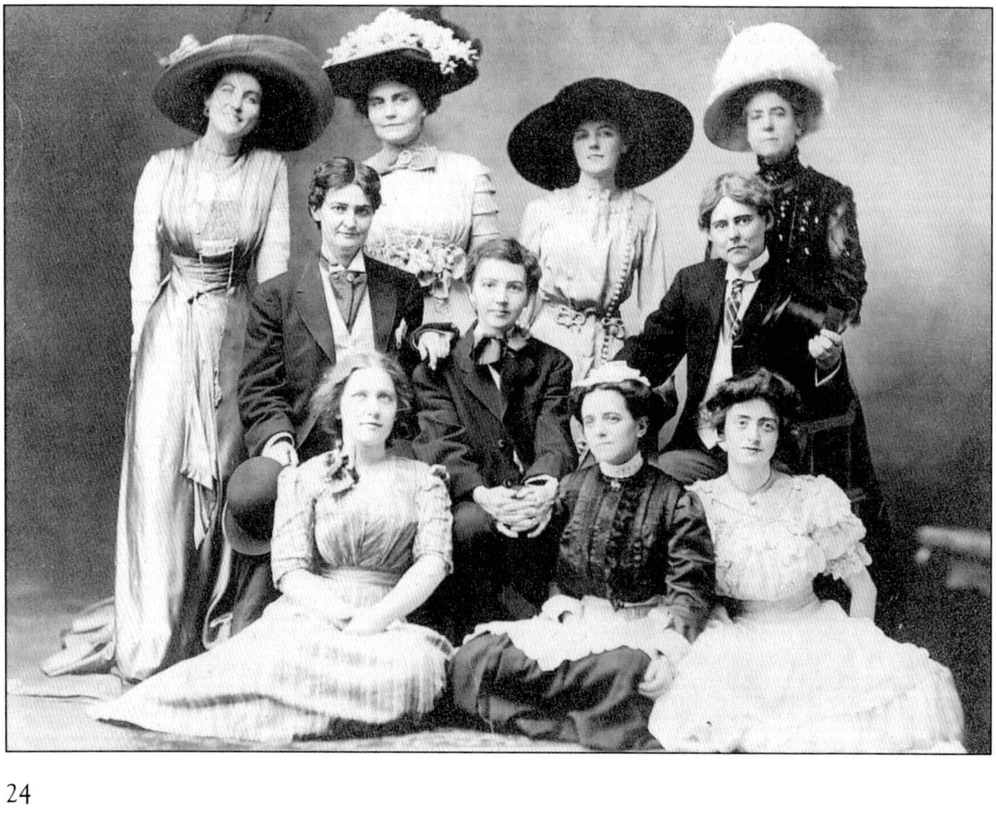

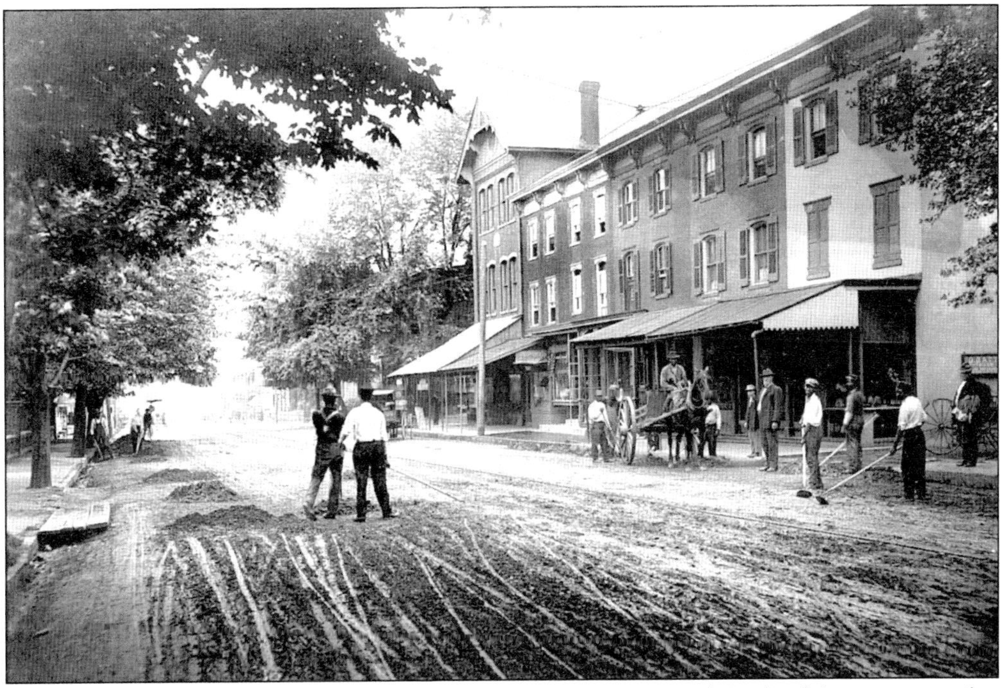

As Coatesville moved into the 20th century, Main Street improved. Both of the scenes on this page are from 1911. The top view is looking west toward Third Avenue. The Odd Fellows Hall is the tall building on the right at the corner of Third Avenue. The view below is looking east from Third Avenue, with the Jesse Coates residence in the background to the right, next to the W.P. Worth residence.

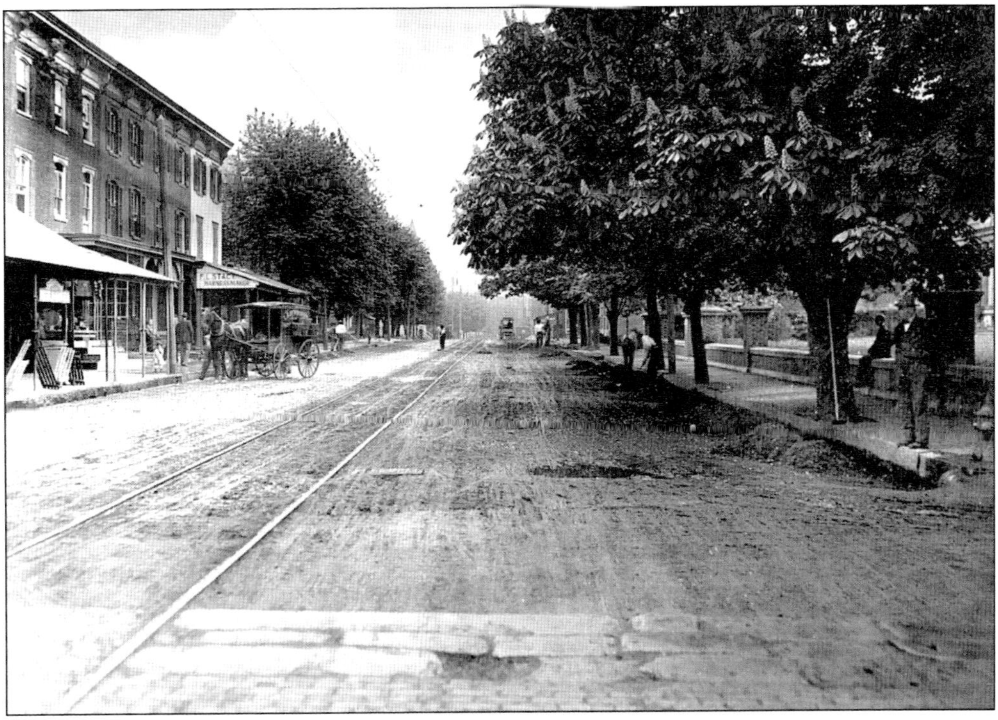

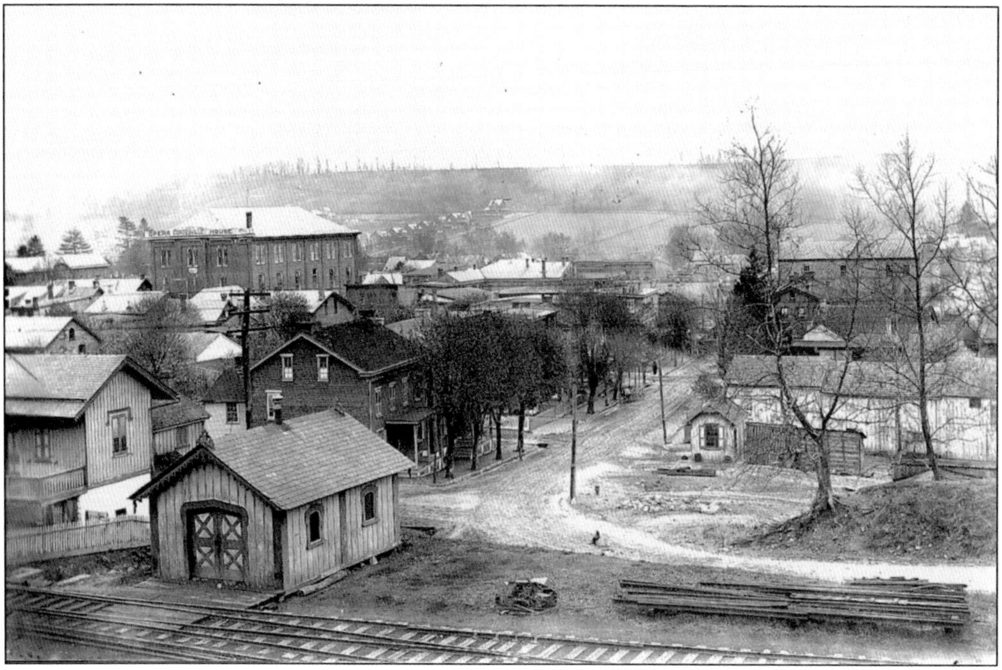

Railroad access made Coatesville a thriving community in the 1860s. Commuters could make their way to the borough, but more importantly, the mills of the area were able to ship products and receive necessary raw materials. Both of theses photographs were taken in the 1890s. The image above clearly shows the tall Coatesville Opera House building. The image below depicts the Pennsylvania Railroad station.

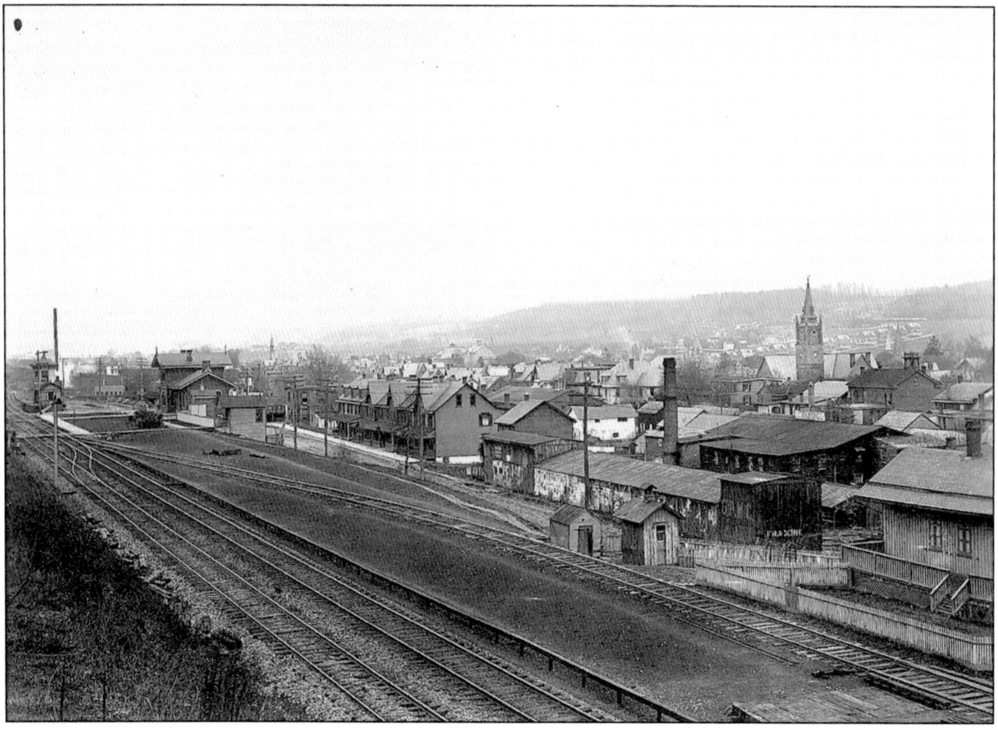

Two

EARLY INDUSTRY

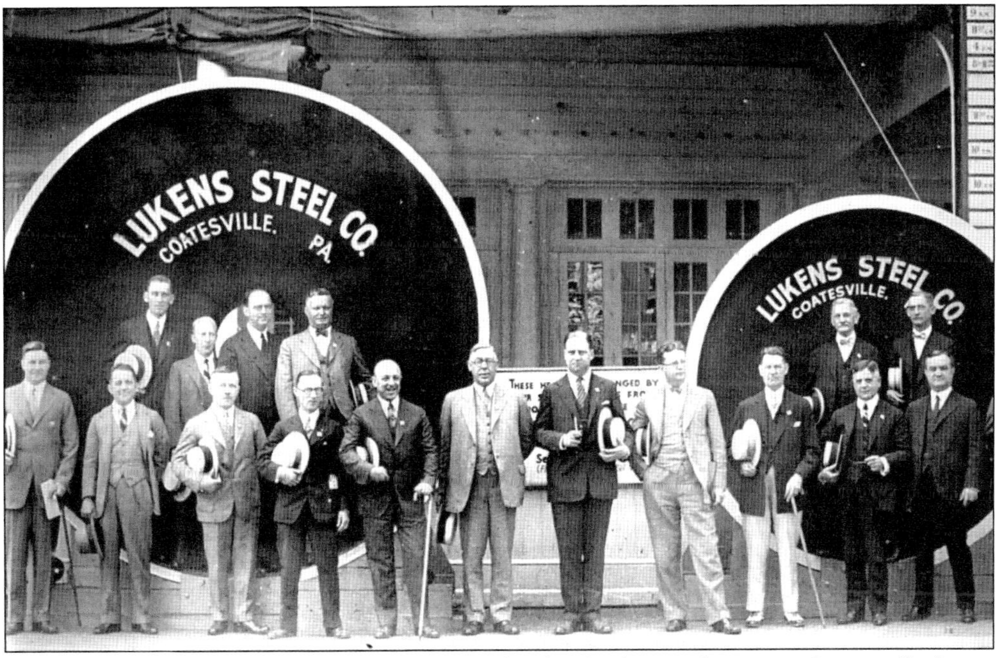

The Lukens Steel Company became not only the leading industry in Coatesville but a major U.S. corporation as well, known as the leading manufacturer of specialty steel. In this photograph, Lukens Steel executives are shown in front of a display of spun heads. Lukens was the first company in America to make boilerplates, used in ships and steam locomotives.

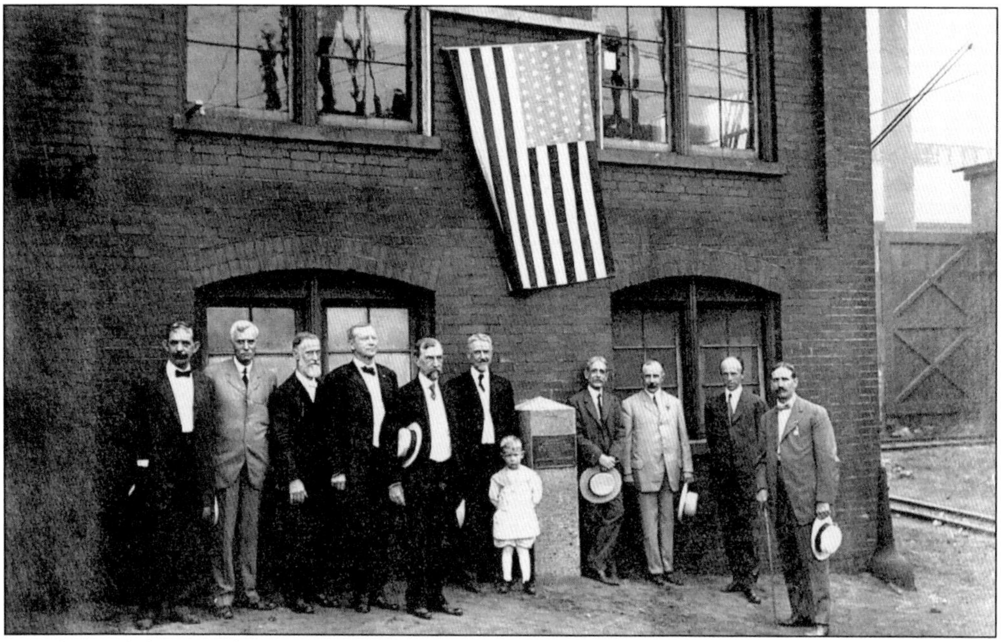

Members of the Worth and Huston families, company executives, and dignitaries from across Chester County are shown gathered on July 2, 1910, at the dedication of a marker in front of a company building to commemorate the 100th anniversary of the founding of the Lukens company. In the *c.* 1895 photograph below, company office workers take a break from a hard day of work to pose in the old office building.

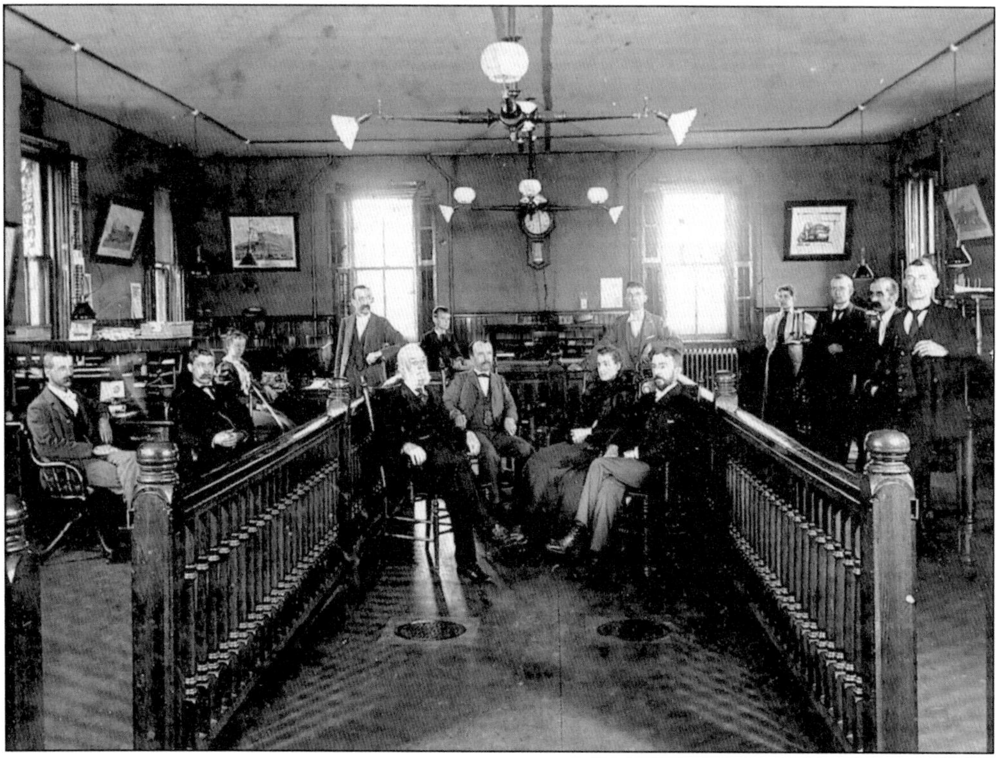

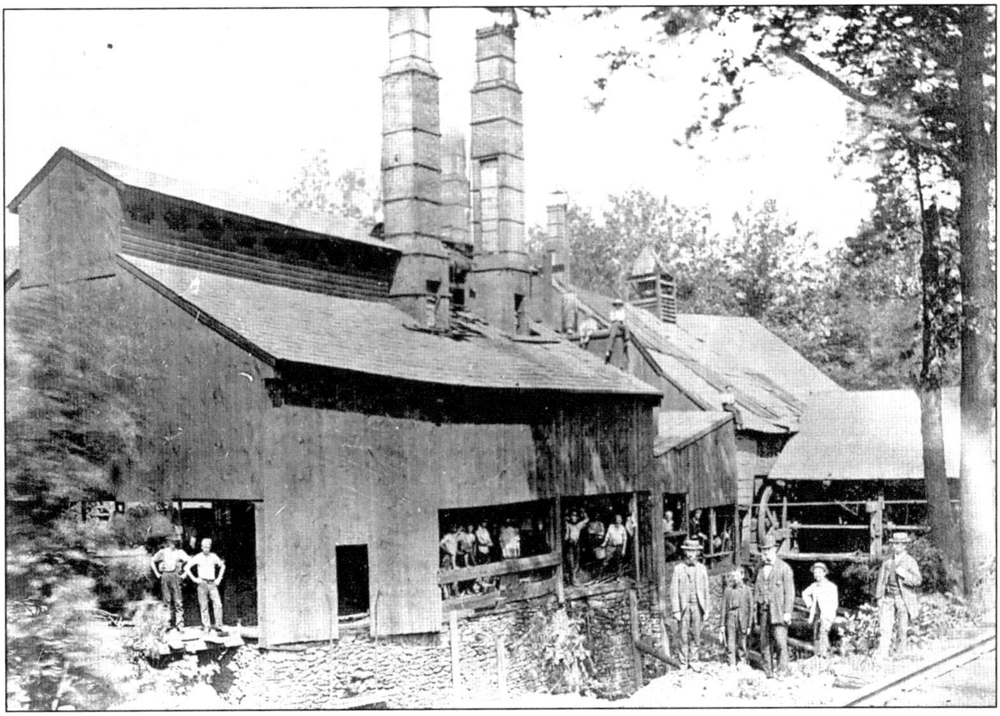

During the lifetime of Rebecca Lukens, "the Woman of Steel," the Brandywine Rolling Mills appeared as depicted in these two *c.* 1887 photographs. The image above shows the east side of the Brandywine. Notice the workers seated on the roof. The photograph below shows the workers on the west side of the Brandywine.

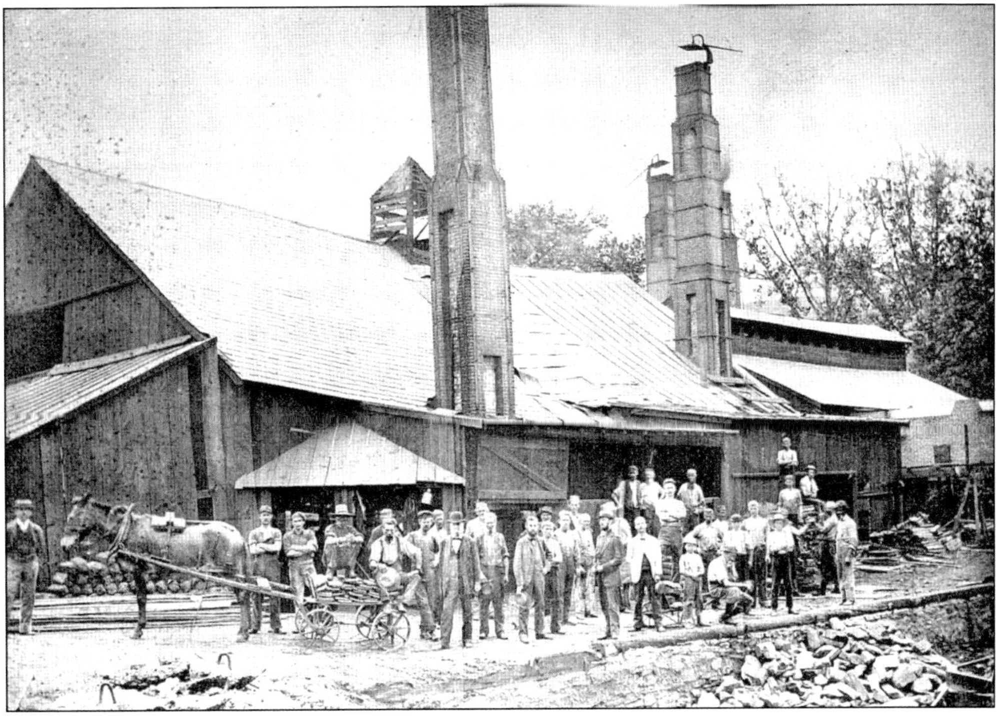

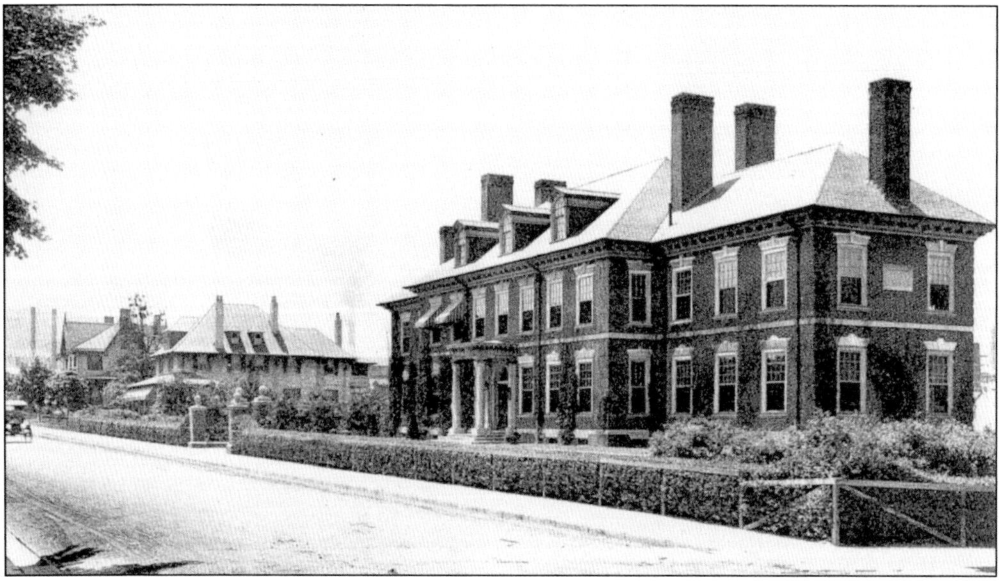

The hub of operations of the Lukens Steel Company was the main office building on South First Avenue, just south of the Lincoln Highway. The above photograph, taken c. 1910, shows C.L. Huston's home, Terracina (far left), and the main office building. The photograph below was taken from the residence of Lukens Steel Company president A.F. Huston.

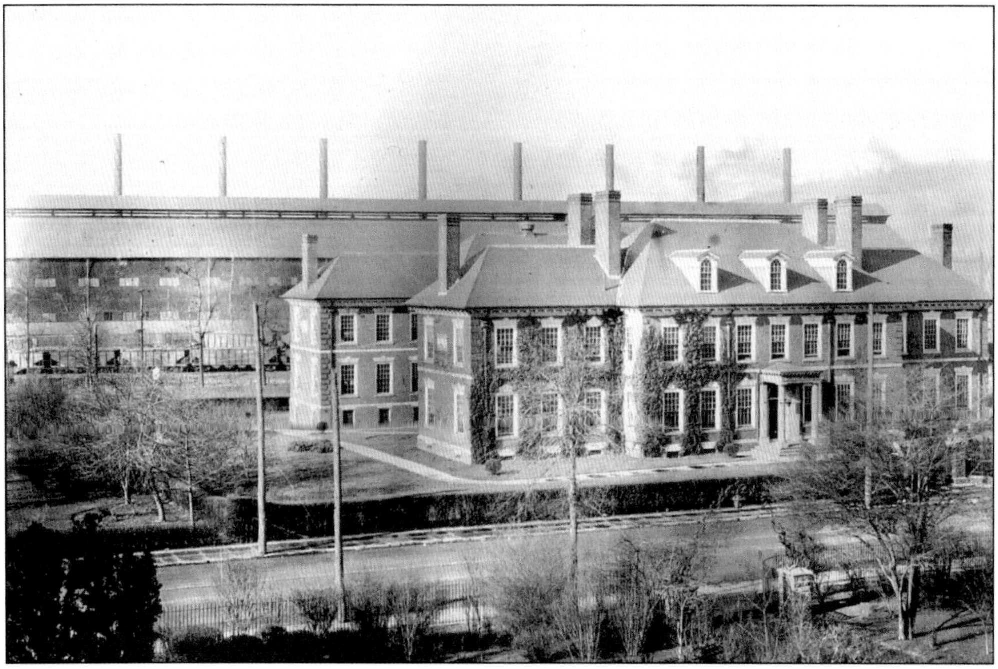

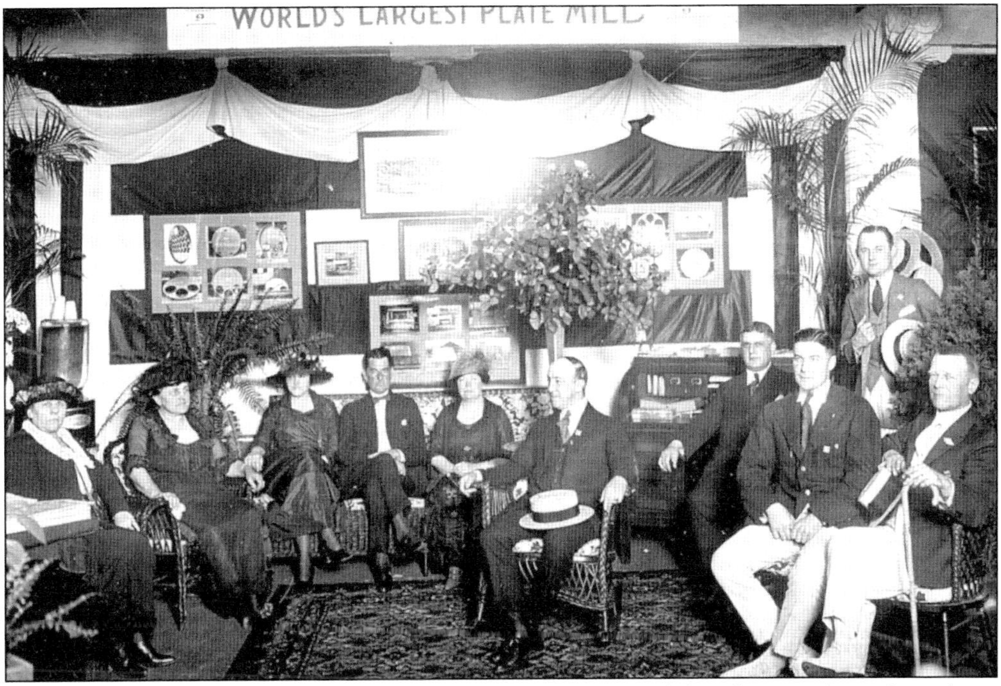

During the early 20th century, the Lukens Steel Company exhibited its products throughout the country. In the above photograph, representatives of the company sit under a banner denoting Lukens as the "World's Largest Plate Mill." Lukens rolled the largest steel plate in the world. The photograph below depicts a large steam boiler made with steel from Lukens.

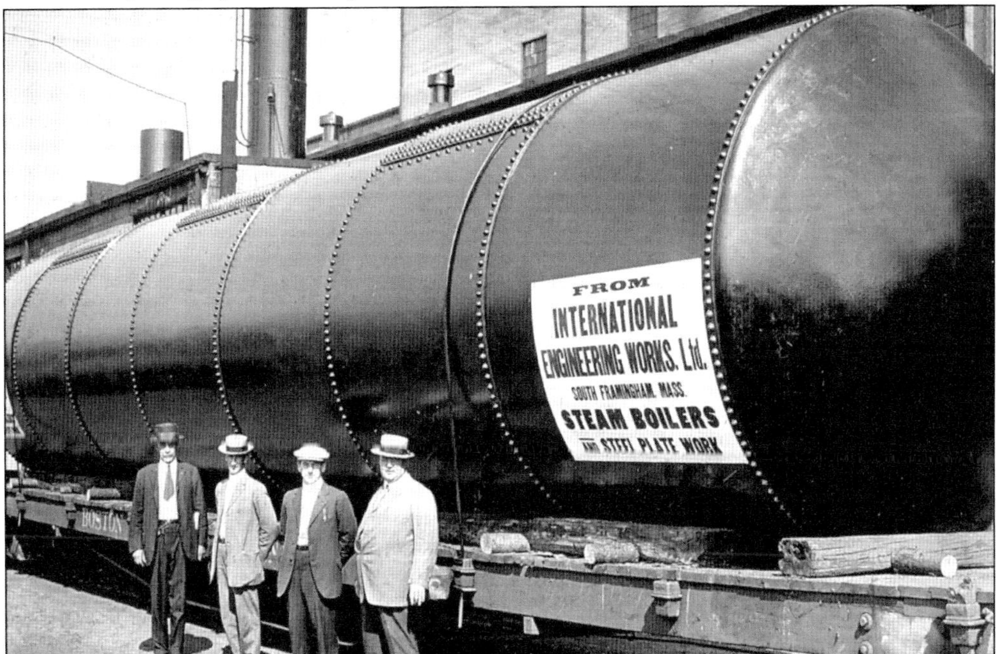

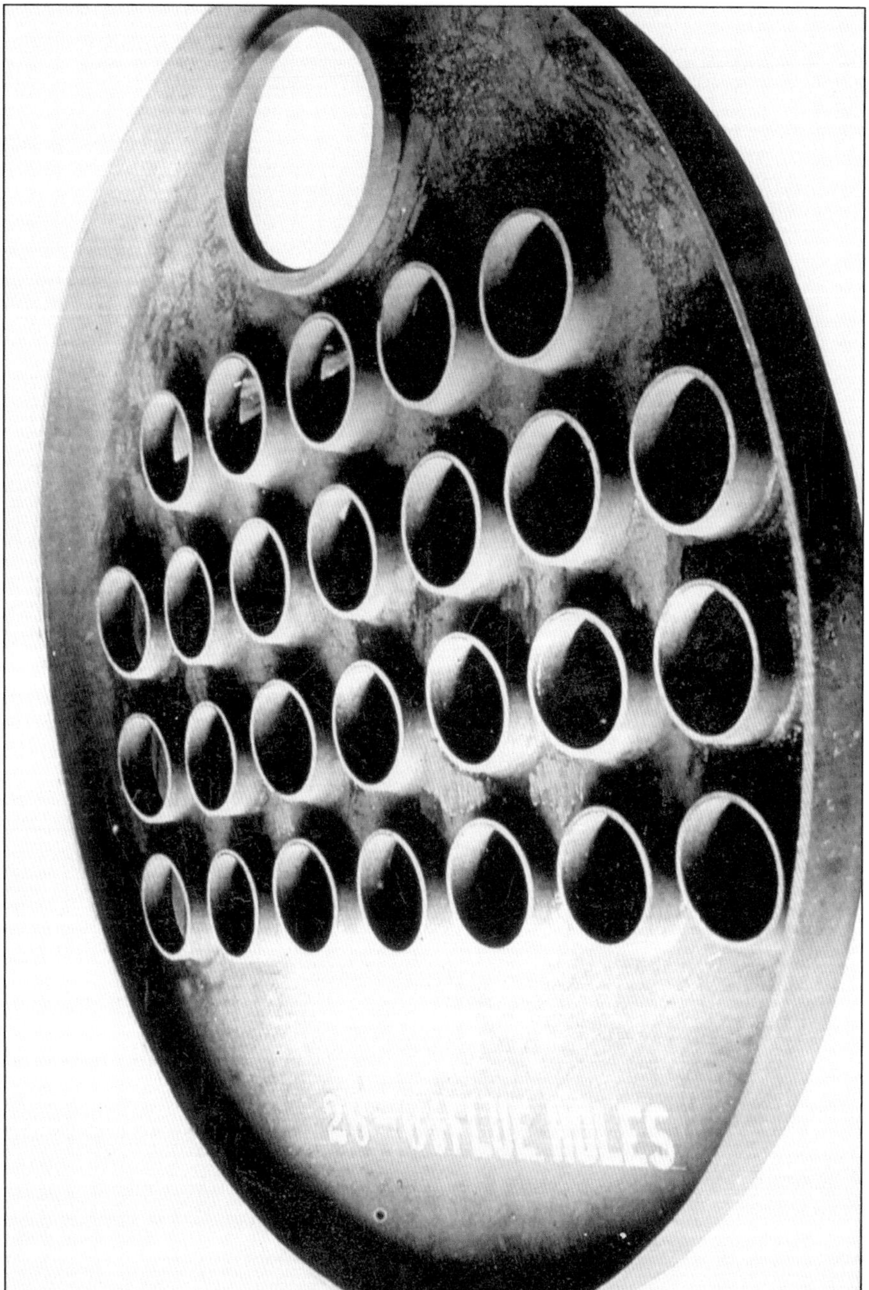

This photograph shows a large boiler head made at the Lukens Steel Company. Lukens supplied boilerplates for many locomotives of the railroads of America and also supplied boilerplates for maritime engines and other types of products. As the years passed, the types of products produced by Lukens increased along with the size of the products. Lukens first made its reputation with the production of boilerplates in 1810. As the times changed, so did Lukens, and the company's products were later used in a number of modern buildings, including the World Trade Center and a number of ships for the U.S. Navy. The Lukens Steel Company was a major supplier of material to the U.S. armed forces during both world wars.

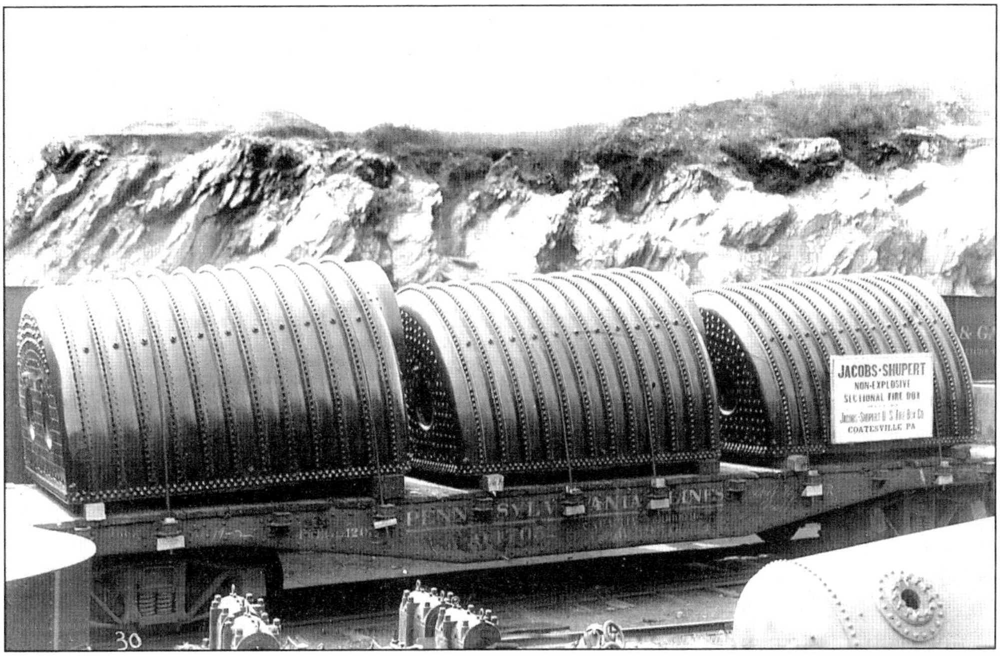

The fireboxes loaded onto the Pennsylvania Railroad car in the photograph above were made with Lukens steel by the Jacobs-Shupert U.S. Firebox Company of Coatesville, for the Lehigh Valley Railroad. At the time, only the Lukens Steel Company could produce a flanged head, depicted in the image below.

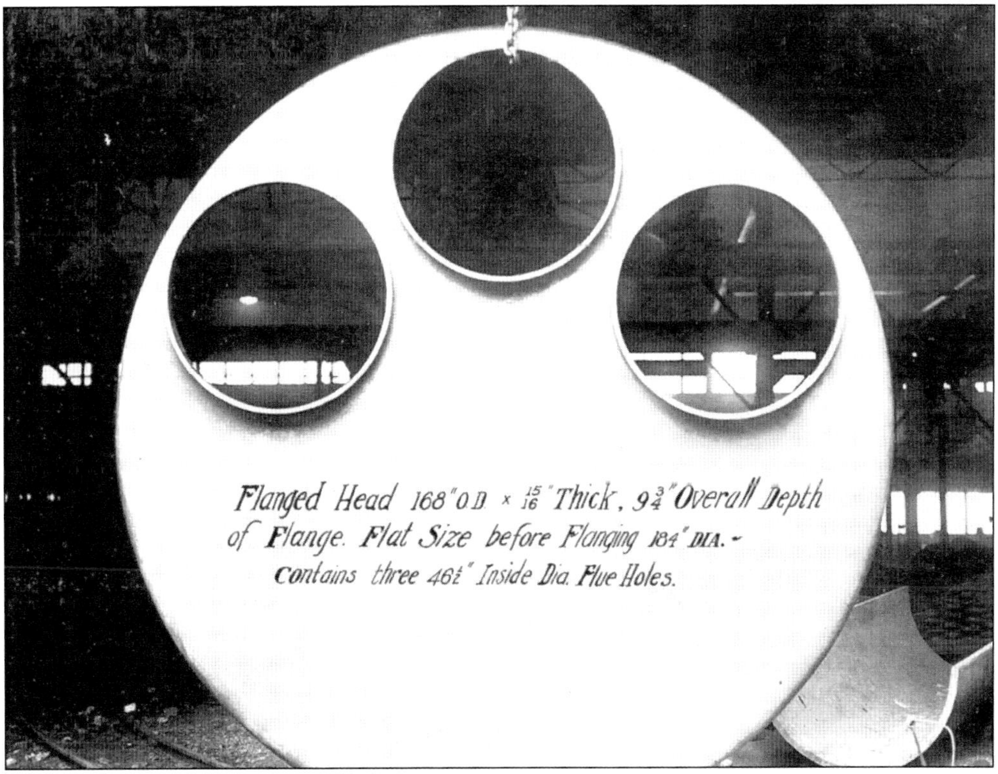

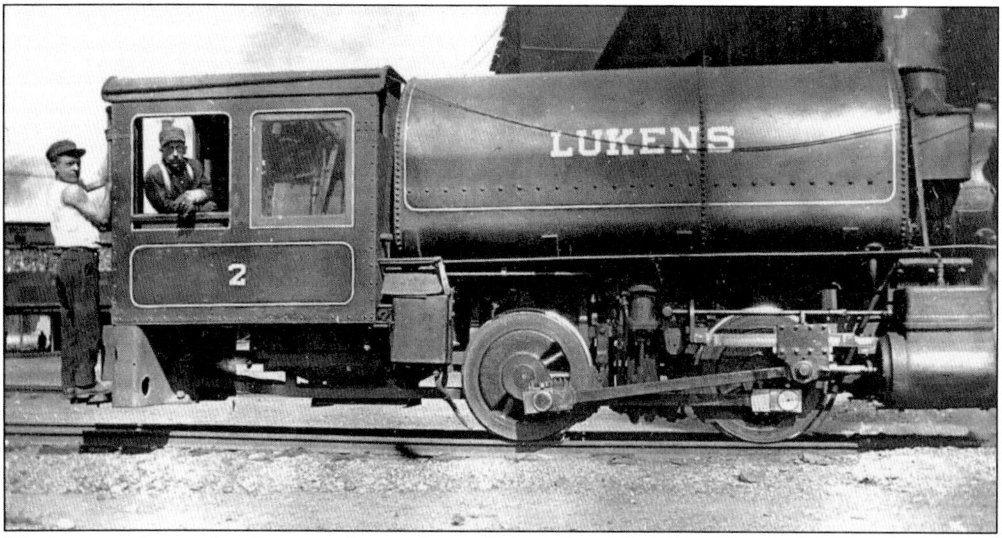

Working in the steel mills was a demanding job, but the railroad system used by Lukens helped to move materials from one section of the mill to another. The above photograph shows two of the mill workers on Lukens Engine No. 2. The photograph below shows the railroad, engine, workers, and material in one of the yards.

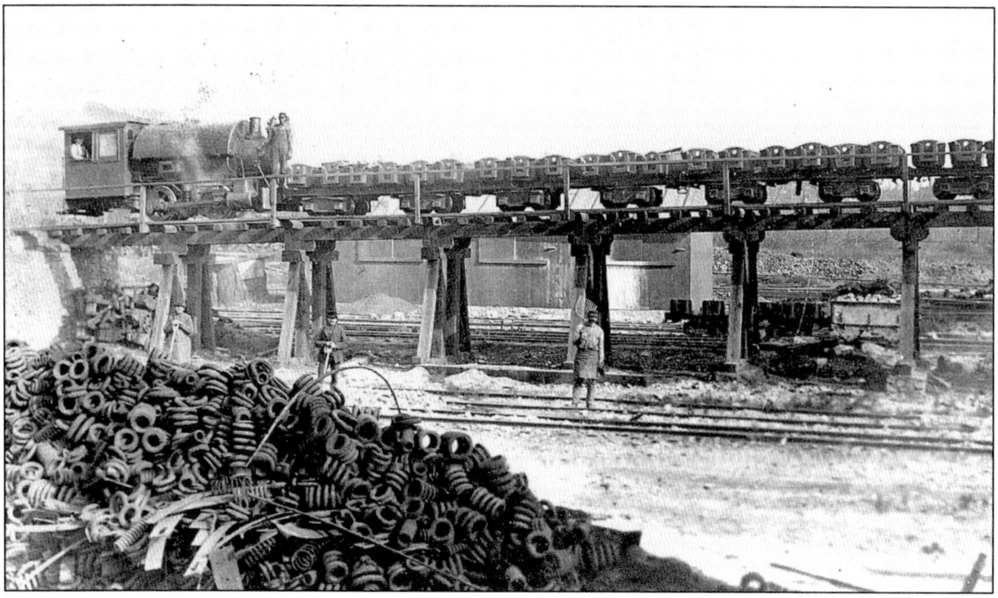

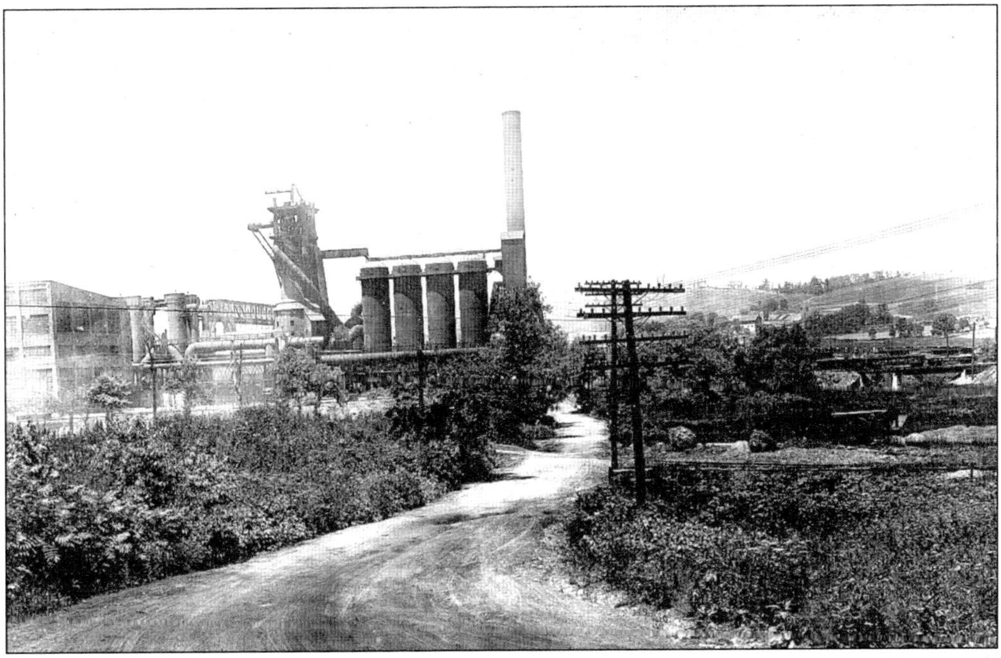

The steel industry in Coatesville grew with the years, as plants expanded. The above photograph shows the blast furnaces of the Midvale Steel and Ordnance Company. The photograph below shows the then-new Lukens 84-foot rolling mill with the rotary side shears visible. At the rear, the end shears are visible. To the left is the table from the annealing furnace.

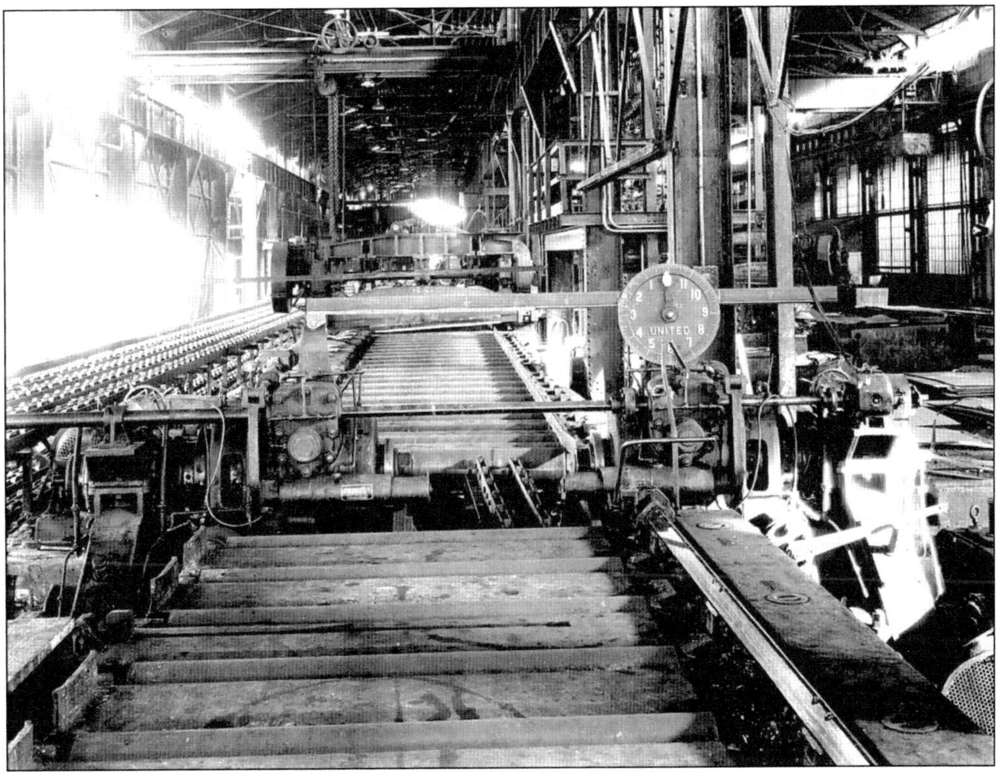

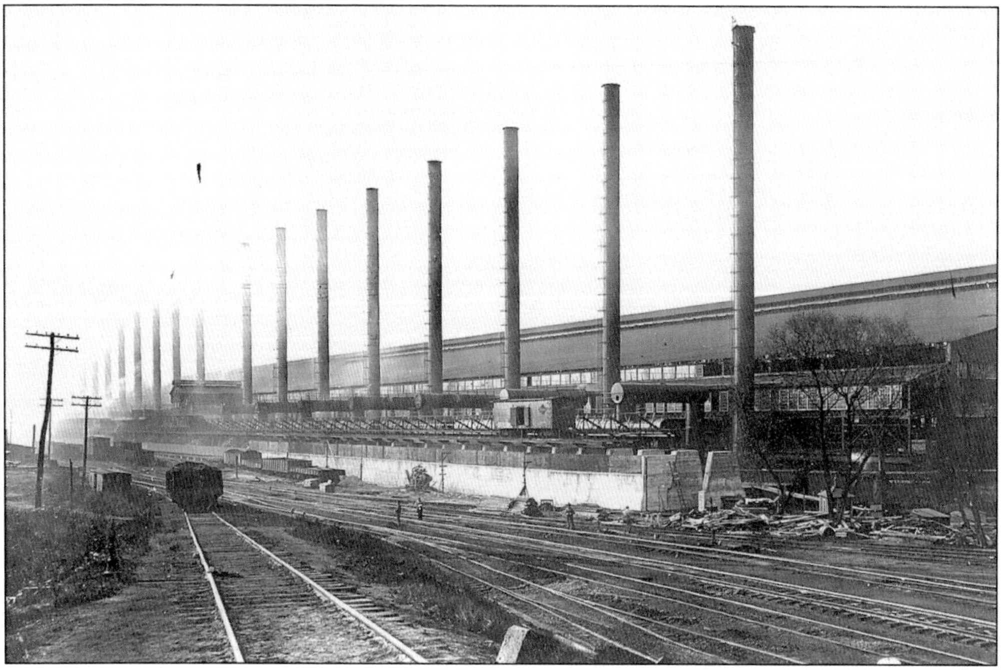

Other local businesses thrived during the time that Coatesville was known as "the Pittsburgh of the East." The above photograph is a view of Worth Brothers Company's new steel plant. The photograph below shows the Coatesville silk mill owned by the Aronson family. A notation on the photograph observes that the mill was exclusively using central station power.

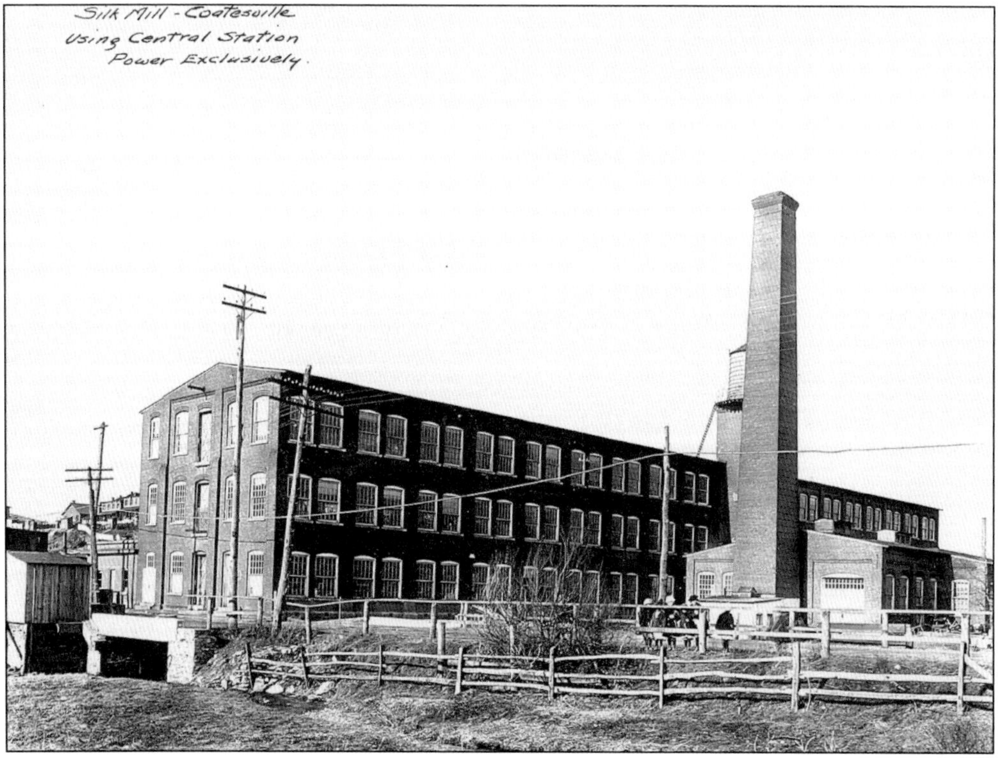

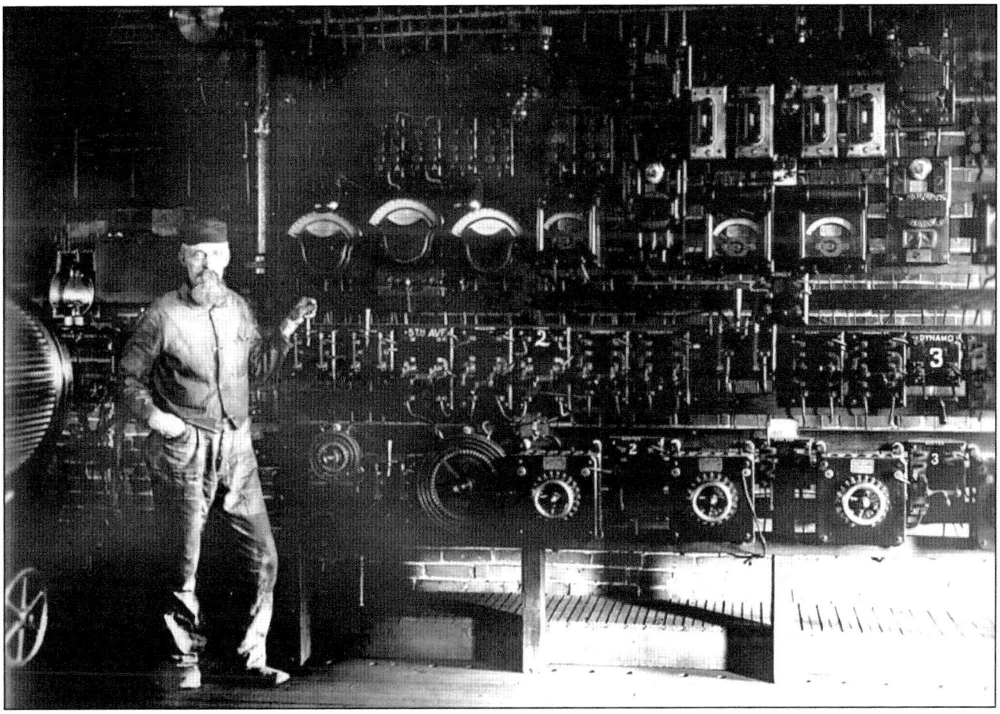

The first electric plant in Coatesville, the Chester Valley Electric Company, was located at Fourth Avenue and Fleetwood Street. One of the early employees is shown in the above photograph. Below is a photograph of the town's Clegg Mill, also home to the Rowe Manufacturing Company.

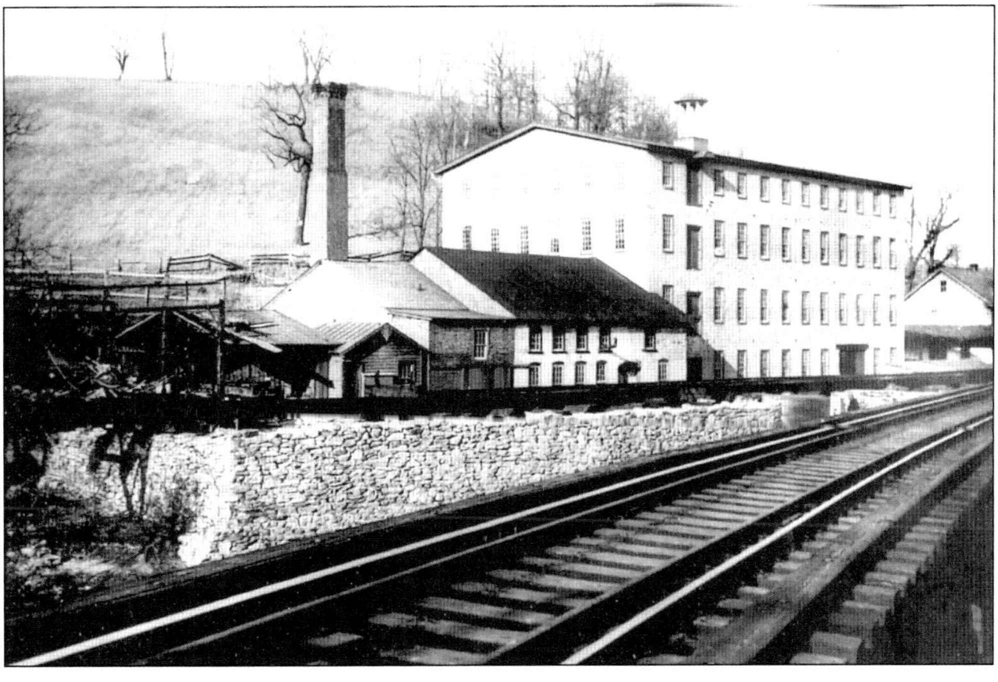

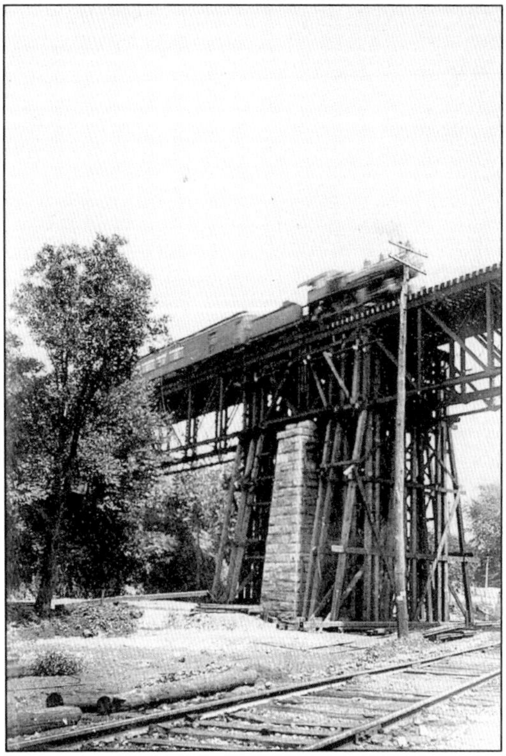

The Railroad High Bridge has been a Coatesville landmark since 1834, when the first bridge was erected. The third bridge is shown as it appeared in 1896. In the photograph to the left, a New York and Chicago Limited speeds across the viaduct on May 29, 1896. The photograph below was taken on the same day.

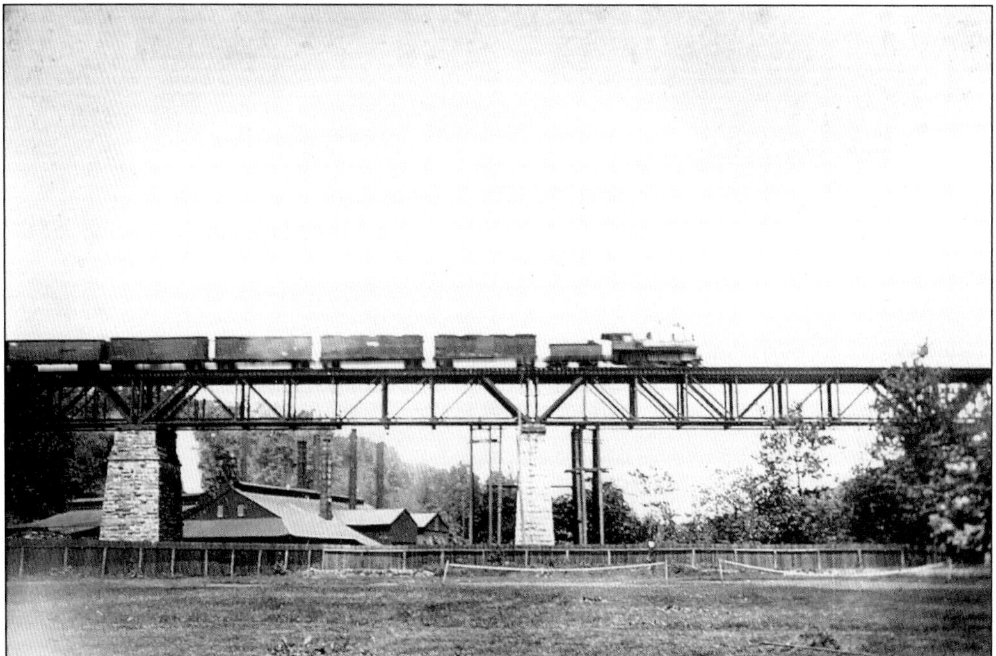

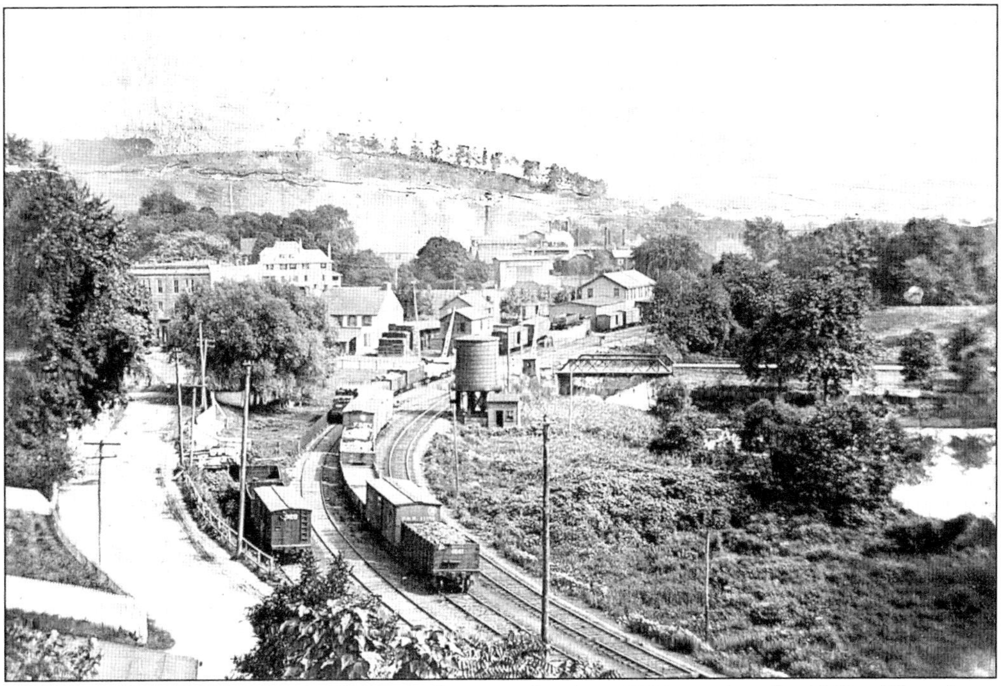

The railroad yards in Coatesville were busy in the late 1800s and early 1900s. The above photograph shows loaded cars awaiting an engine. The view looks south to Coatesville and depicts the Wilmington branch of the Reading Railroad. In the photograph below, steel plates are loaded onto Reading Railroad cars on tracks at the Lukens Steel Company plant.

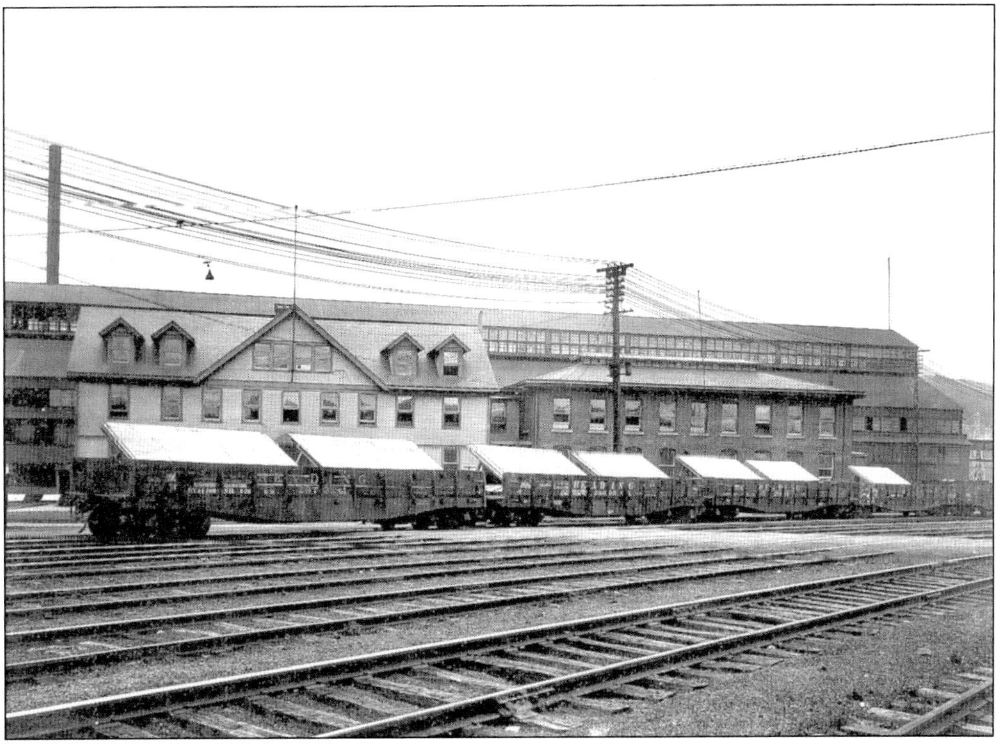

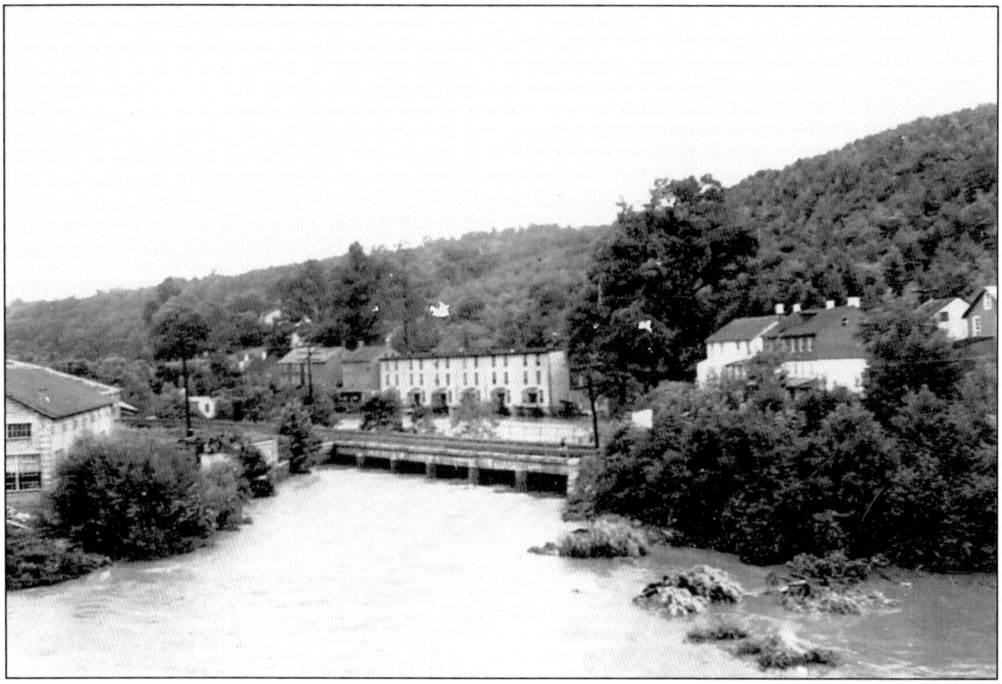

The Brandywine River supplied power to the mills of the Coatesville area, but it could also rage out of control. The above photograph shows the Brandywine flooding north of Coatesville at the Reading Railroad Bridge. The photograph below shows another use for the water of the Brandywine—helping to grow vegetables in a garden behind the Lukens and Huston family homes.

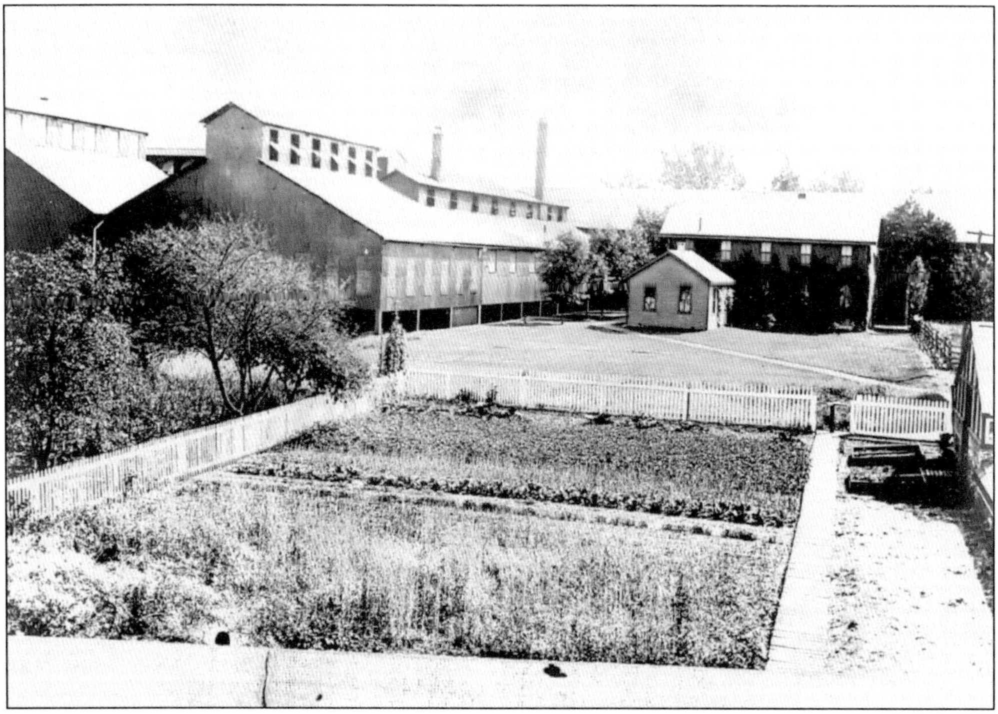

Three

EARLY COMMERCE

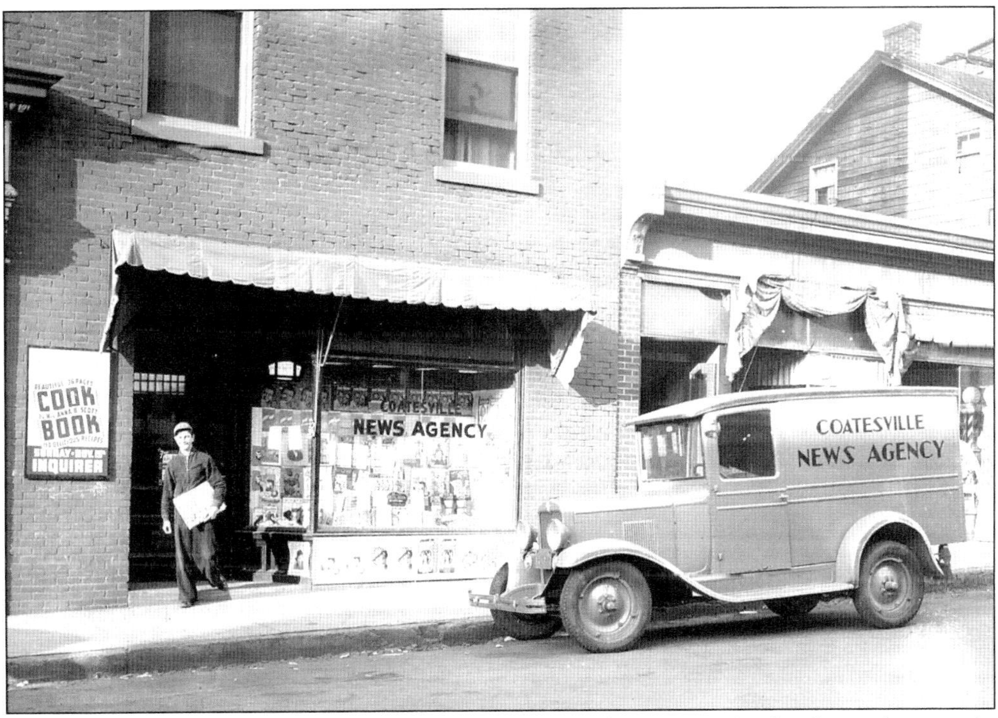

As the mills of Coatesville prospered, so did other types of commerce. In the above photograph, a Coatesville News Agency delivery truck is seen in front of the agency. Several newspapers, including the *Coatesville Record*, were published. The *Record*'s first edition was published on October 7, 1908. The sign to the left promotes a cookbook to be delivered with an edition of the *Philadelphia Inquirer*.

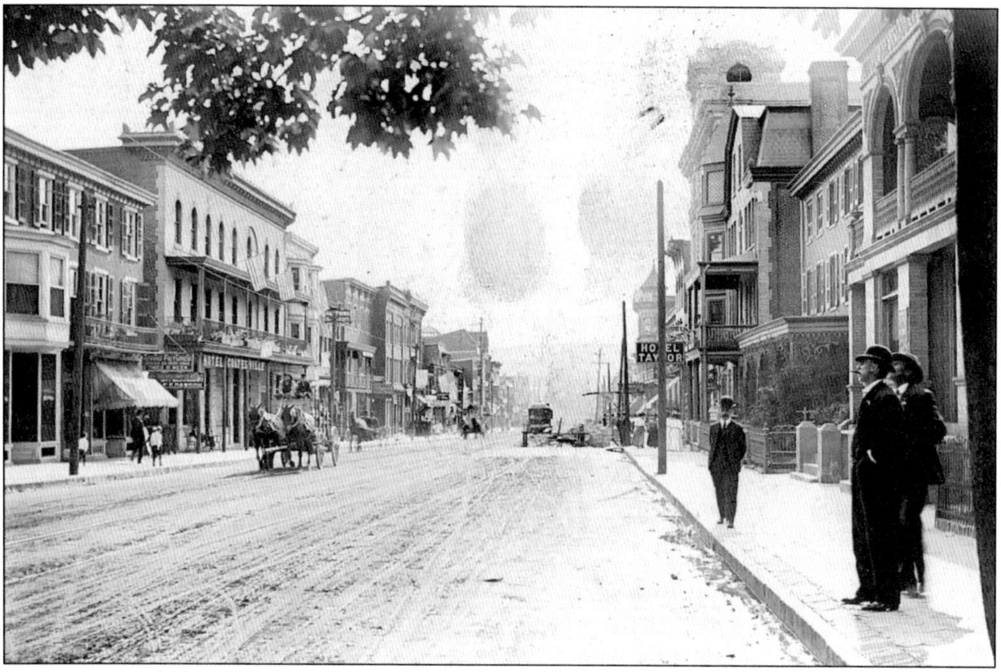

Businesses, including hotels, prospered along the Main Street section of Coatesville. The above photograph, taken in 1907, shows residents and a horse and carriage. The photograph below shows Heck Brothers at 152 Main Street, where the store's delivery wagon and horse, along with some of the store's employees, can be seen.

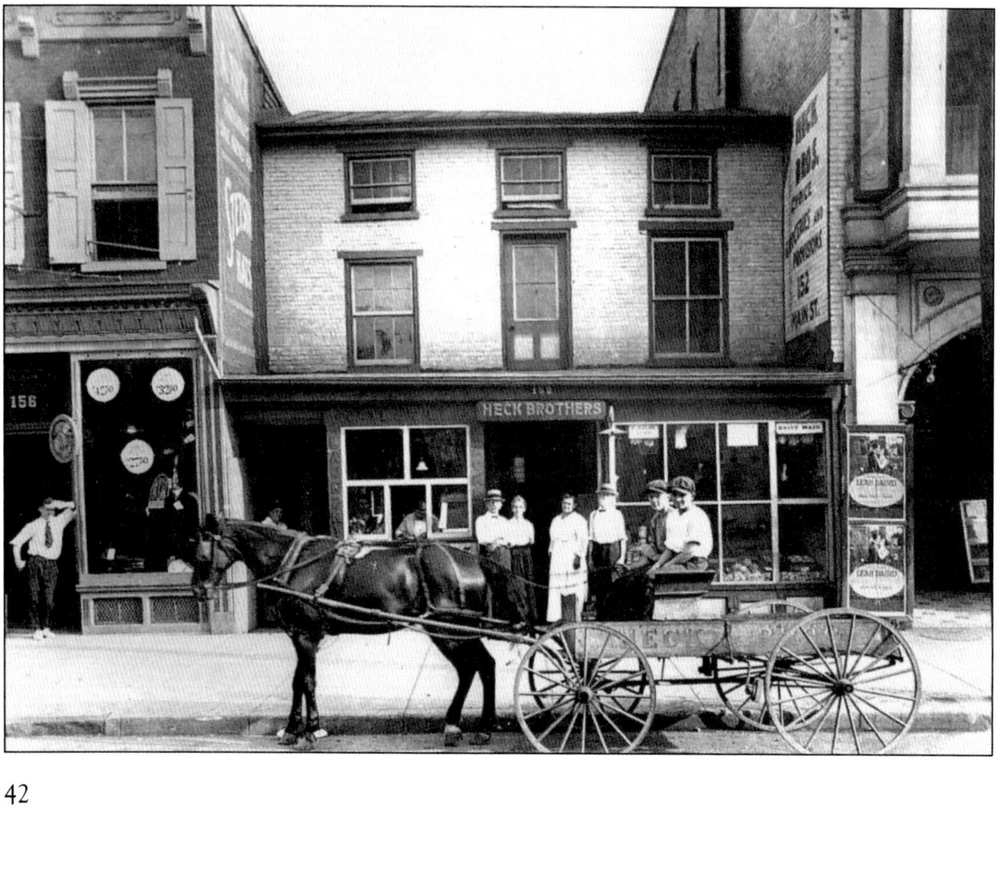

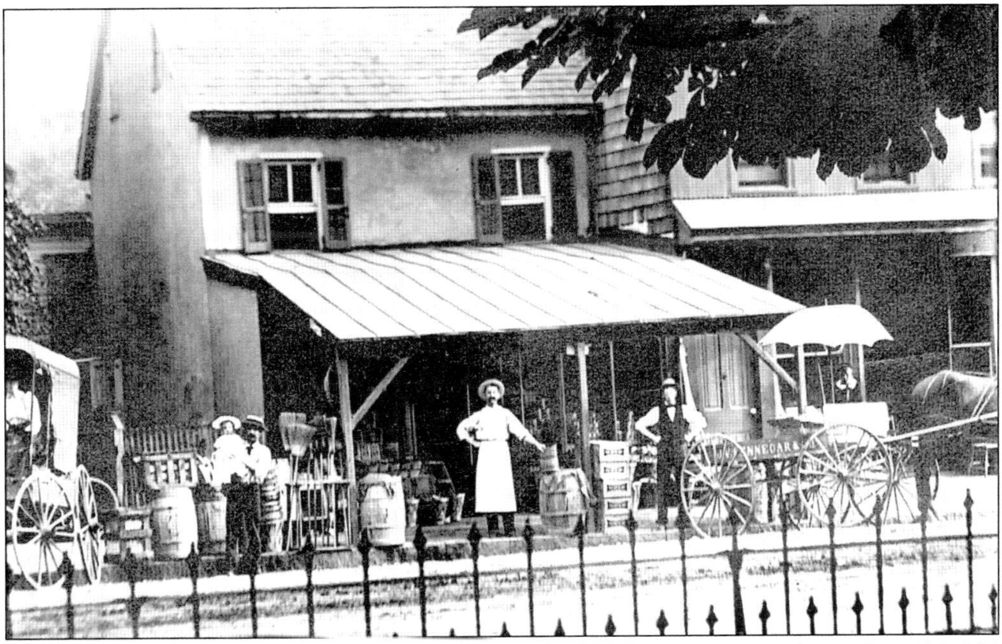

One of the stores for shoppers in Coatesville was the J.V. Pennegar store, located at 242–244 Main Street. The shop contained a little of everything. The above photograph is from the Frank P. Pennegar Collection, housed at the Chester County Historical Society. In the photograph below, Young's Drug Store is selling Coca Cola for a nickel. To the left of the drugstore is a laundry.

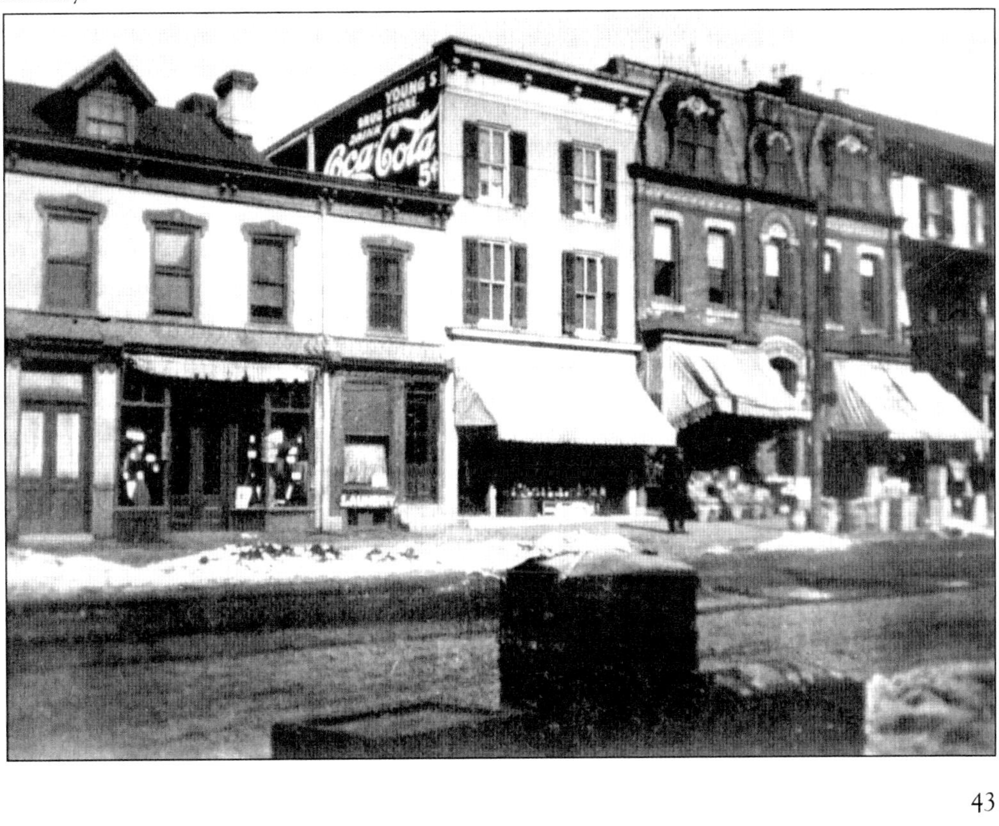

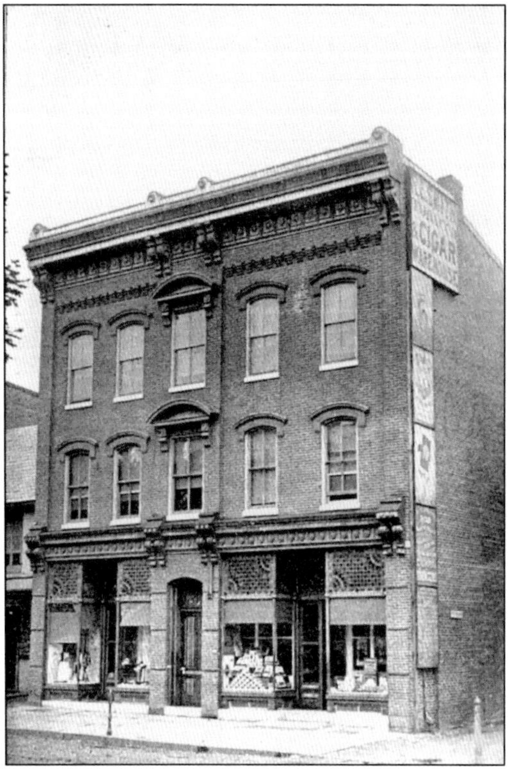

A tobacco and cigar warehouse owned by R.E. Smith stood on Main Street between 1870 and 1970, after which time it was demolished. The structure was late Victorian Second Empire in design. The photograph below shows residents in front of the Taylor House Hotel on Main Street. Also shown are the Pennock House and the Mutual Insurance building.

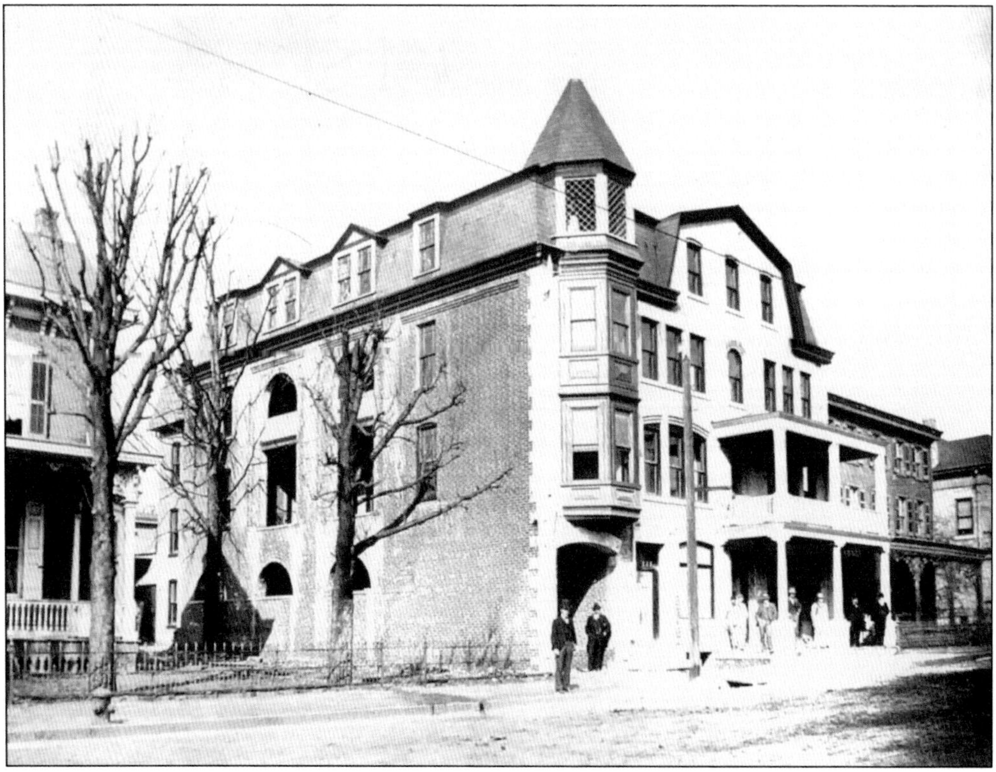

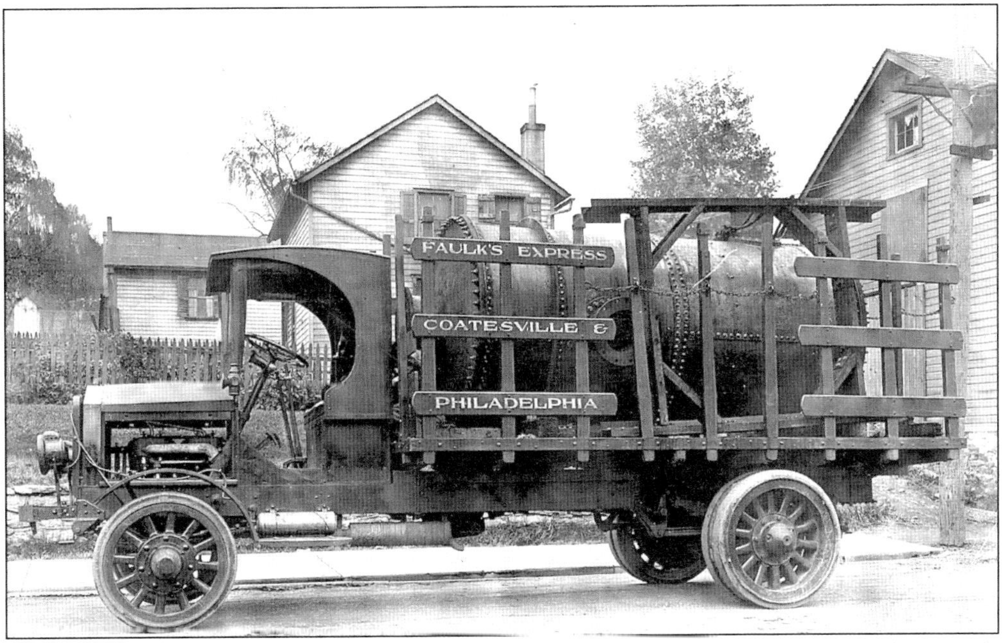

Coatesville is about 35 miles from Philadelphia, and the truck in the above photograph belonged to Faulk's Express, a company with offices in both cities. The photograph below shows an interior view of A.G. Luebert's Drug Store, on Main Street just east of the Washington Hose Company. The Coatesville Flower Shop and then Bell Telephone Company later occupied the building.

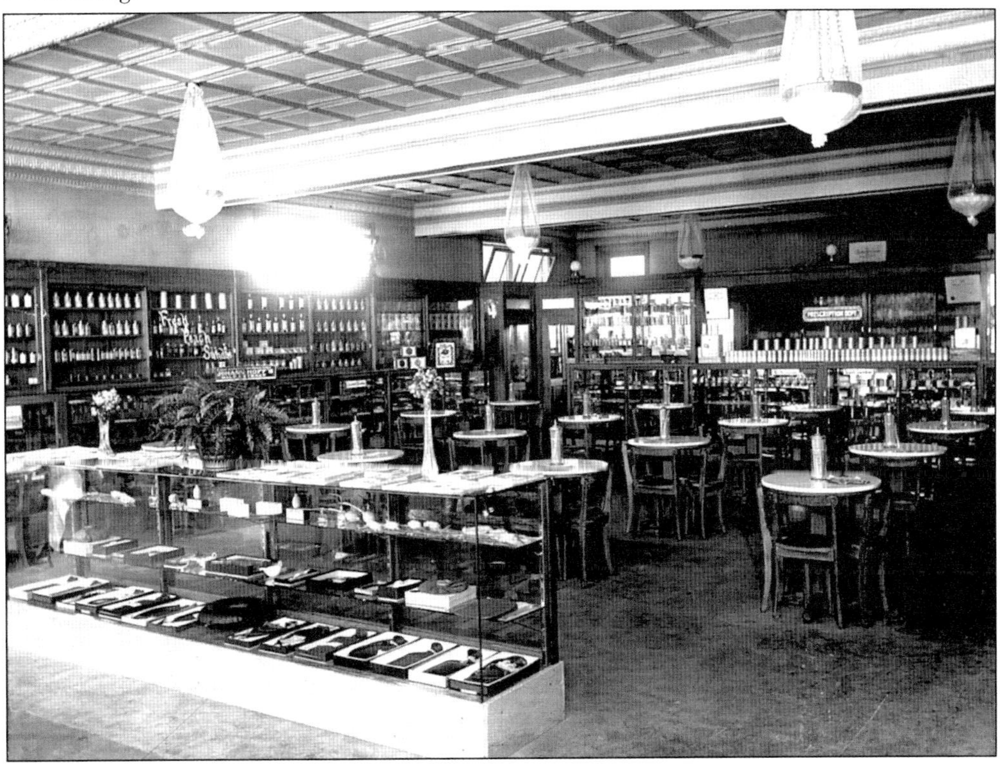

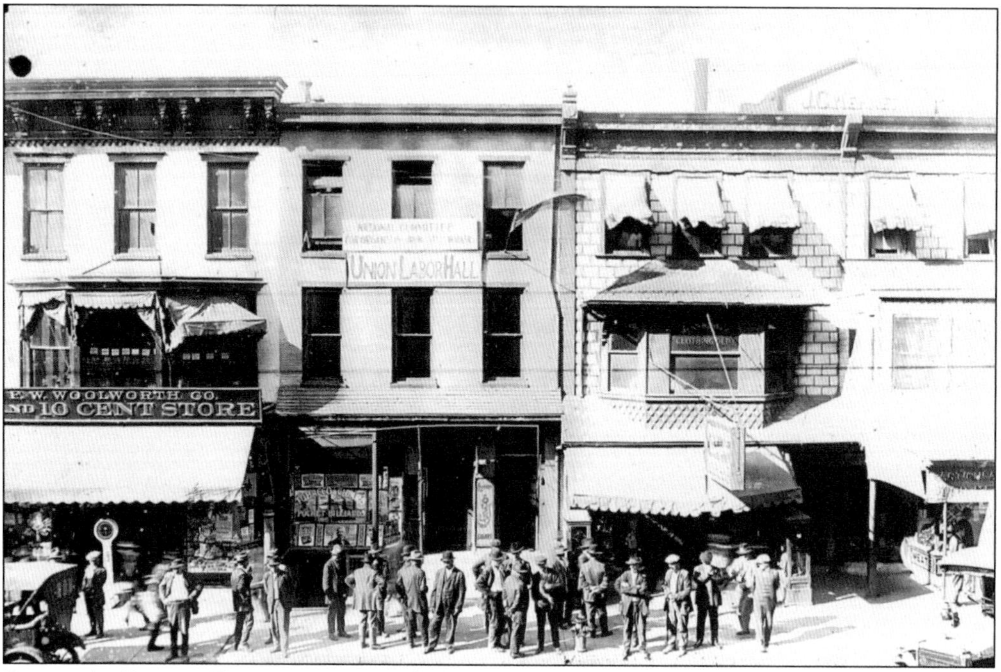

During the Roaring Twenties, Coatesville had a cigar store and pocket billiards business next to the F.W. Woolworth store on Main Street. Above, men are lined up at the curb. The photograph below shows the interior office of the Richard Scully lumberyard. Contractors could purchase building blocks, masons' supplies, and plastering and roofing supplies.

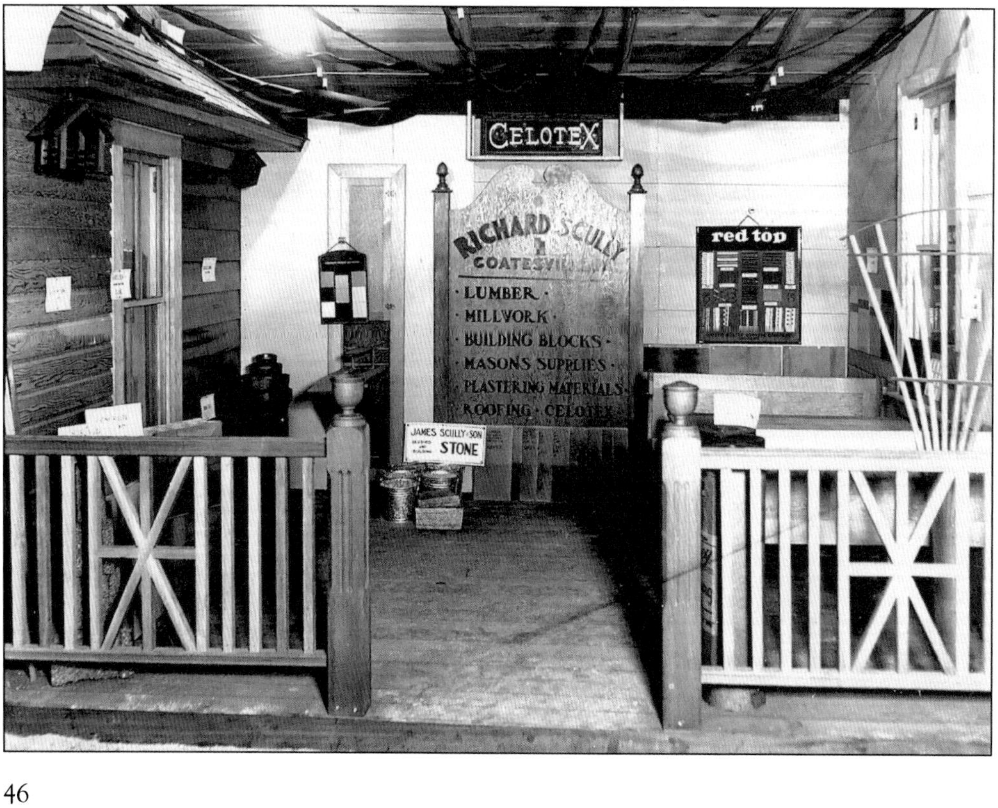

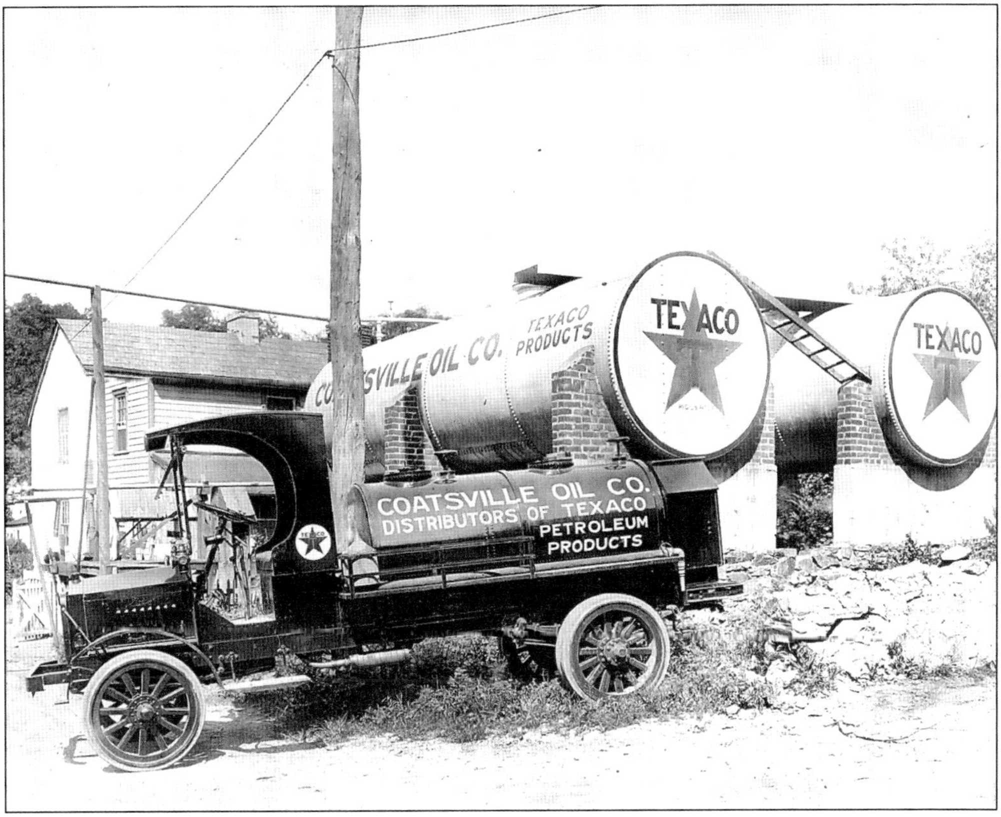

As the automobile started to change the lives of Americans across the nation, the automotive industry took hold in Coatesville. Above is a photograph of the Coatesville Oil Company, distributor of Texaco petroleum products. Below is a photograph of the N. Harlan Slack and Graham Brothers motorcar business. A. Duie Pyle delivery trucks are seen in front of the building.

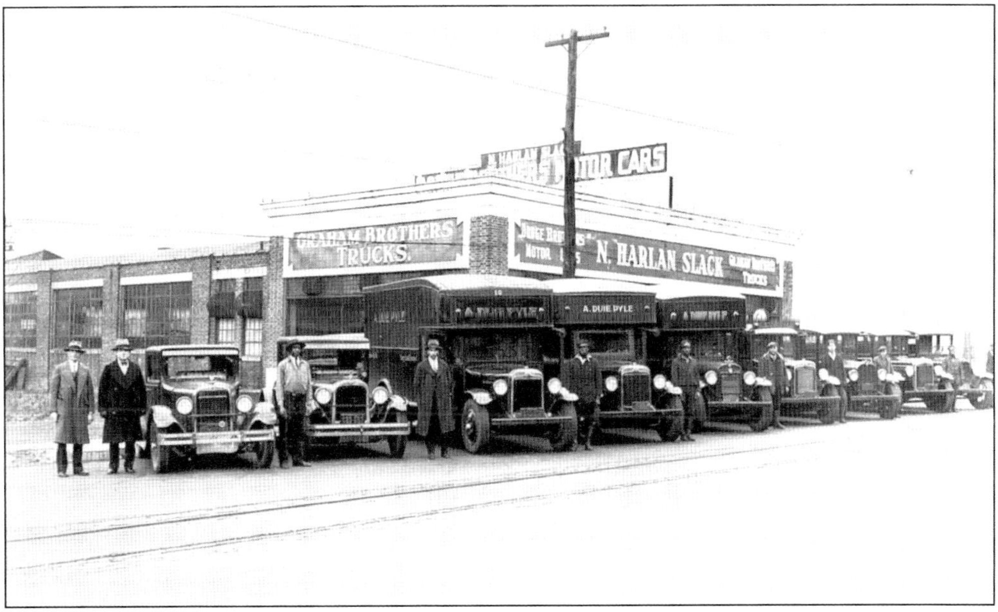

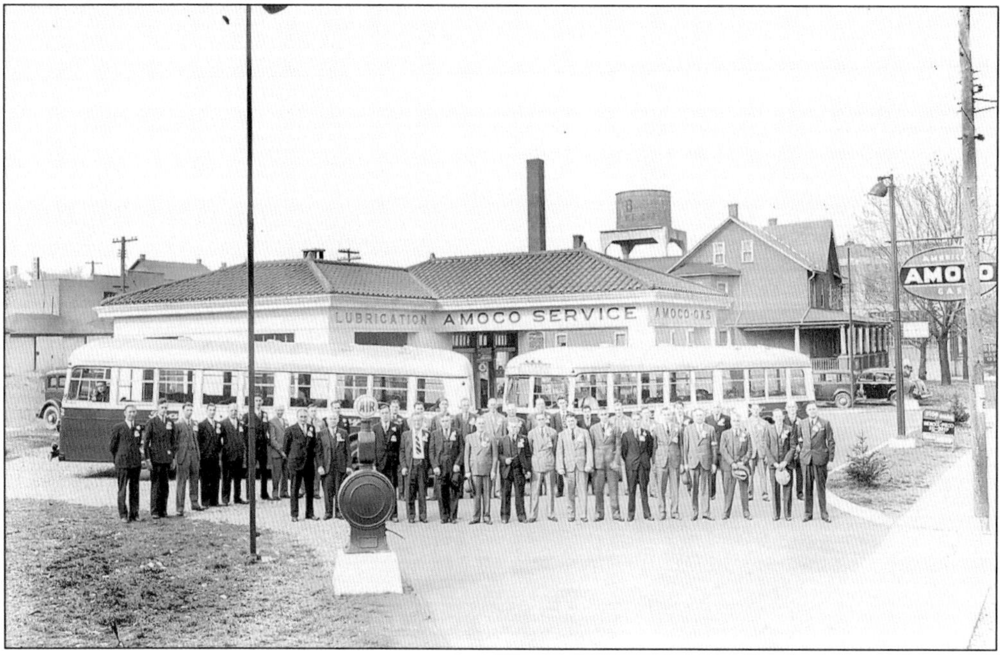

The Amoco station shown above was located on East Lincoln Highway (Main Street) near 10th Avenue. Below is the Charles D. Sensenig coal and building material company, located at 601 Merchant Street. In this view, one of the owners is writing up an order at the truck to the right. One of the signs announces that Sensenig sells the "celebrated Lackawanna Anthracite."

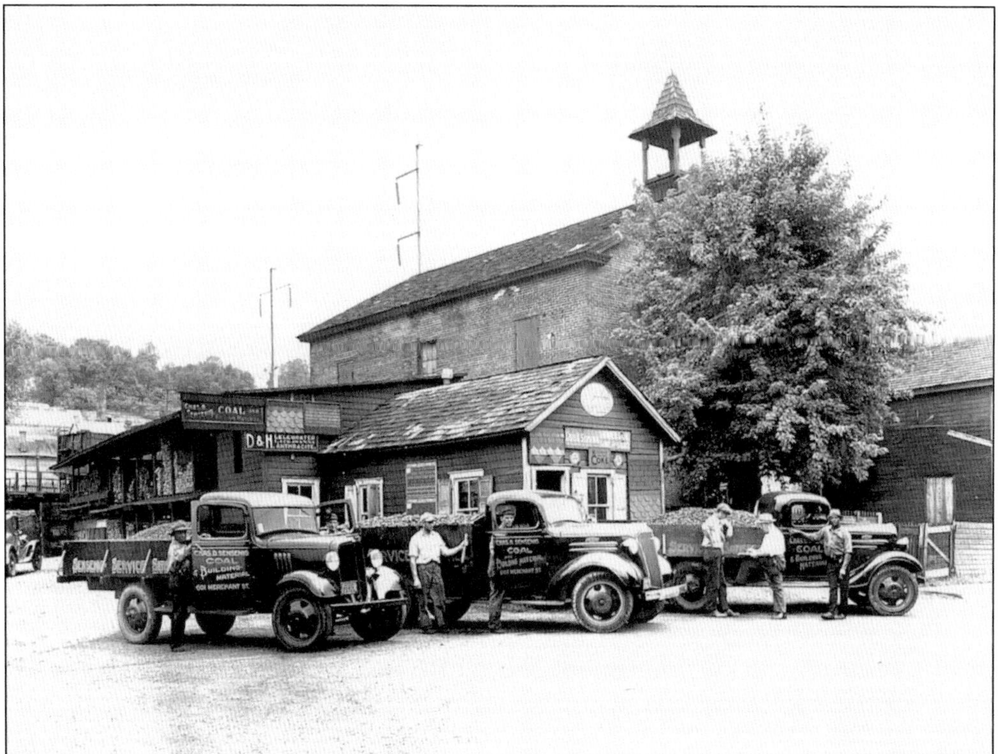

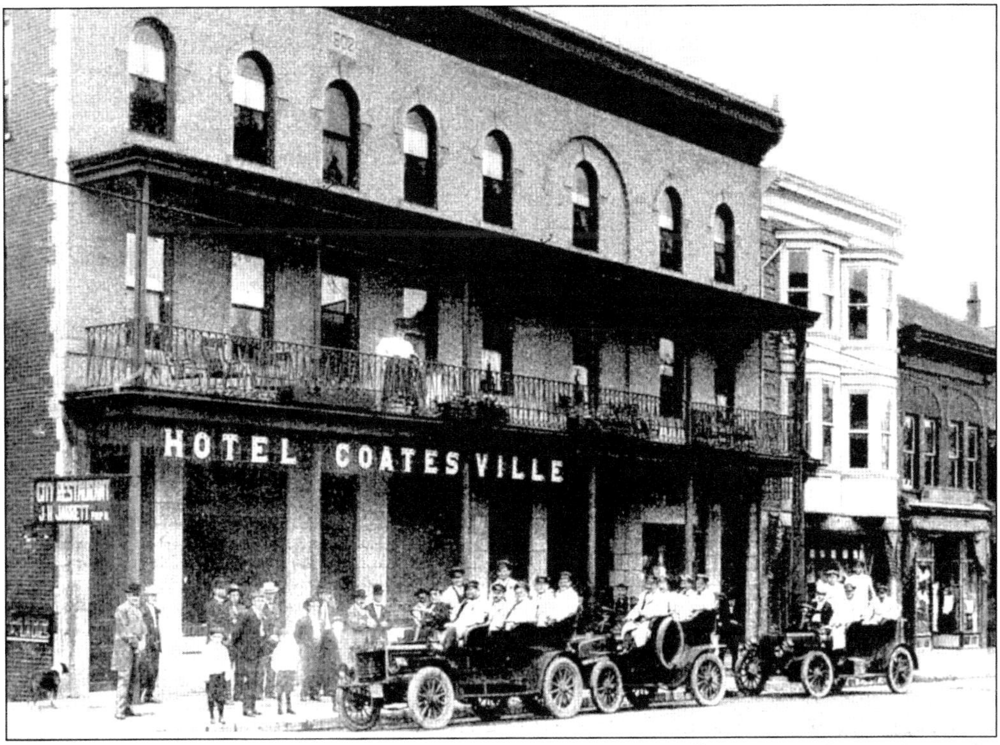

Three carloads of passengers gather in front of the Hotel Coatesville on Main Street. A sign for the City Restaurant, J.H. Jarrett proprietor, is visible to the left. One of the guests of the hotel enjoys a seat on the second-floor balcony. If the cars were heading west toward Lancaster, they could stop at the gas station at the west end of Coatesville on Lincoln Highway, just before reaching the city's border.

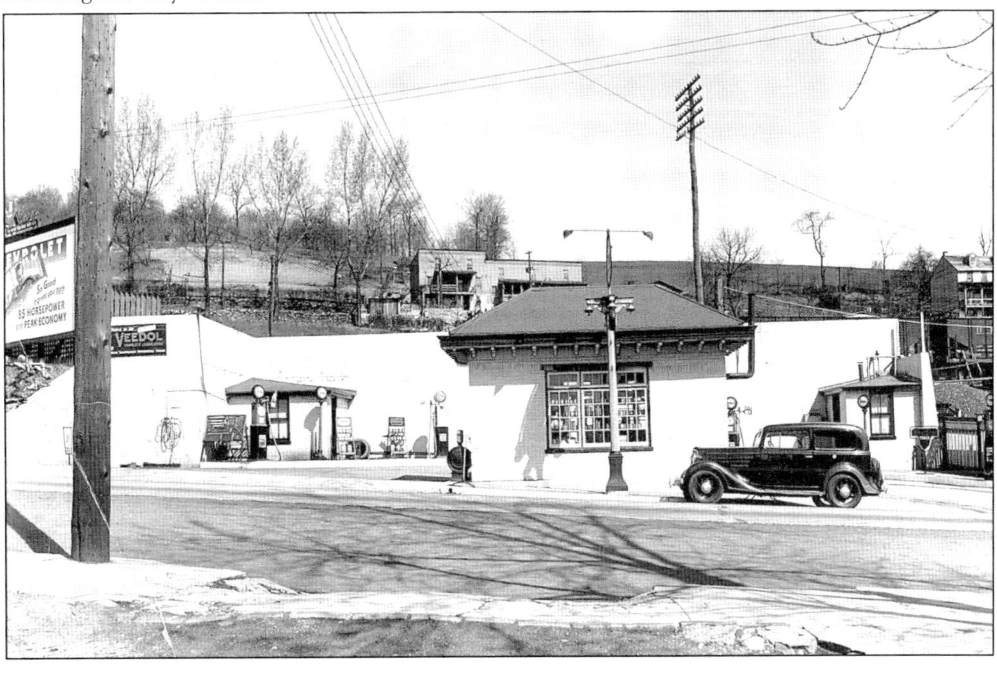

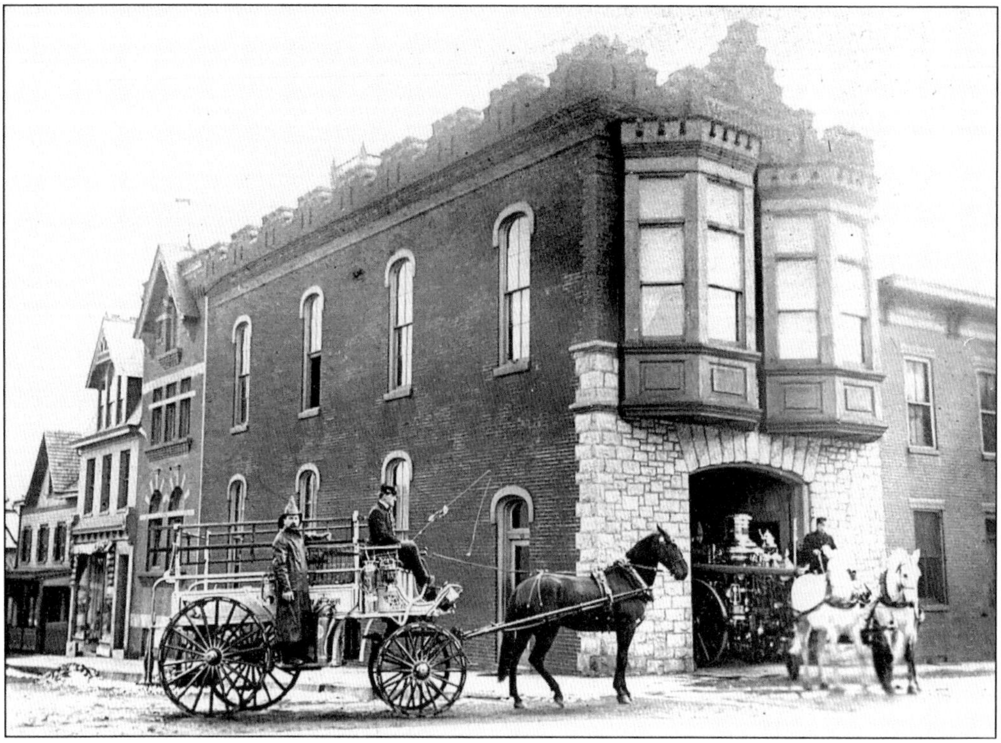

The stores of Coatesville needed protection from fire. The above photograph shows the Washington Hose Company in the Nagle building at Third Avenue and Chestnut Street. The photograph below shows a crowd gathering to view firefighters battling a fire in the buildings along Third Avenue. Hoses and fire apparatus are shown in the center of the image.

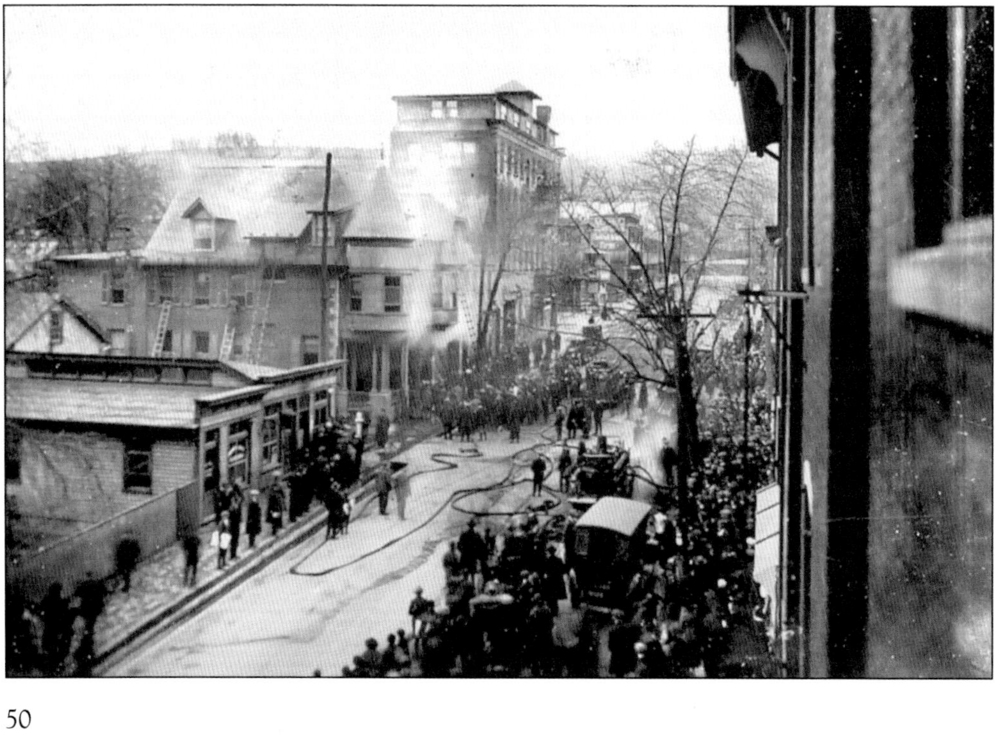

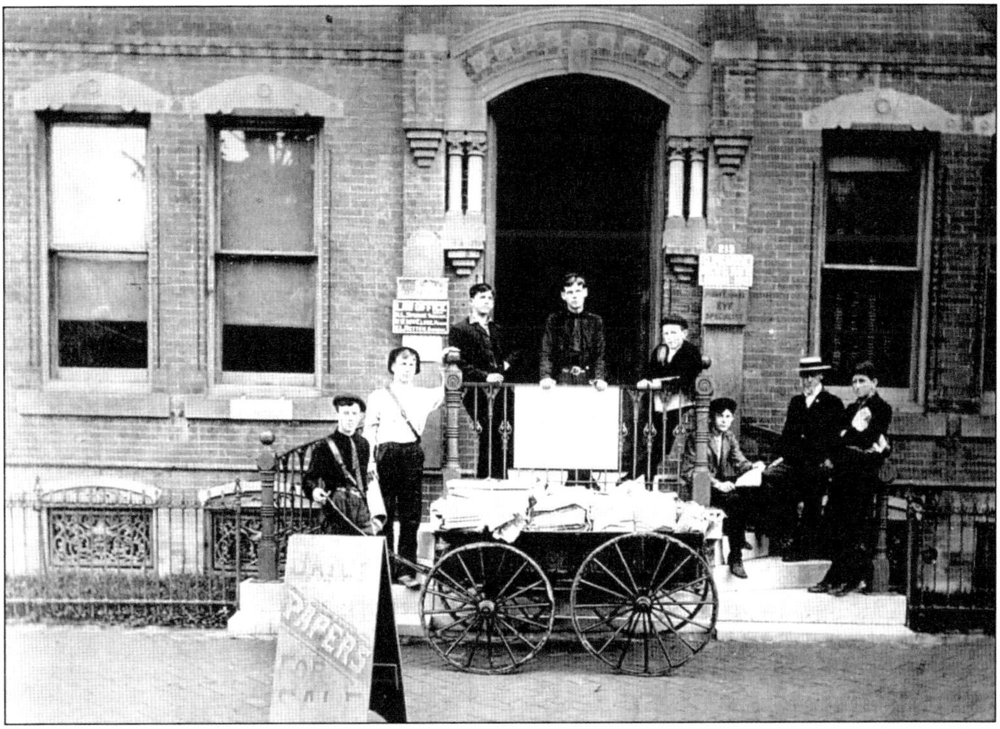

Some of the young entrepreneurs of Coatesville were newsboys. Above, young hawkers gather with their papers and their wagon in front of the C. Pearce News Agency. The McClure building, on Main Street between Second and Third Avenues, also housed a law office, where noted writer and attorney W.W. McElree worked. Below is a 1906 view of Main Street, showcasing a bicyclist.

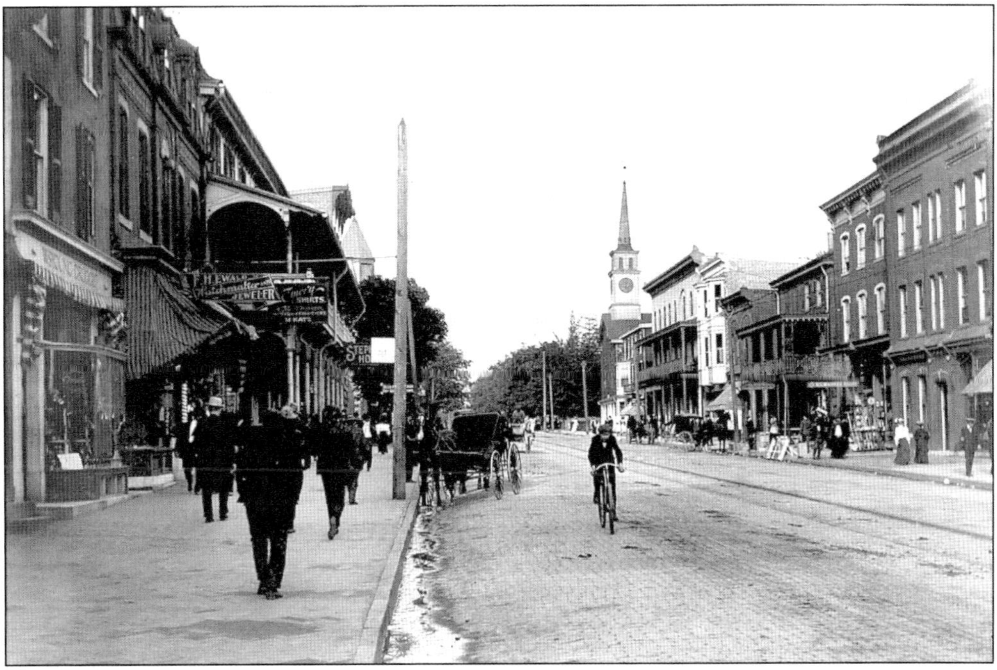

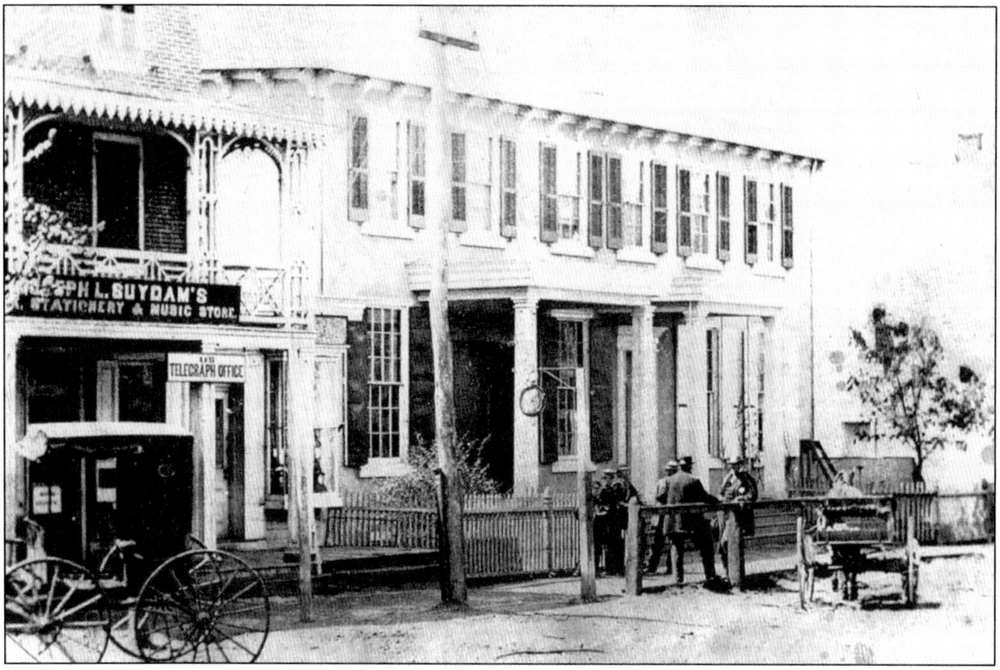

Some buildings housed a number of different services. In the photograph above, the store to the left has signs for a stationery and music store and also a telegraph office. The men and the buggy to the right are in front of the first building used by Chester Valley Bank. The photograph below shows the Chester Valley Academy, on the north side of Chestnut Street between First and Second Avenues.

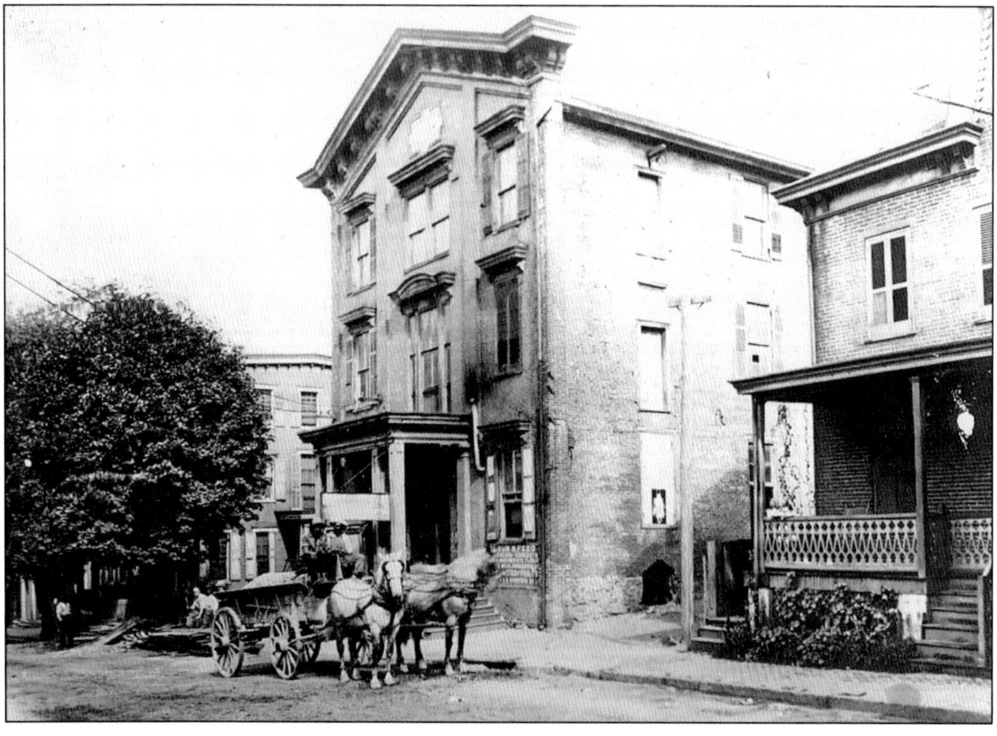

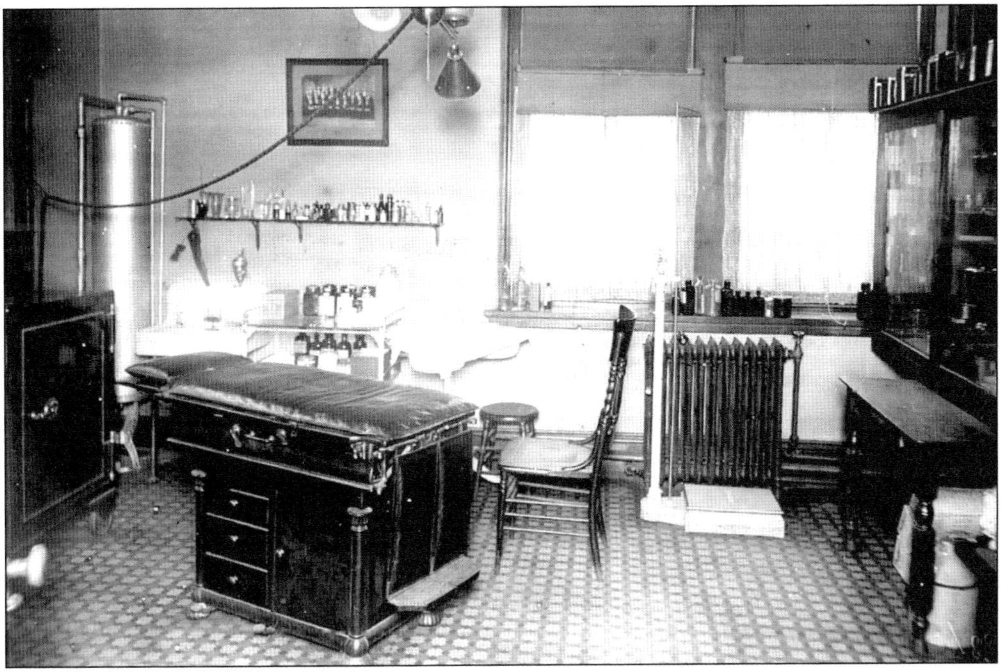

An early doctor's office in Coatesville, as seen above, included a well-lighted examination table, medicines along the walls, and a safe. For those involved in the sporting life, Coatesville had a sporting-goods store that sold baseball equipment as well as fishing and hunting gear. An oversized baseball is hung from the ceiling in the image below.

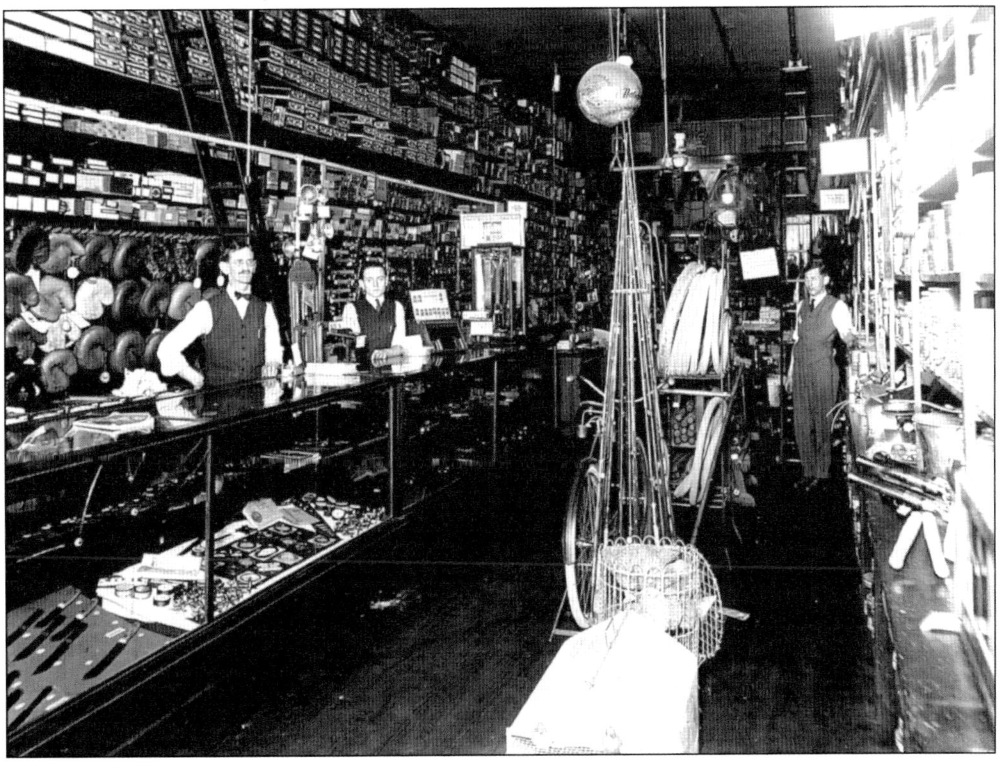

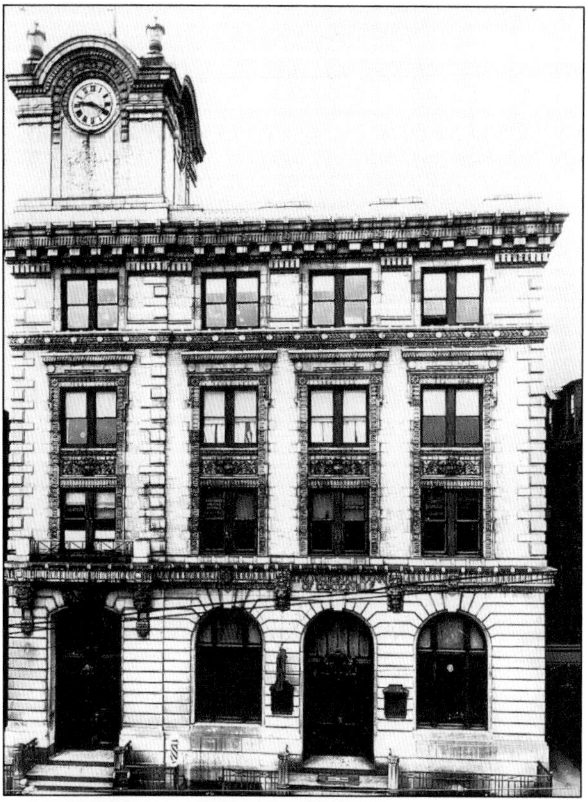

The National Bank of Coatesville building, with its clock, was a landmark in Coatesville for years. Designed by Watson and Hucker Architects, the building was constructed in 1906. It is listed on the National Register of Historic Places. The photograph below shows an interior view of the Main Street building.

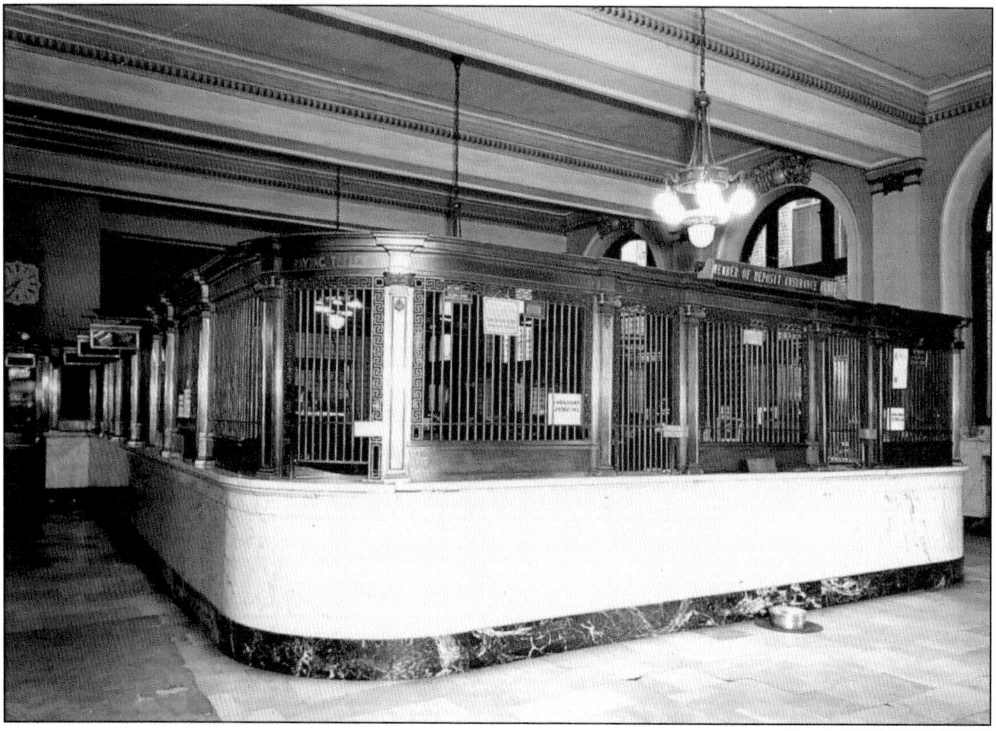

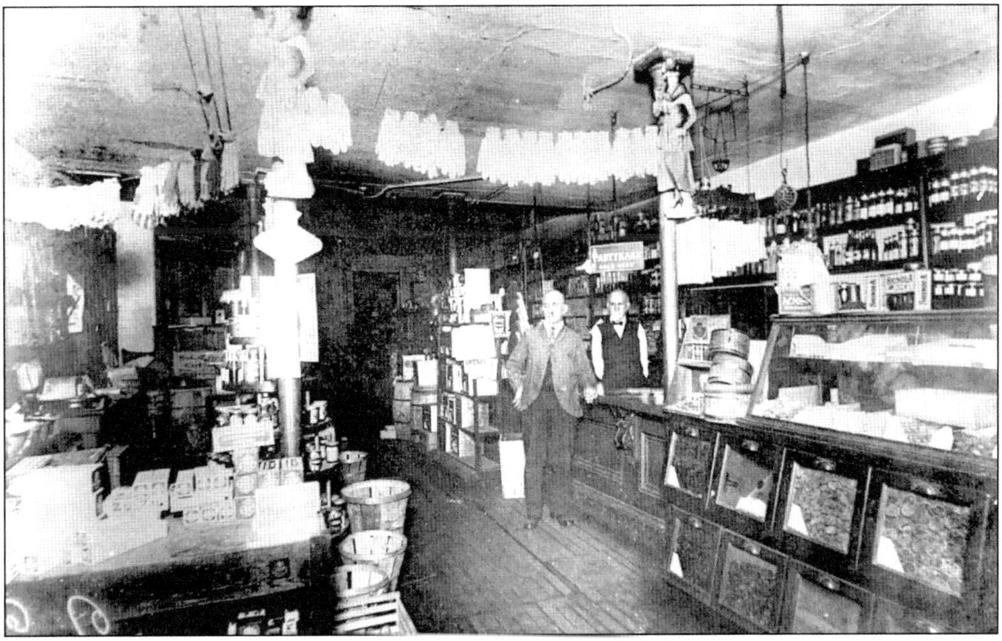

Tastykakes have been a confectionary staple of the Philadelphia area for years. In the photograph above, an early display sign in a Coatesville grocery store advertises Tastykakes. The view below of Main Street shows both the Hotel Taylor and Hotel Coatesville, on opposite sides of the street.

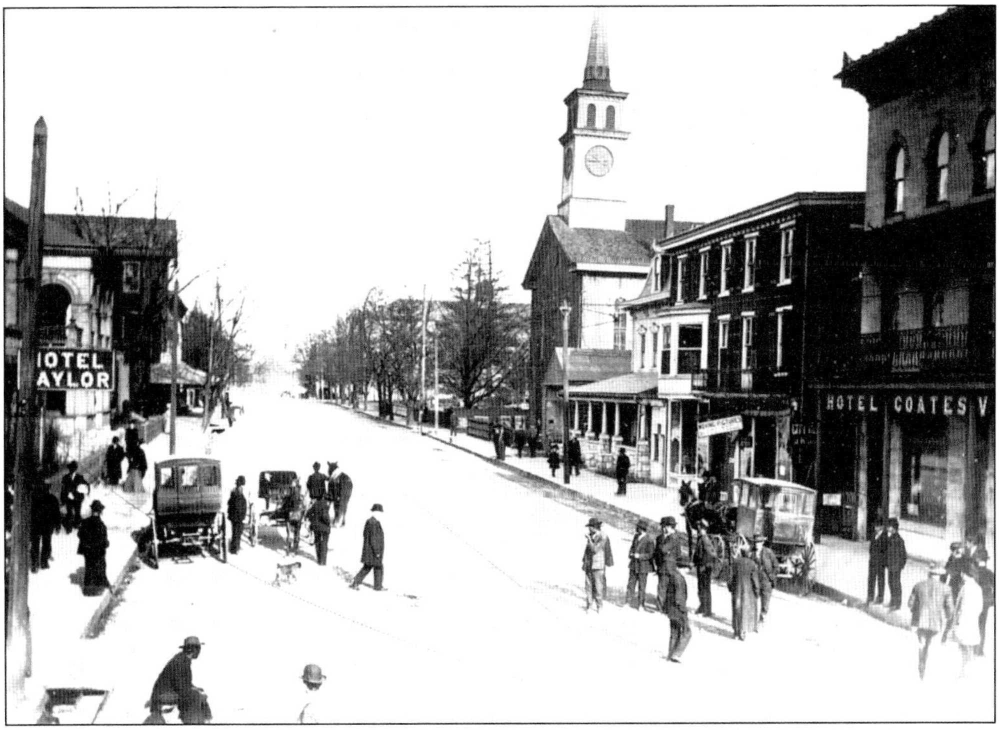

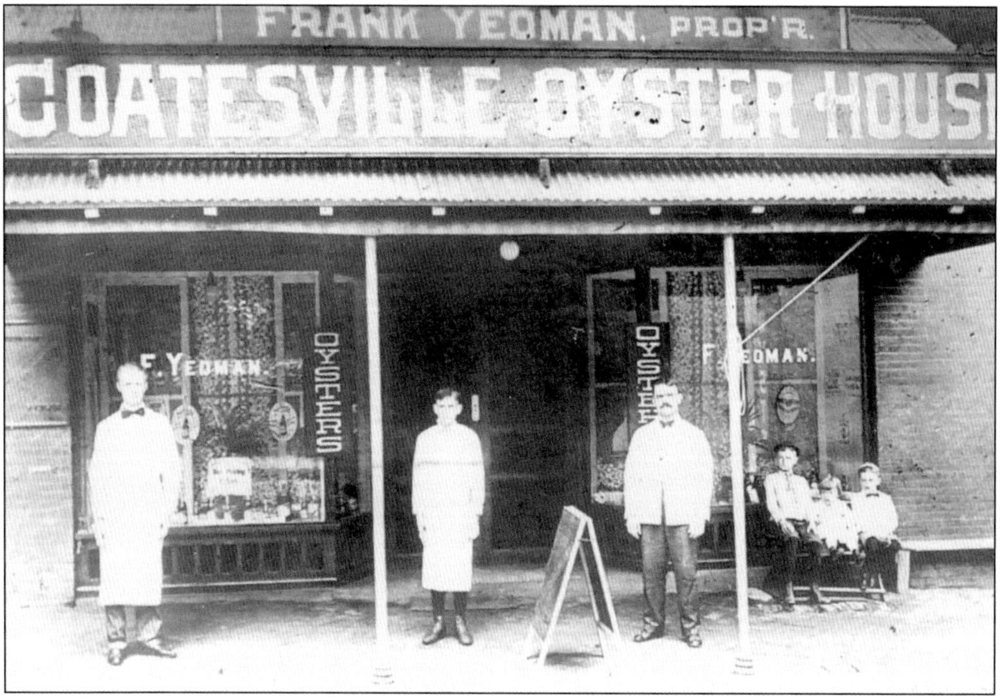

The Coatesville Oyster House, under the proprietorship of Frank Yeoman, prospered in the town. Shown above are some of the employees and children outside the eatery. Below is the Victorian-style building that once housed Mast's Department Store. It is now home to the Coatesville Cultural Society.

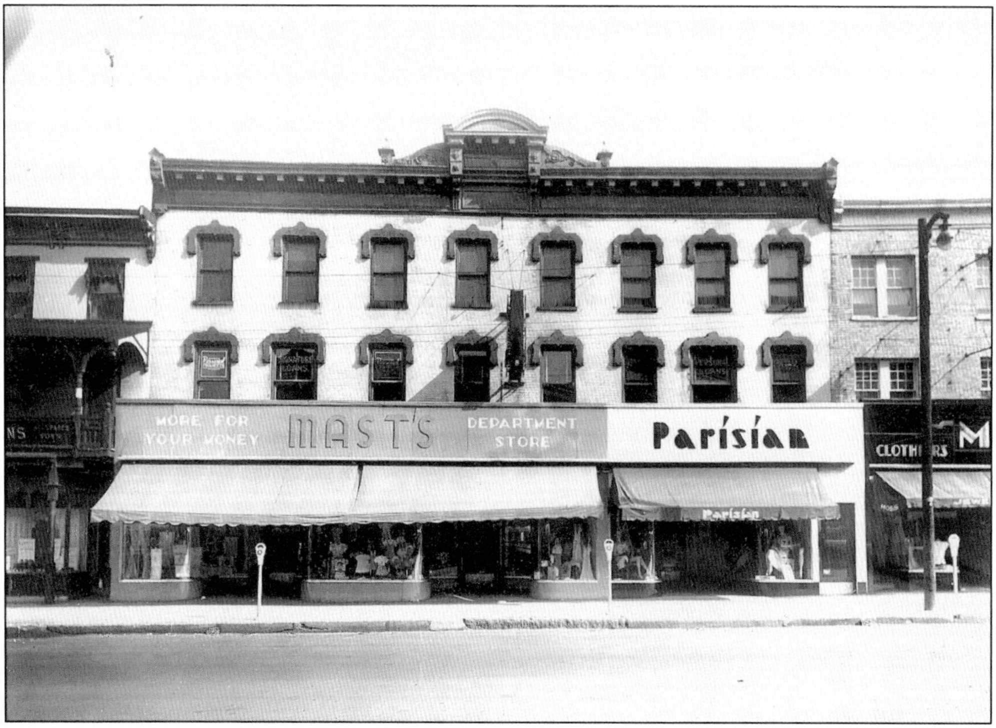

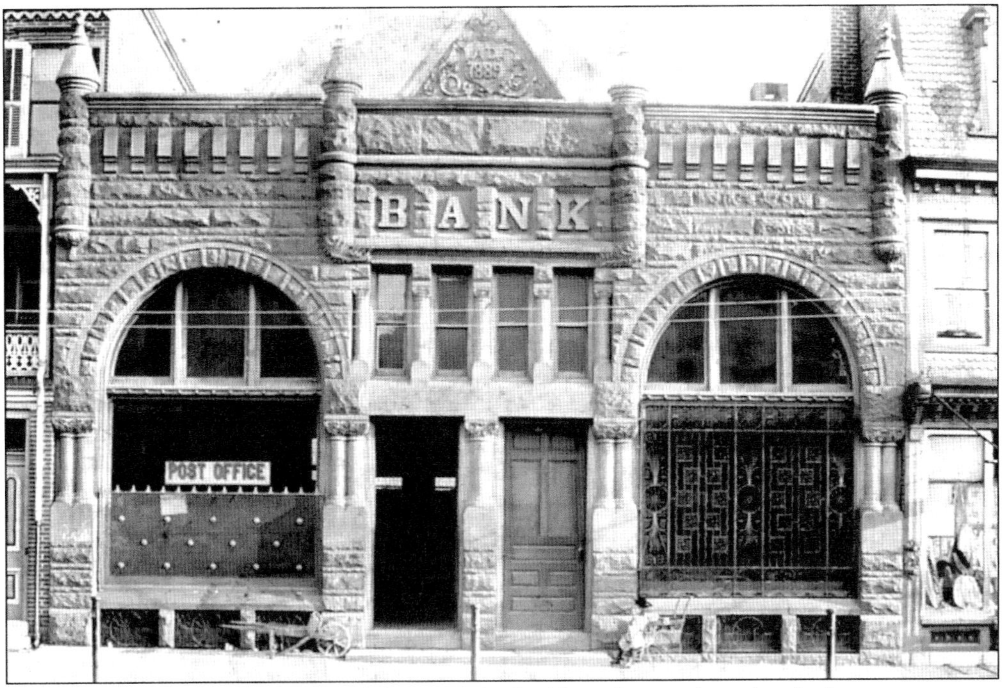

Located on Main Street at Second Avenue, the building shown above has had many uses over the years. It has housed the post office, the National Bank of Coatesville, and the *Coatesville Record*, the city's daily newspaper. The photograph below shows the Chester Valley Bank building on Main Street, near First Avenue.

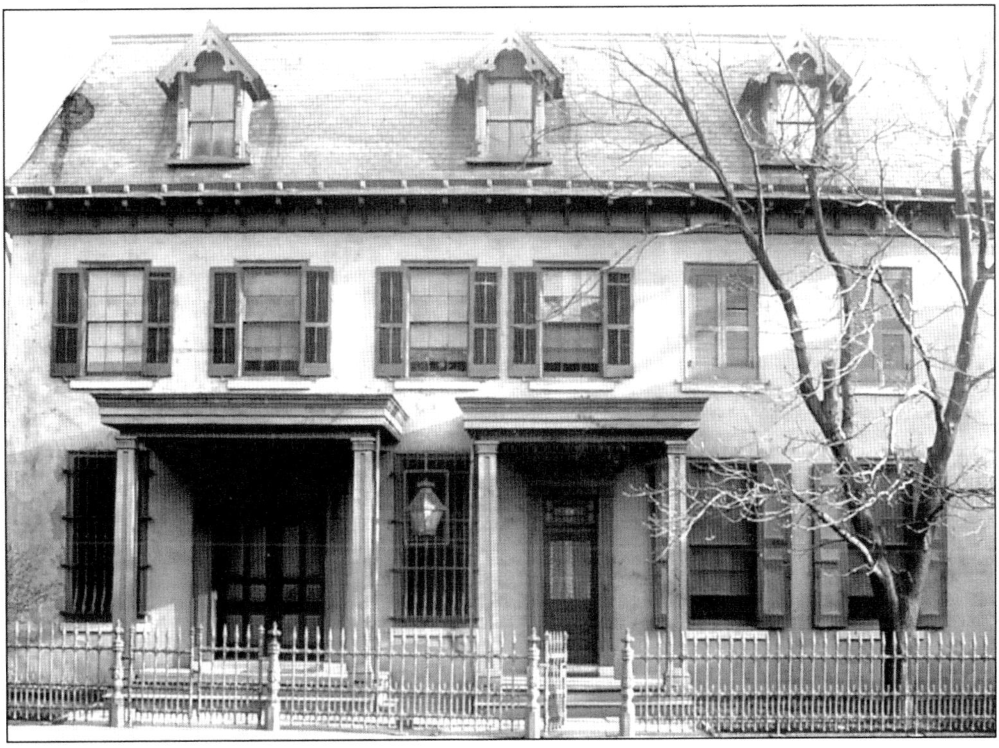

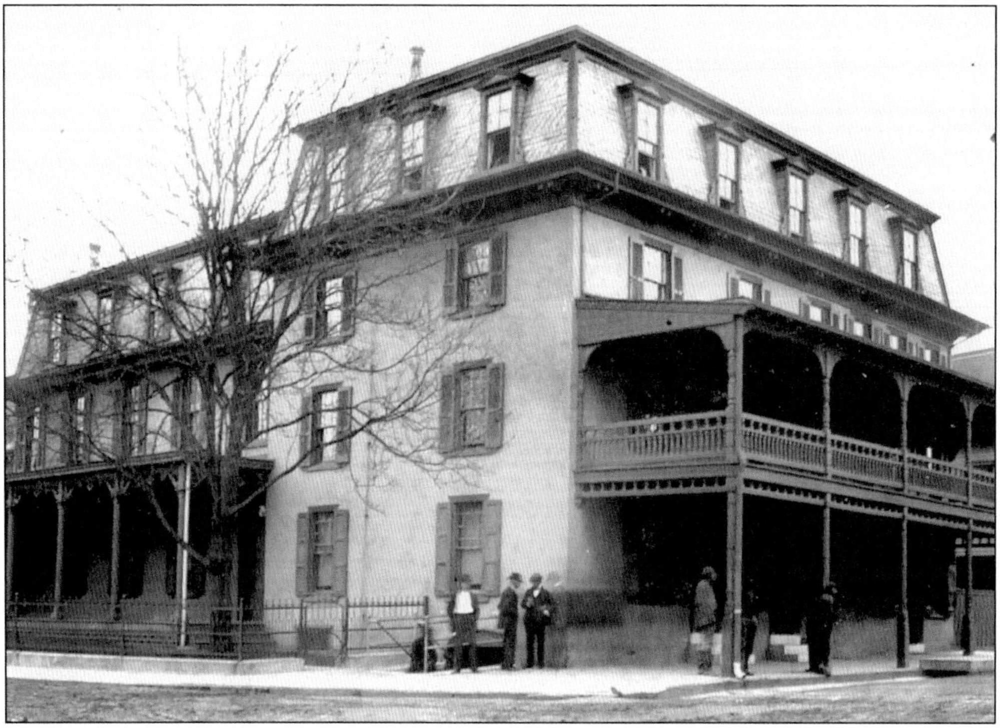

During the early days of Coatesville, the Speakman House, pictured above, was a popular hotel and gathering place. It was located at the northeast corner of Main Street and First Avenue. Shown below is the Grand Hotel, which stood on the north side of Main Street.

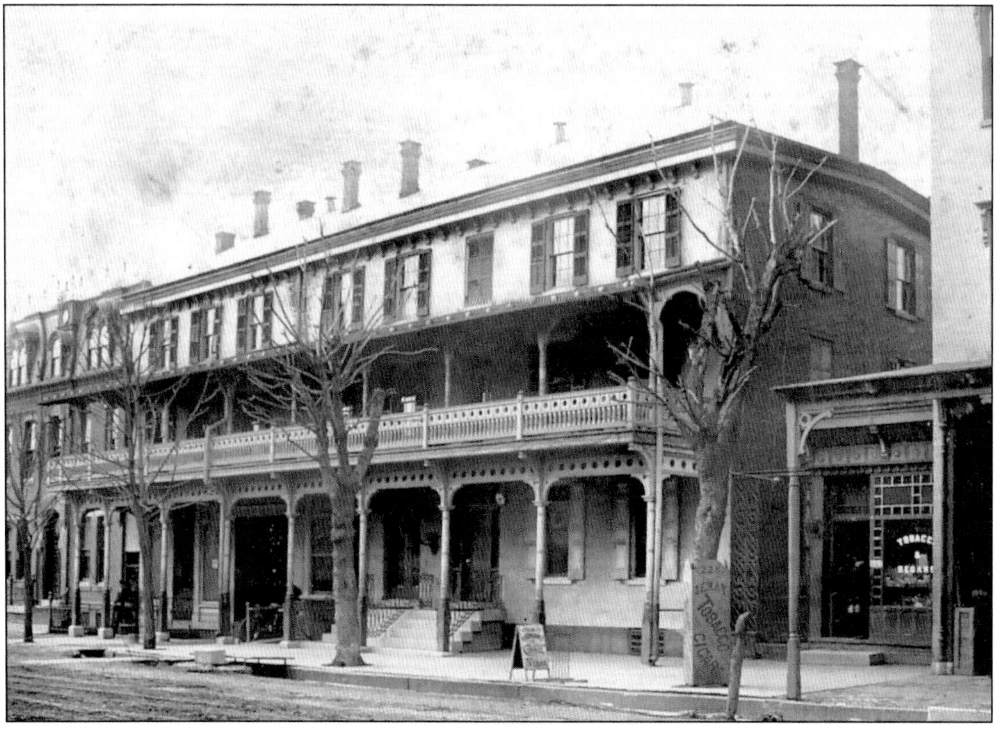

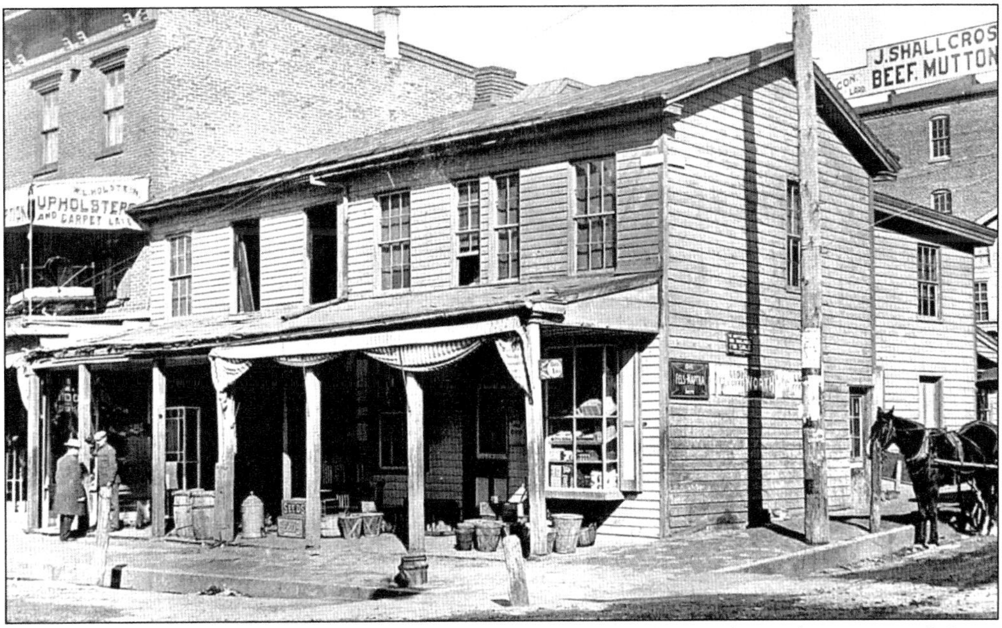

In the image above, signs on the corner of the building of the Heck Brothers General Store advertise hot coffee and Fels Naptha soap. Above Wickersham's Notion Store was the W.L. Holstein Upholsterer and Carpet Layer store, to the left of Heck's. Russell Brothers Restaurant and Jackson and Weaver Shoe Store are both visible here. Next to Heck's is the J. Shallcross Beef and Mutton business. The photograph below shows Main Street *c.* 1910.

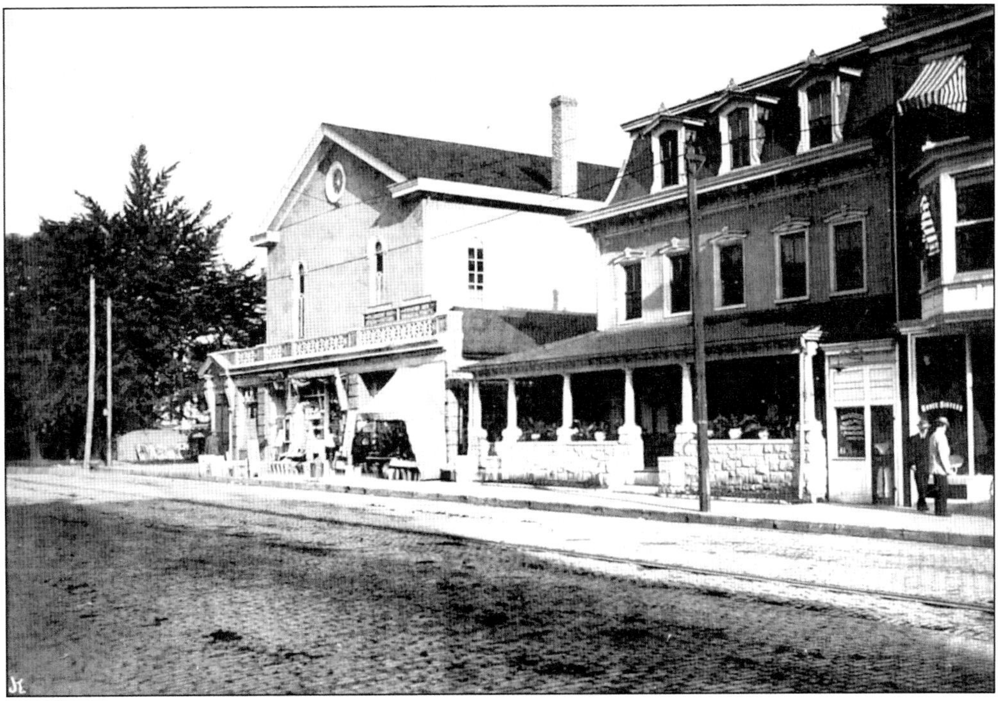

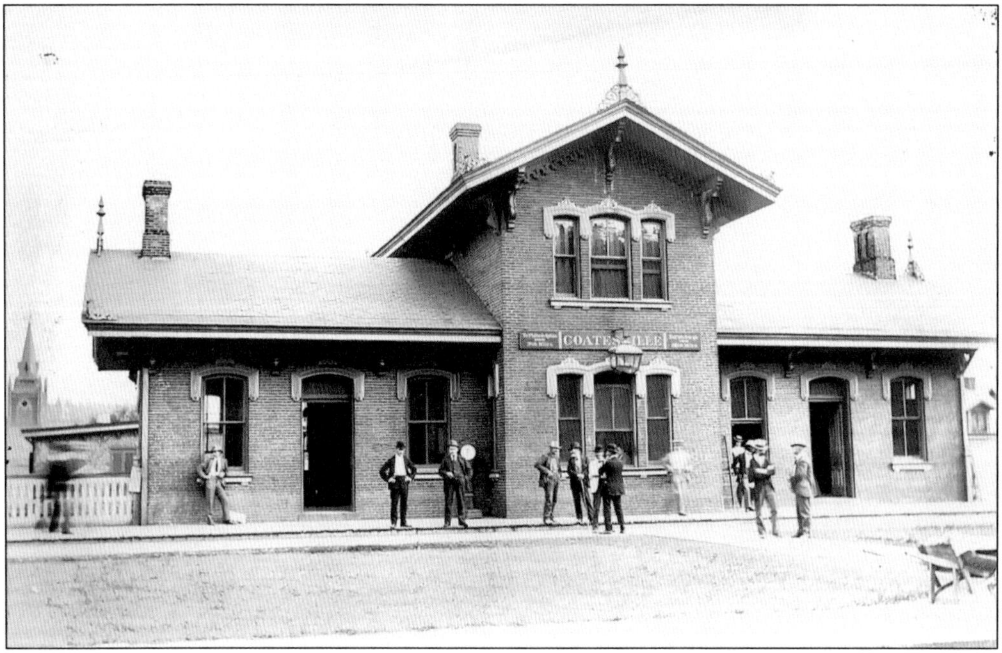

The Pennsylvania Railroad passenger station was a busy place during Coatesville's commercial days, as it brought riders to the city. The Pennsylvania Railroad also had a freight station in Coatesville, as shown in the photograph below. Railroad lines played an important part in the development of Coatesville, especially its businesses.

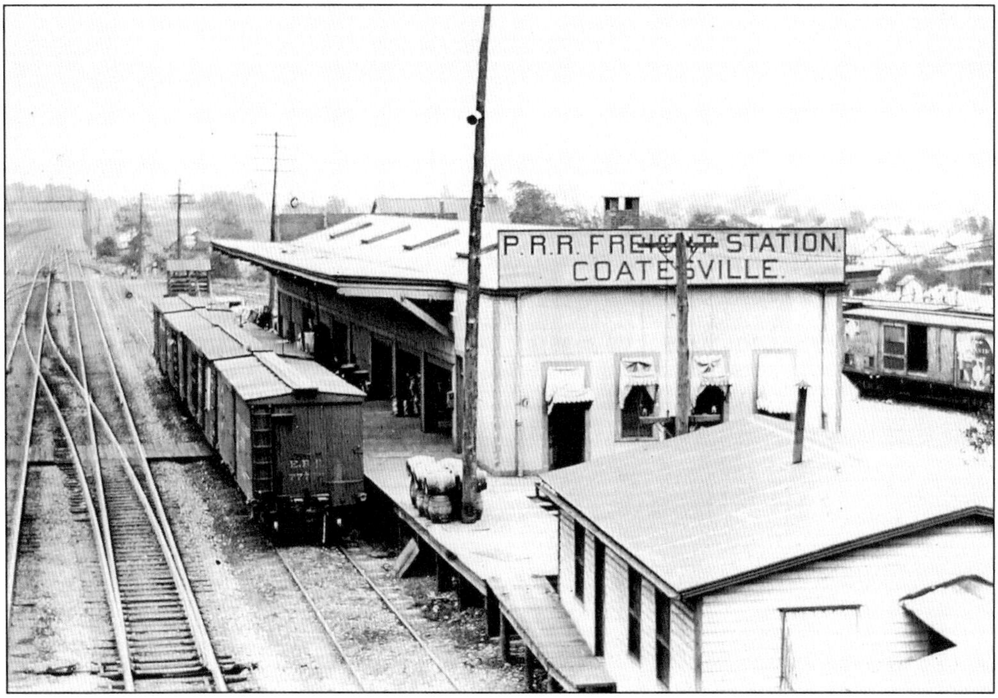

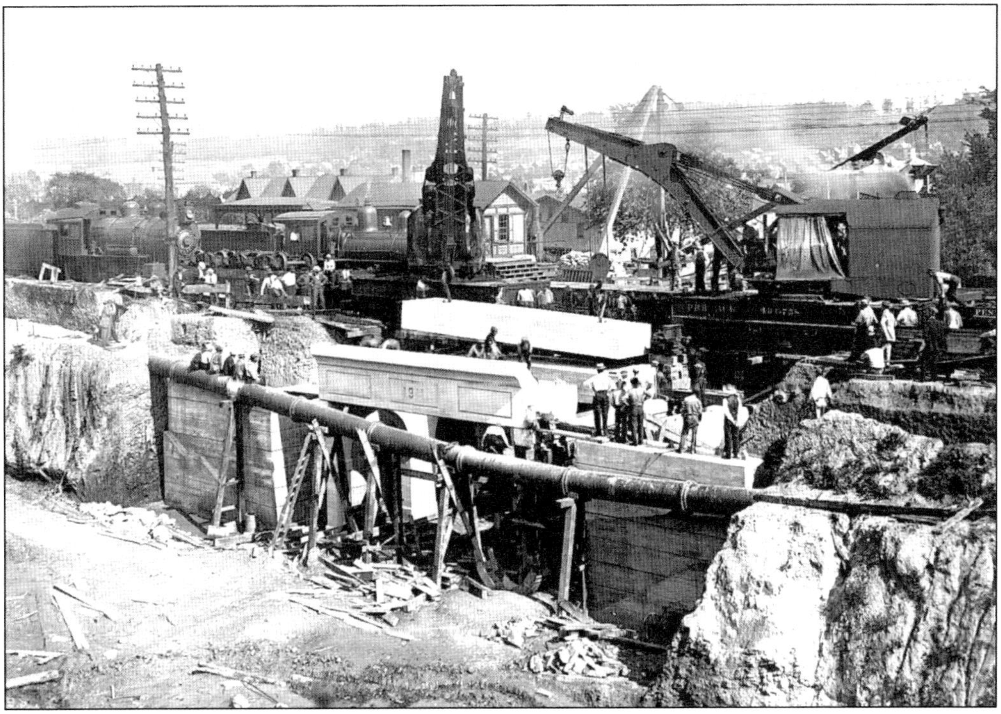

As Coatesville's commercial and residential sections expanded, both the road and railroad systems needed improvement. Both of the photographs shown here were taken in 1911. Above, a 50-ton slab is being put in place as the Third Avenue subway, an underpass, is under construction. Below, the subway at Seventh and Chester Avenues is visible.

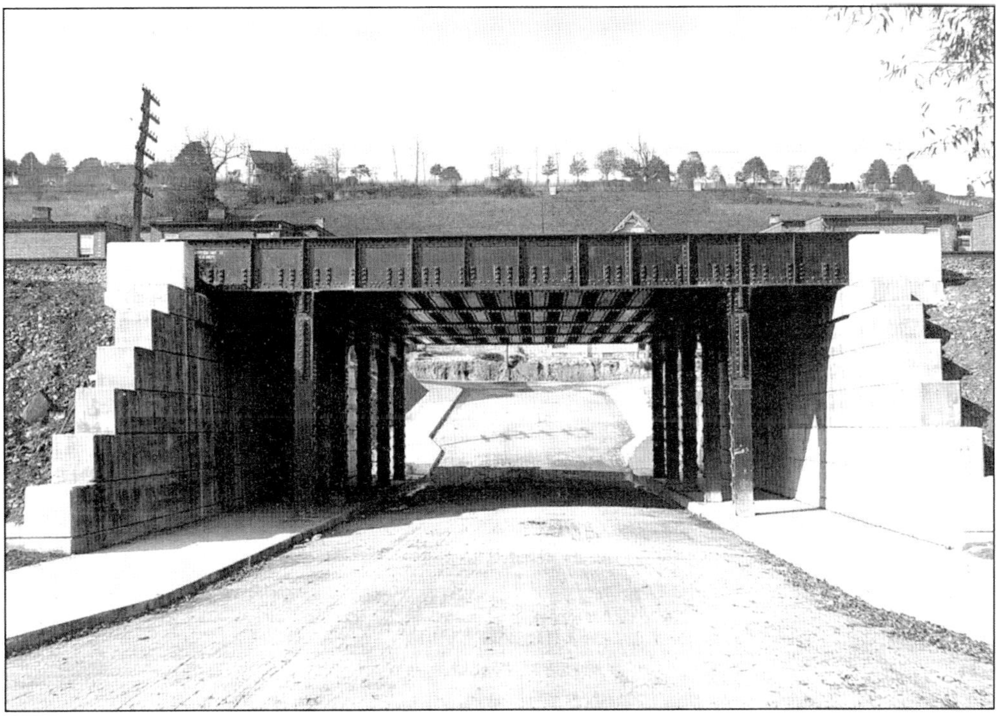

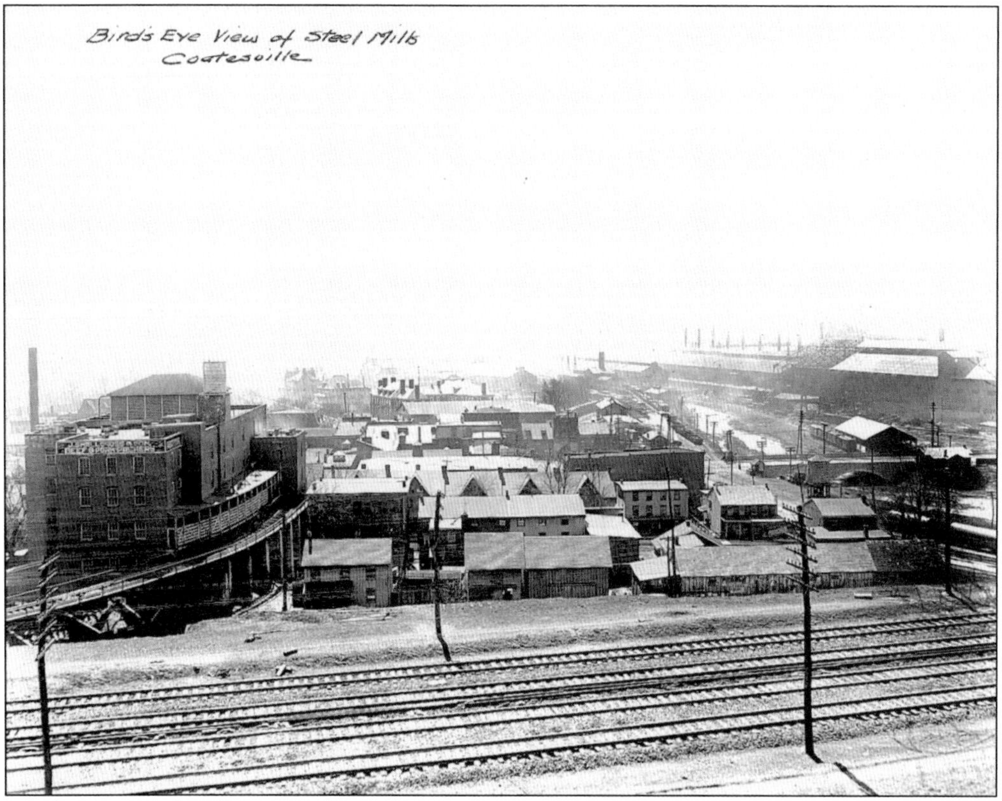

As the steel mills of Coatesville and the various businesses shown in the above photograph thrived, the town's need for public services increased. The photograph below depicts an ambulance belonging to the Washington Hose Company.

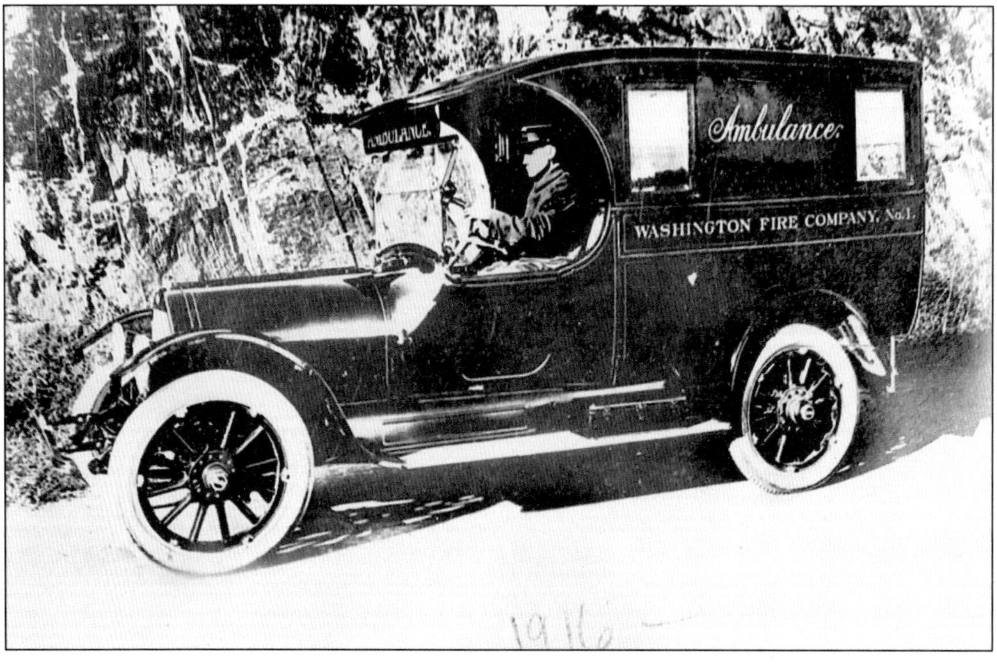

Four

COMMUNITY LIFE

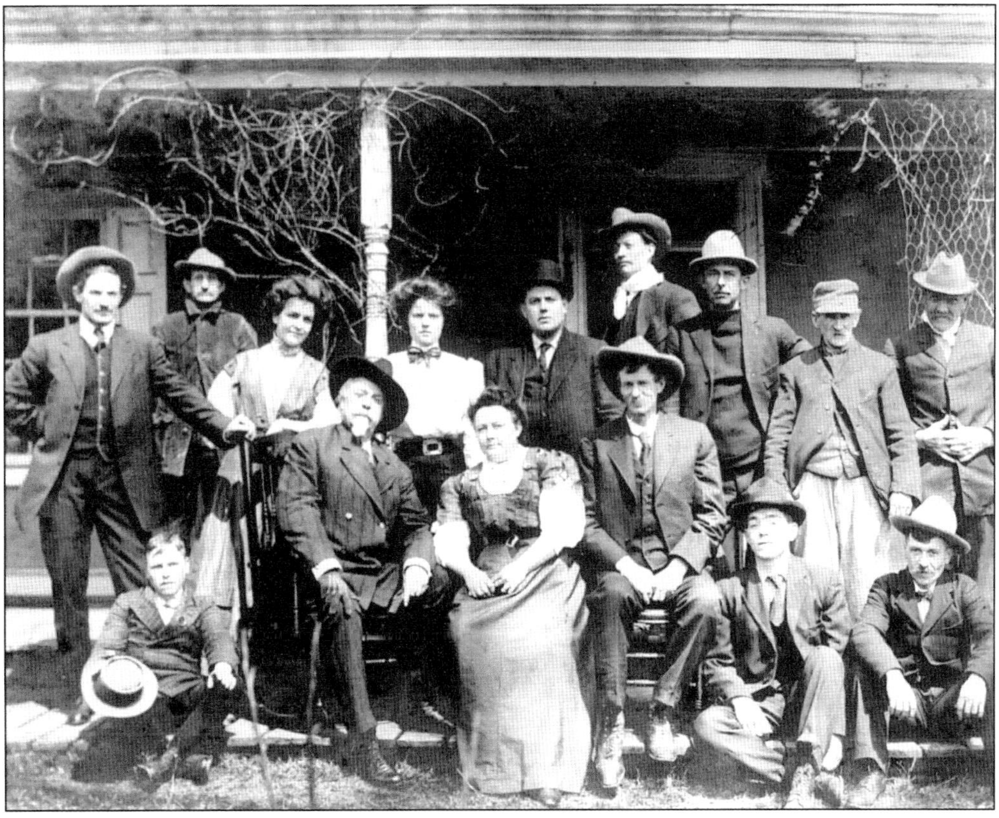

Buffalo Bill Cody and his Wild West Show called Coatesville their winter home during the 1890s. Cody (sitting in a chair to the left in the front row) was only one of a number of celebrities who lived in and around Coatesville or visited the town. Former president Theodore Roosevelt made an appearance in Coatesville in 1912.

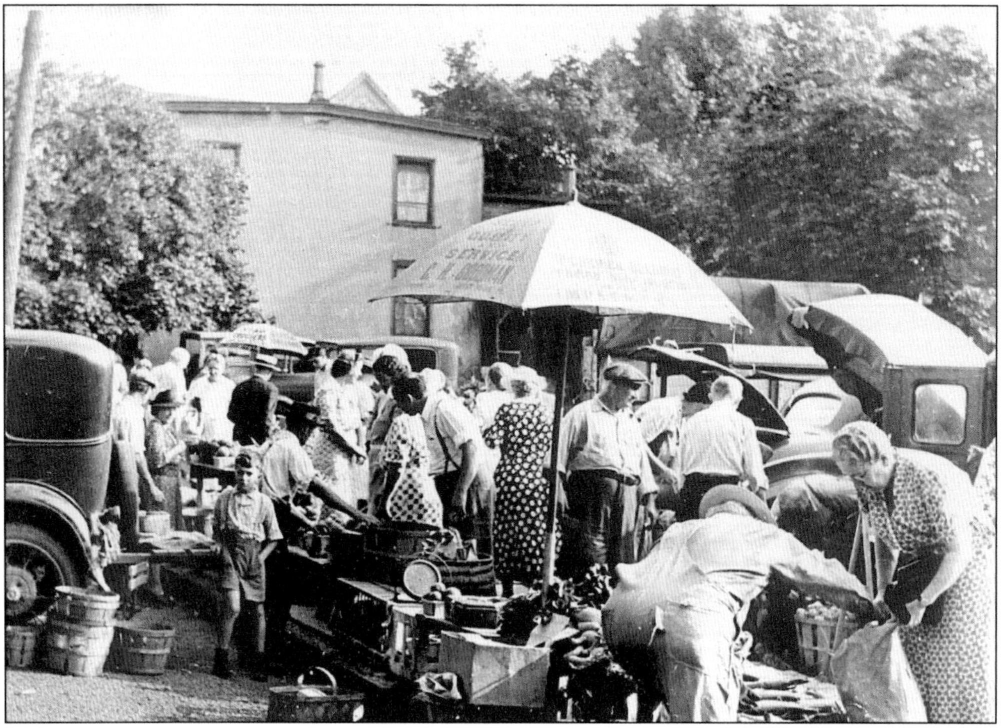

As seen in the above photograph, an open-air curb market at Fifth Avenue and Main Street in the 1930s enticed many Coatesville residents to buy fresh produce and other goods. In the photograph below, a butcher prepares food in a general store in the early 1900s.

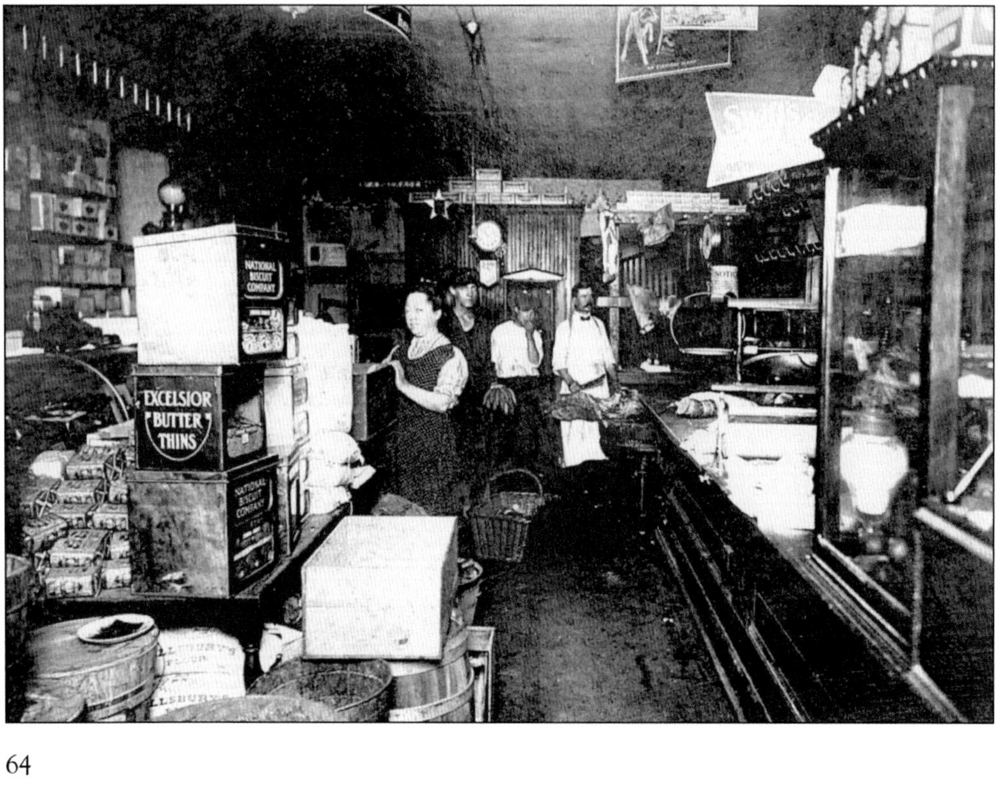

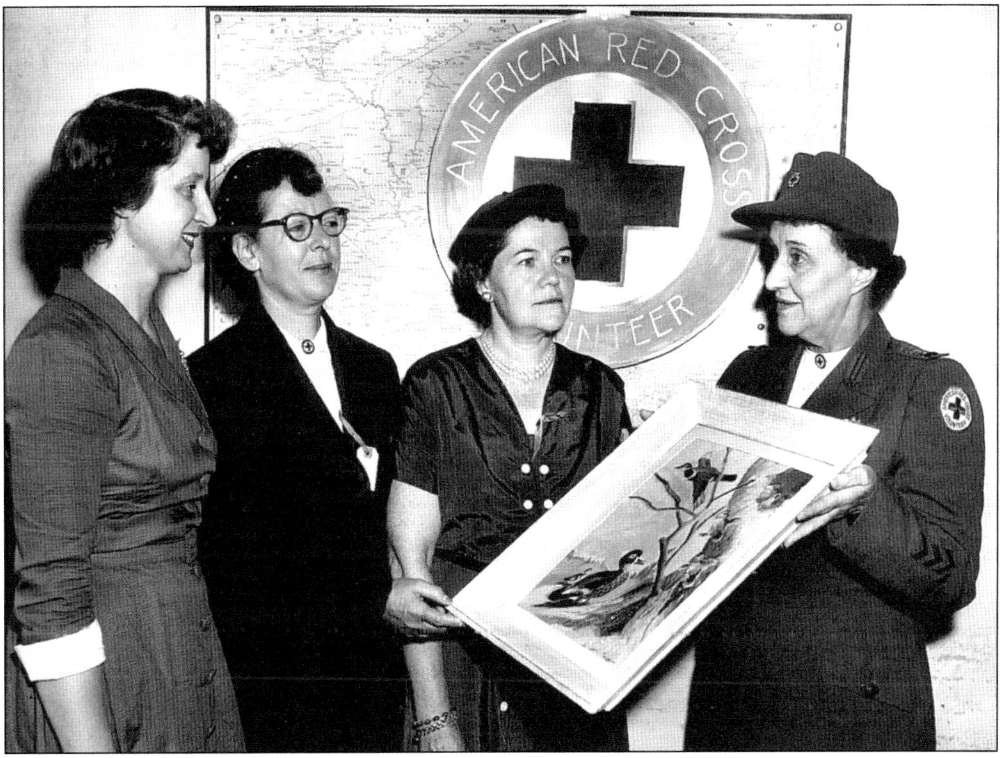

World War II called many Coatesville residents into the armed services. Many residents also served in the American Red Cross. Above, a bird painting is displayed during a volunteer event, and below, members of the local Red Cross chapter gather in front of a station wagon belonging to the eastern Pennsylvania Red Cross chapter.

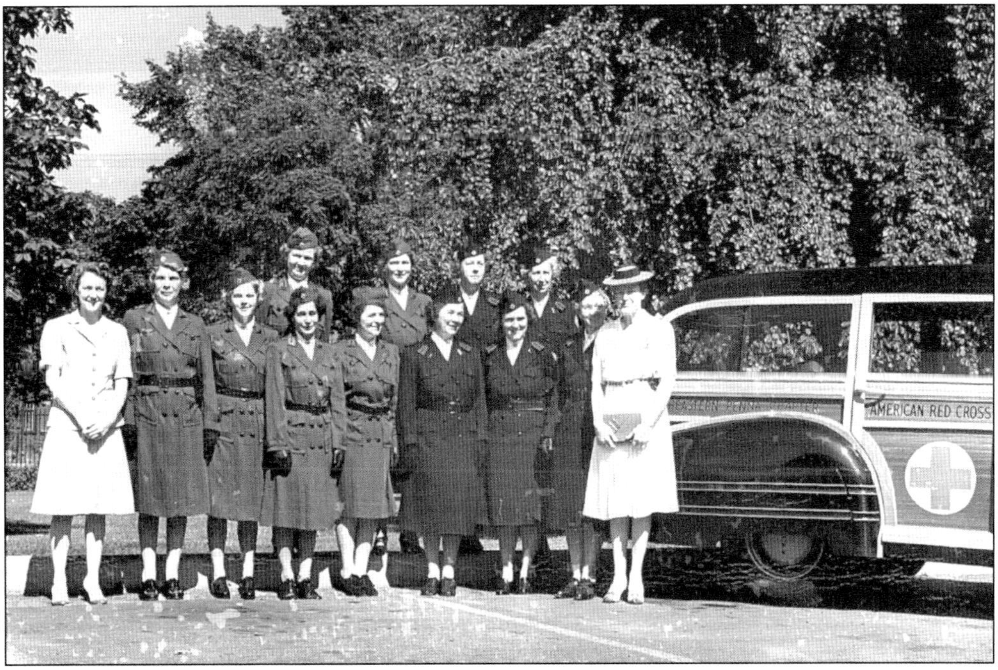

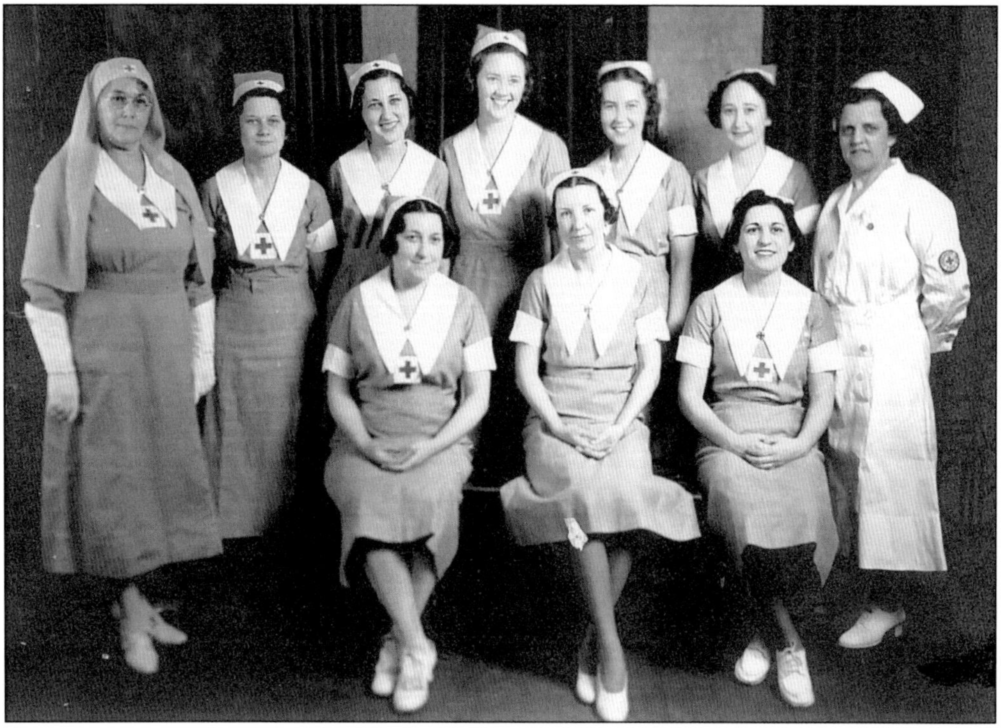

Nurses were needed in the early 1900s to staff the new Coatesville Hospital, on Strode Avenue in the town's west end. A nursing school was founded at the hospital, from which many dedicated nurses graduated over the years. The above photograph shows a group of nurses, and in the scene below, a Christmas event is being readied.

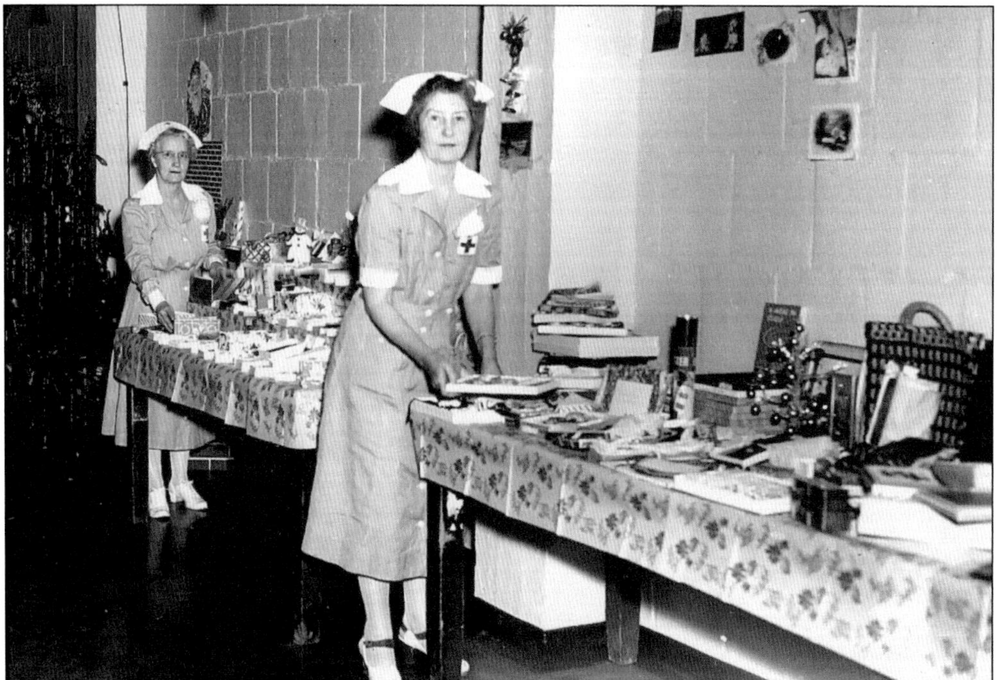

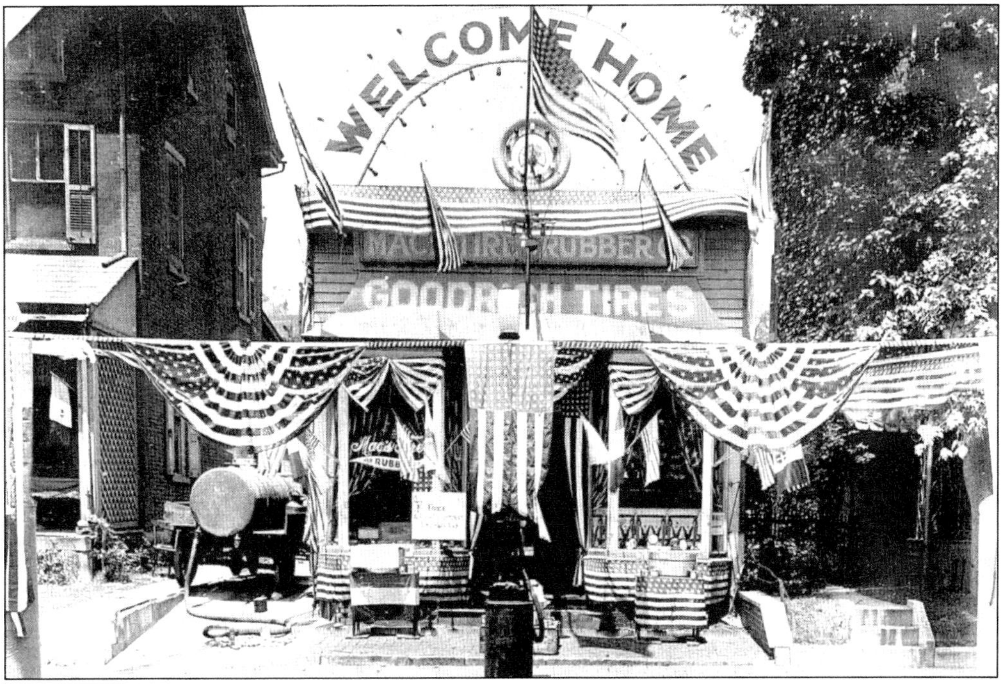

Patriotism was shown in Coatesville during both world wars. The above photograph shows a welcome home display that was constructed in 1918 at the conclusion of "the war to end all wars." In the photograph below, Boy Scouts stand guard over "aluminum donated to Uncle Sam" by the residents of "Coatesville and vicinity."

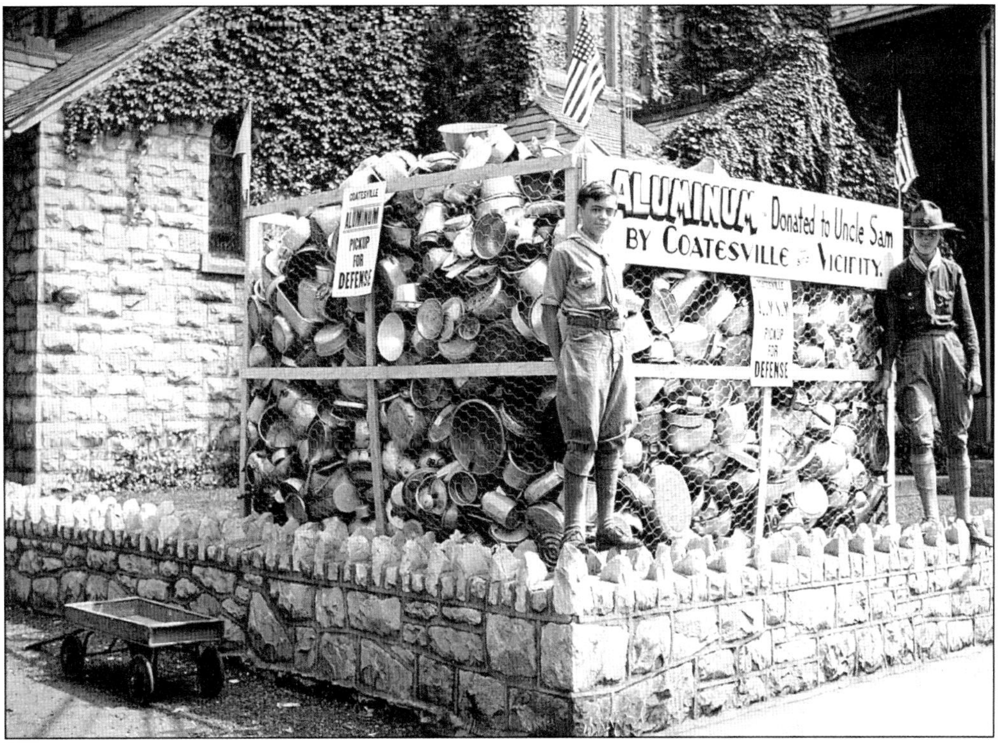

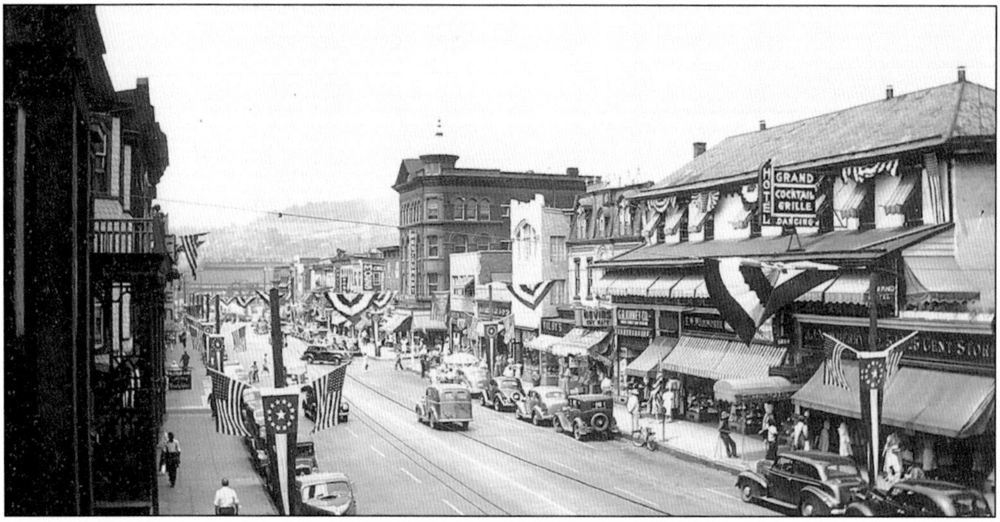

Coatesville turned out for a Fourth of July celebration in 1939 at the beginning of World War II, as shown in the above photograph. In the photograph below, a crowd gathers to hear Maj. Gen. Smedley D. Butler, a Chester County–born war hero, speak at the YMCA auditorium on Main Street in Coatesville in 1931.

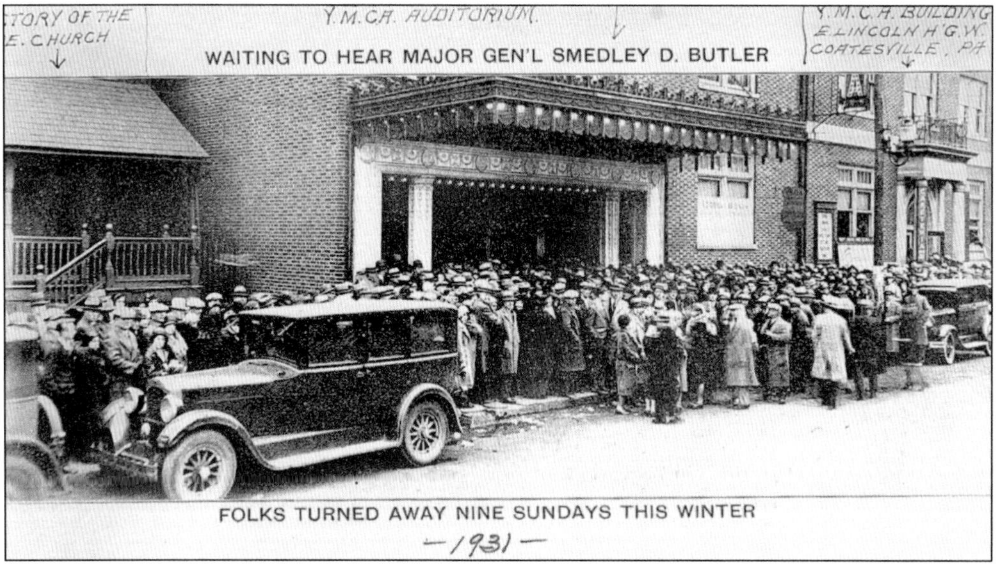

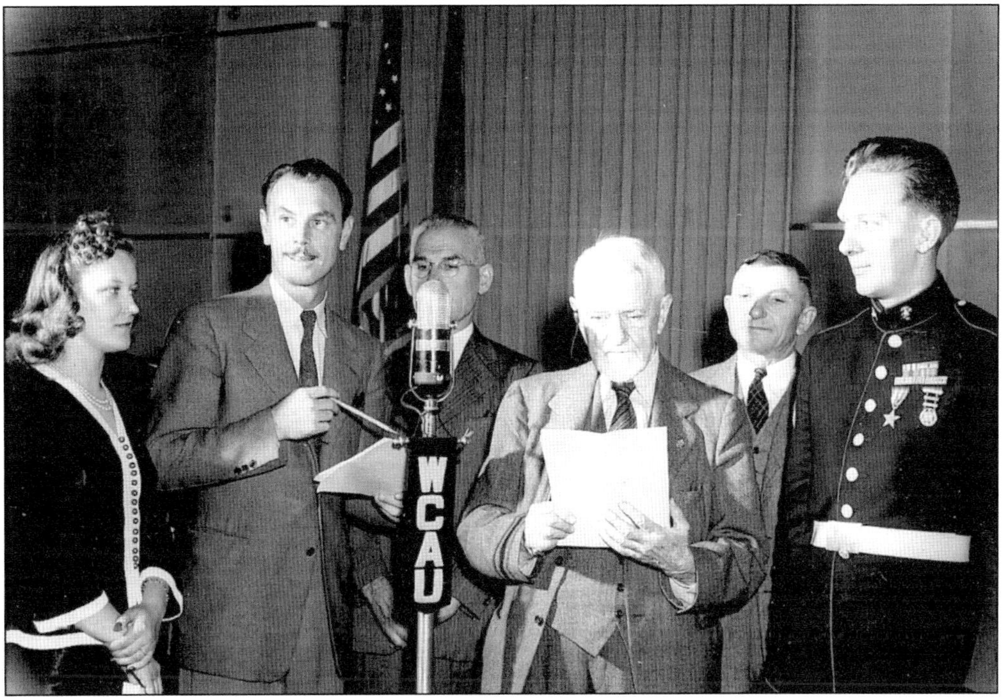

In the photograph above, Lukens senior vice president C.L. Huston takes part in a radio program on station WCAU with a U.S. Marine officer in the 1940s. Lukens was a key manufacturer for the armed forces. The other photograph, showing a U.S. Navy seaman, was taken in Belt's Studio on Second Avenue in Coatesville.

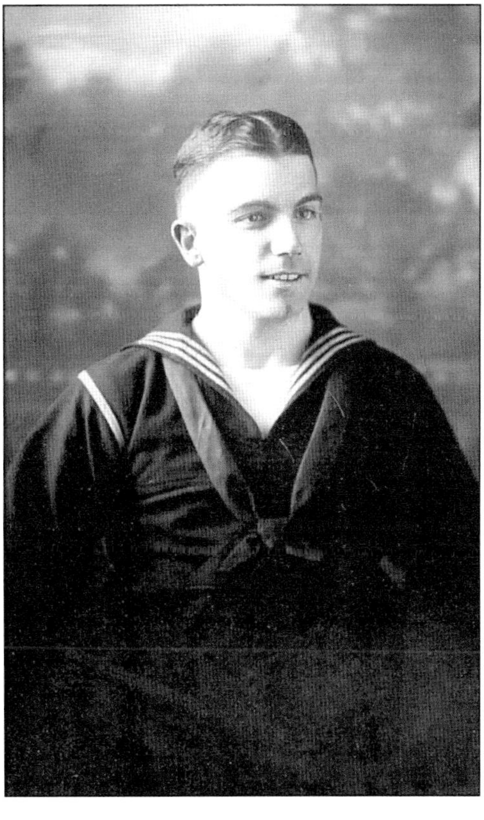

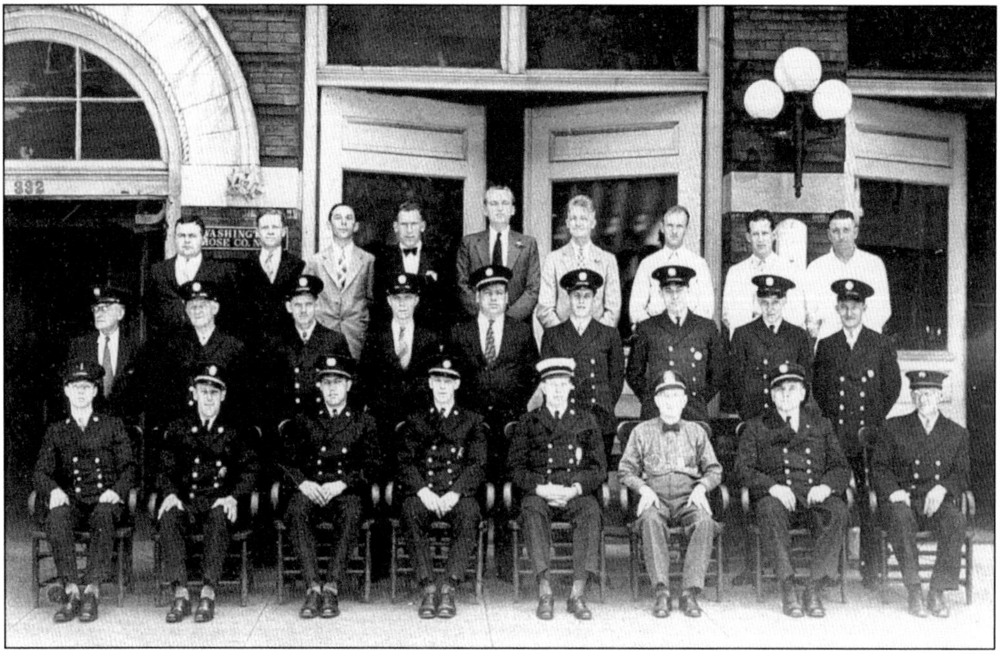

Fire company volunteers were active members of the Coatesville community, with three companies protecting the city for many years. In the above photograph, members of the Washington Hose Company pose in front of their building, while in the photograph below, Brandywine Fire Company members gather for an event during World War II. The Brandywine Fire Company received its charter in 1898.

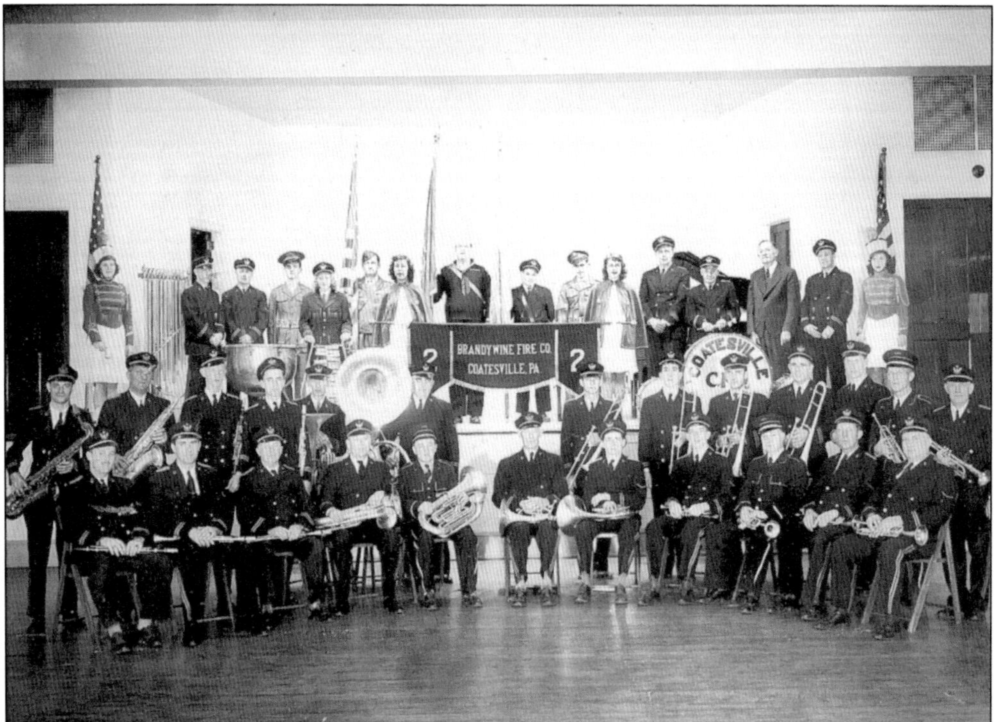

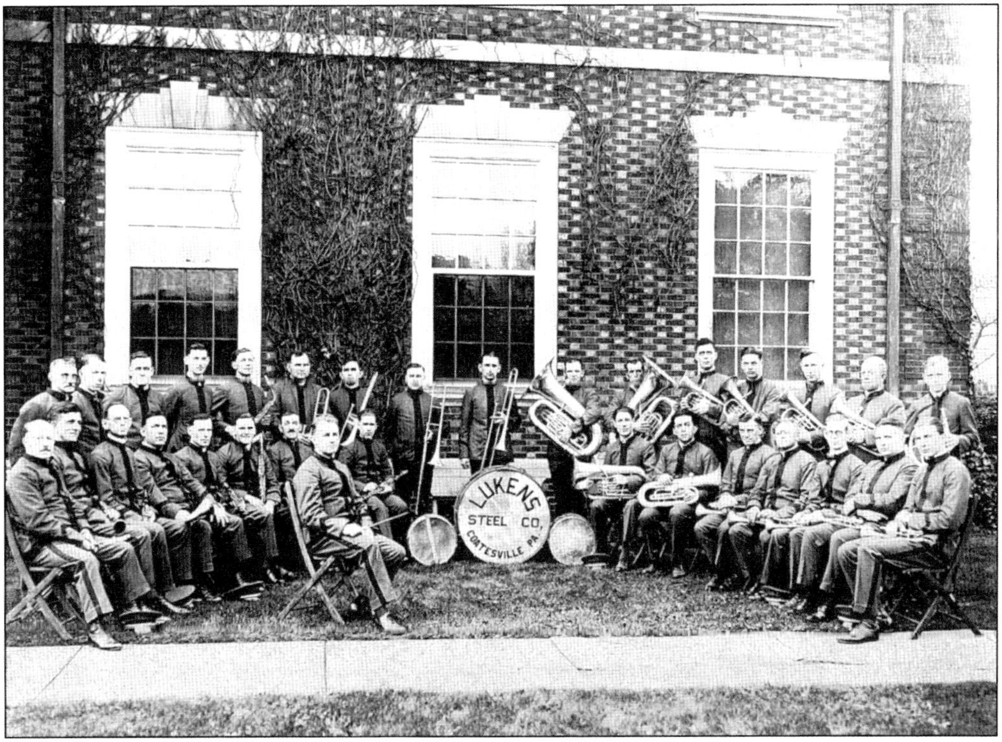

Local bands played at many events in Coatesville over the years. The Lukens Steel Company Band, shown above *c.* 1915, has performed for more than a century. The Star Band, below, was active in the early part of the 20th century.

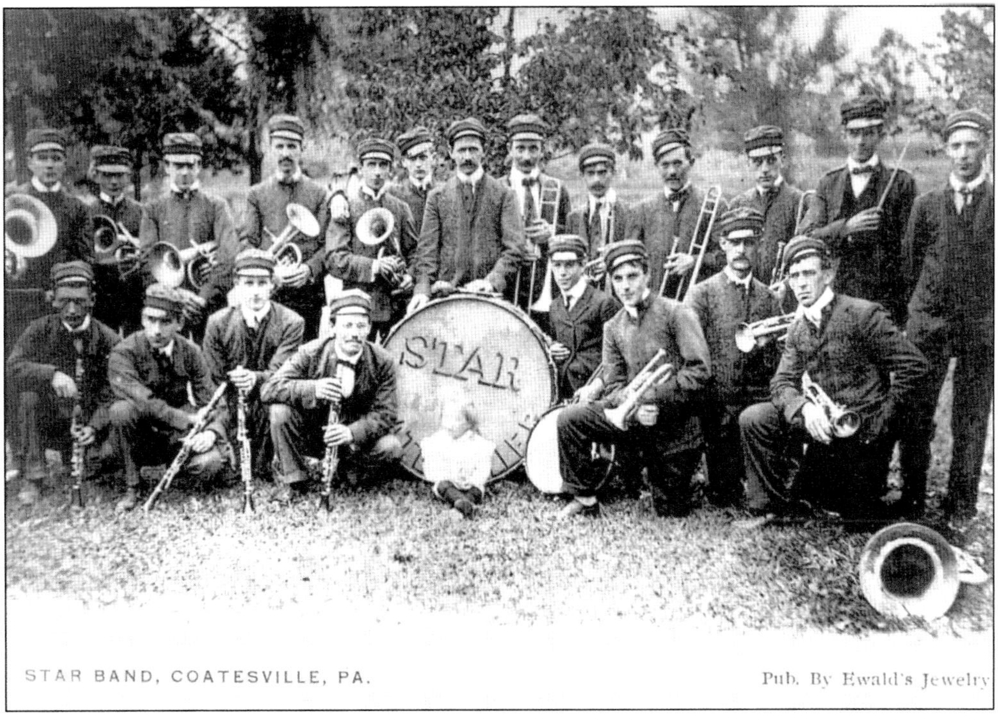

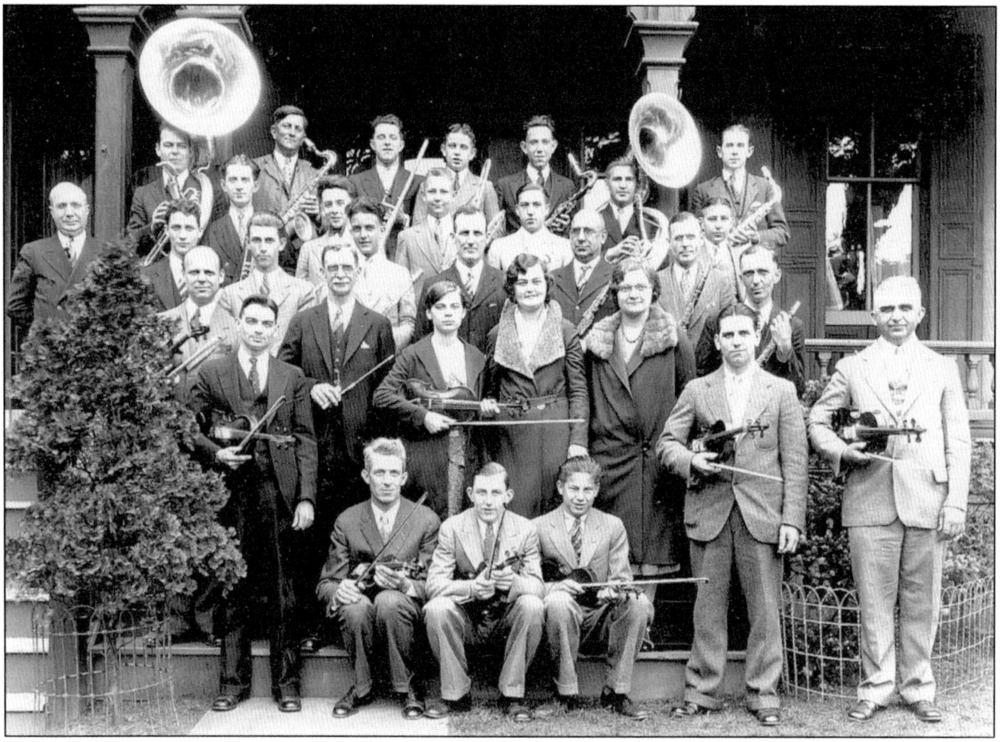

Different organizations formed musical groups in the town. In the above photograph, young musicians pose in front of a Coatesville home, while in the image below, another group, with its leader holding a baton, poses for a photographer. Music was an important part of life in Coatesville.

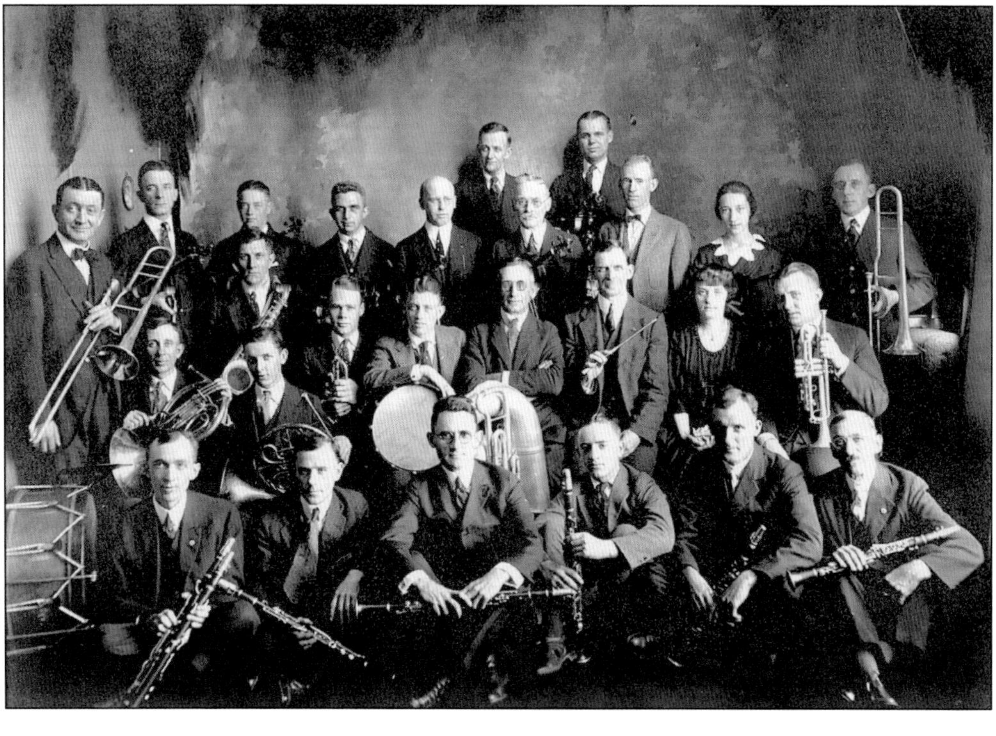

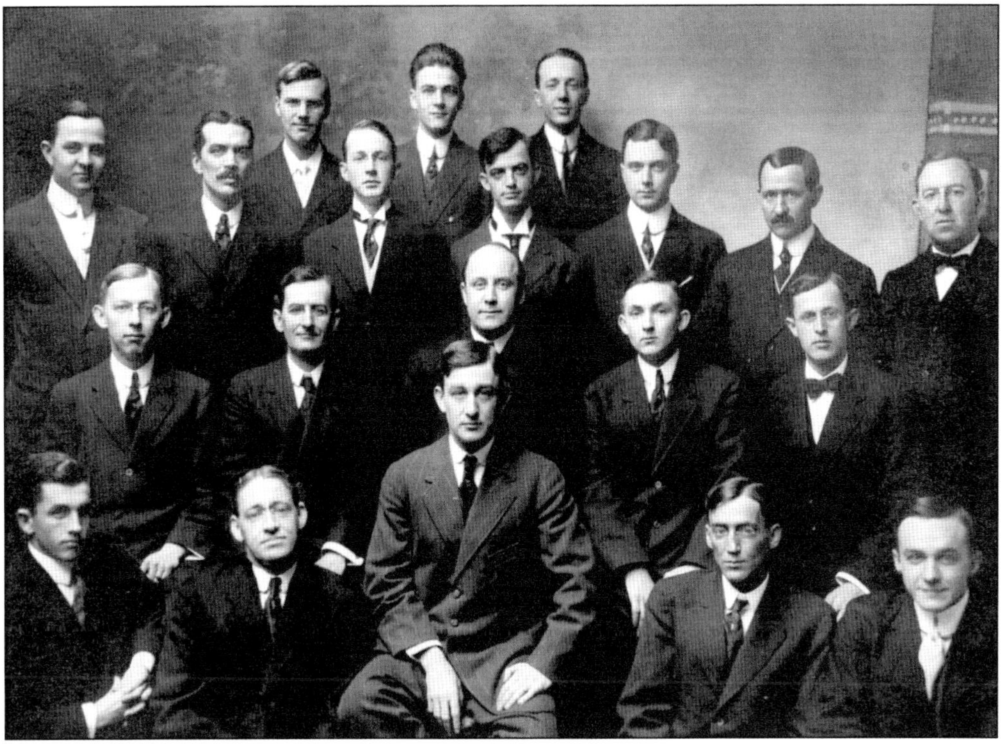

The Washingtonians was a singing group. Its members, from left to right, are shown here: (first row) Sharp Eastburn, Benjamin Fernan, W.G. Gordon, John Maynard, and Earl Neely; (second row) William Manship, Frank Burroughs, Guy Griswold, Ralph Freel, and Frank Penneger; (third row) Minor Ressel, Frank Soule, unidentified, Guy Bailey, Lewis McClain, Norman Steen, and G. Ford; (fourth row) Earl Duncan and Ashmore Johnson. The Mandolin Club is shown in the photograph below.

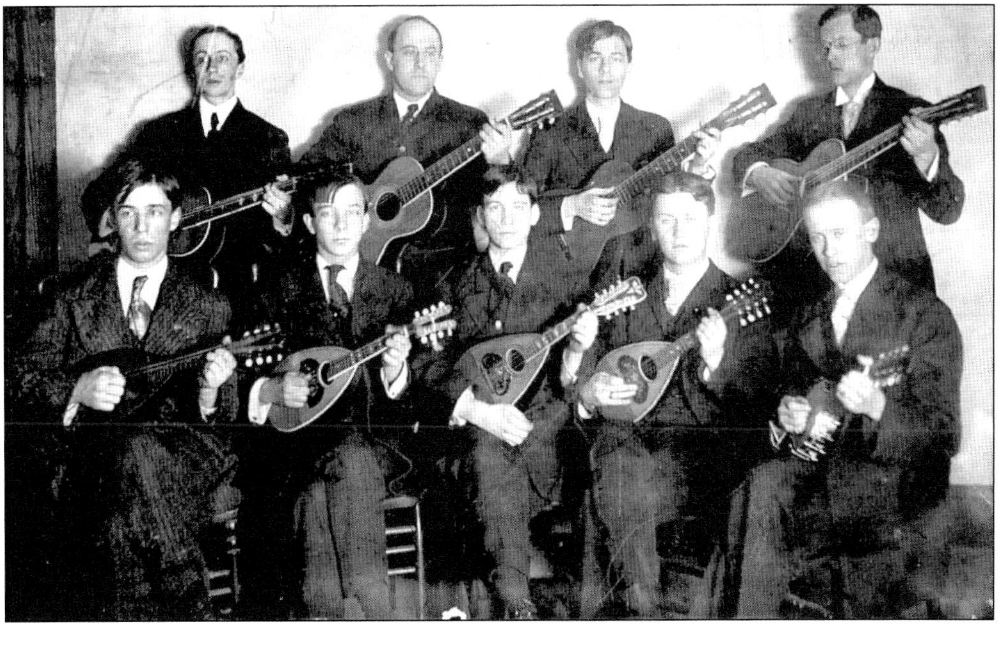

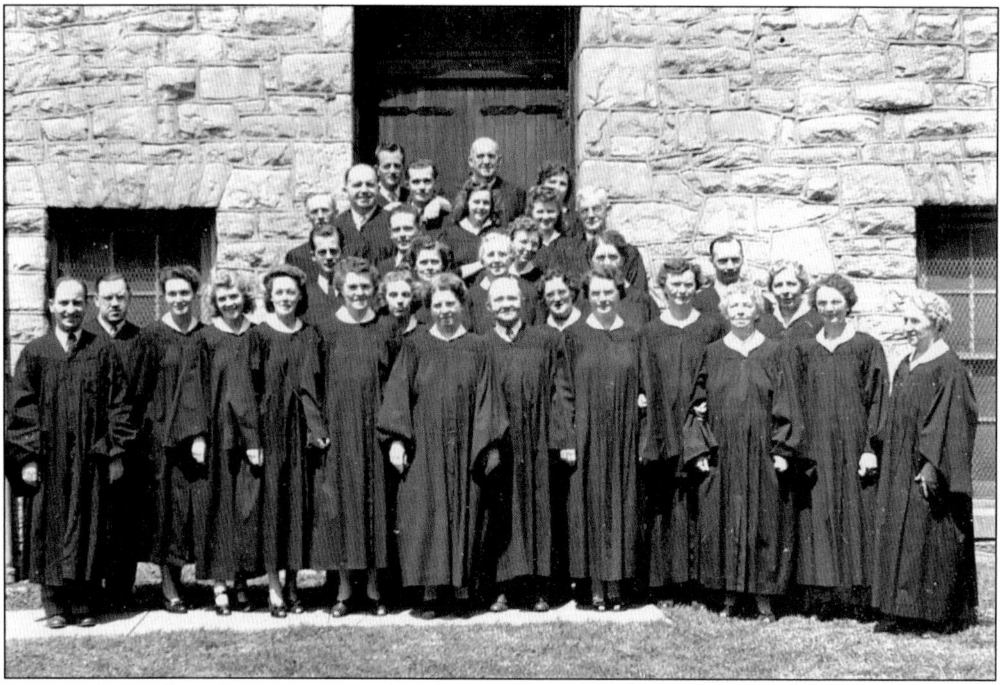

Coatesville has been home to many churches during its history, and each one had a choir to sing during Sunday services. Shown above is one of the church choirs. The town also has a history of having excellent scholastic athletic teams. The photograph below shows the Coatesville High School baseball team with its pet mascot.

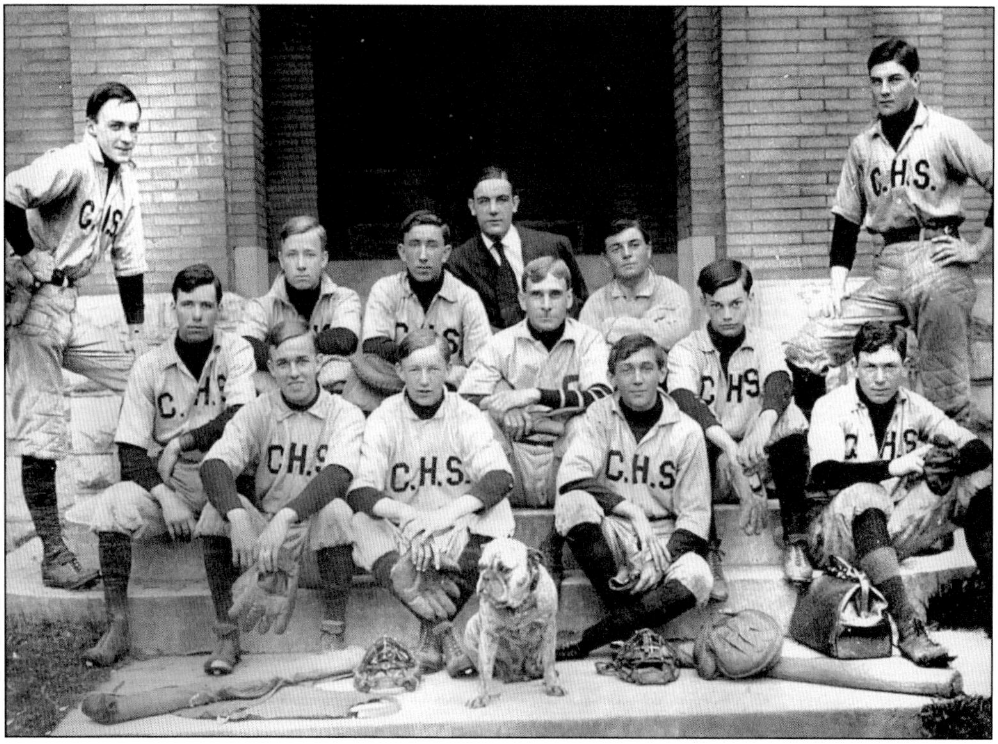

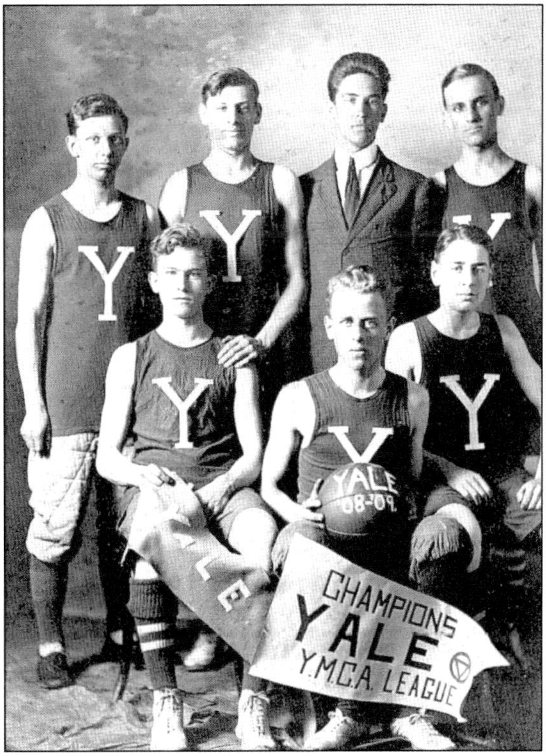

The YMCA was a place where young Coatesville residents played basketball for most of the 20th century. The photographs on this page show the YMCA winners for the seasons of 1908–1909 and 1909–1910. The Yale team is shown to the right. Some of its members appear to have been part of the championship team the next year, as shown below.

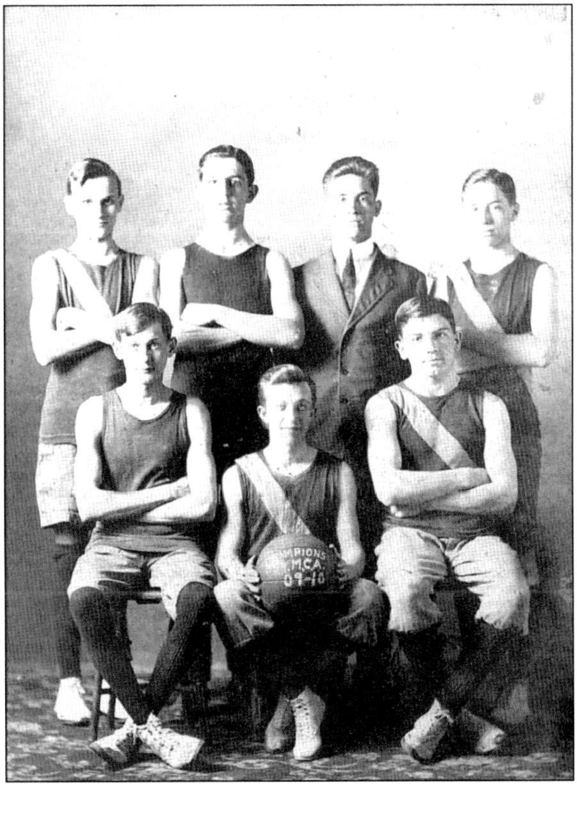

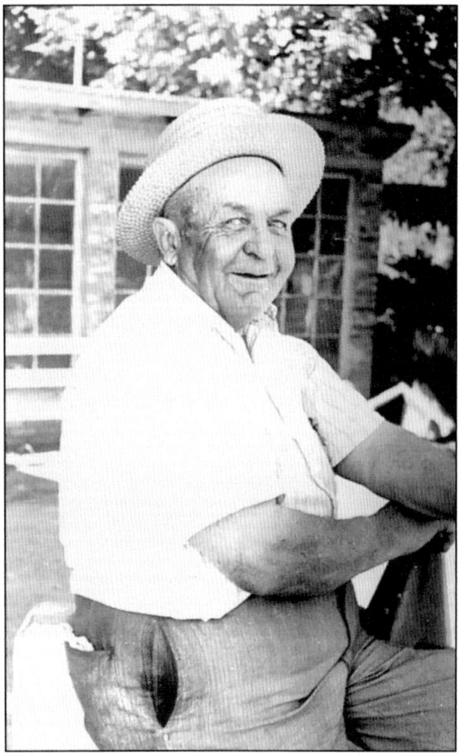

For years, Chester "Pop" Ash was the Coatesville parks director. In honor of the work he had done for the city, Ash Park, located along south Third Avenue, was named for him. The photograph below depicts the "Mammoth Tent" that was erected on Corey Field for "5 Big Nights" of public entertainment during one month of May.

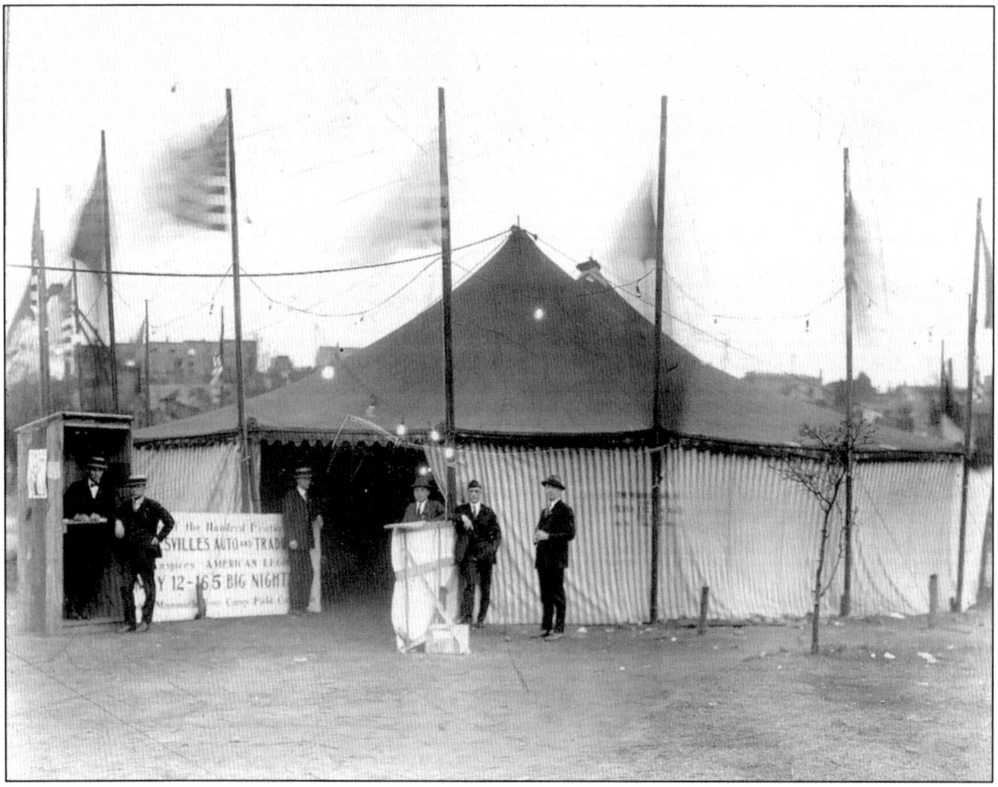

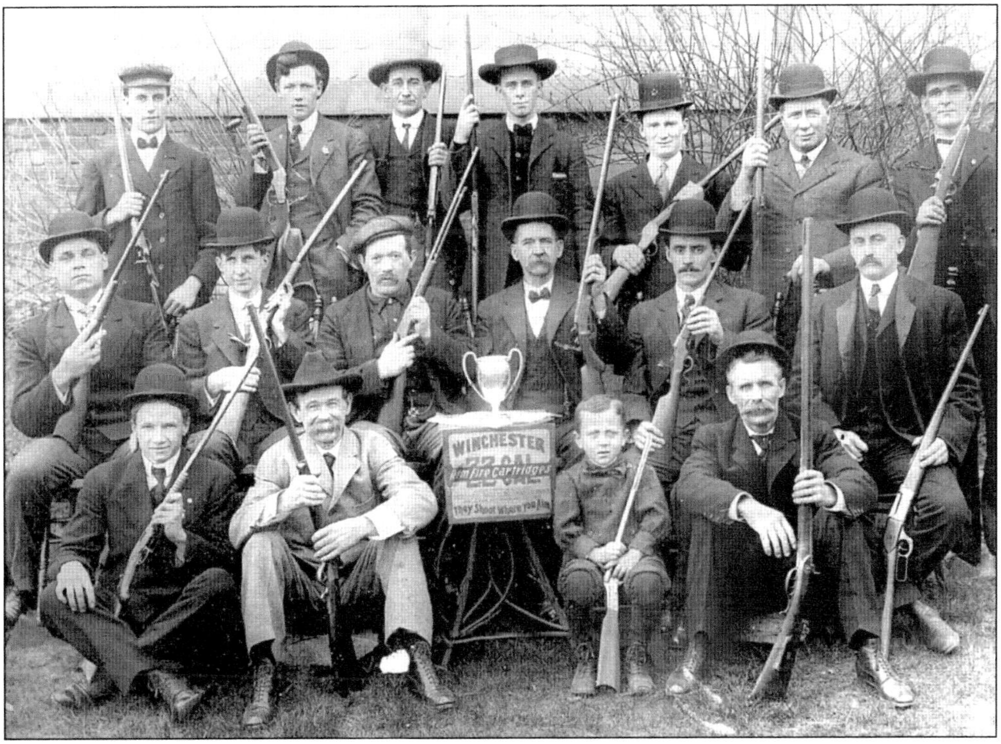

A shooting club was formed in Coatesville. Above, its members pose with a trophy cup they won for their marksmanship. The trophy rests on top of a box of .22-caliber Winchester ammunition that boasts, "They shoot where you aim." The group in the photograph below shows policemen with their cars near Coatesville City Hall.

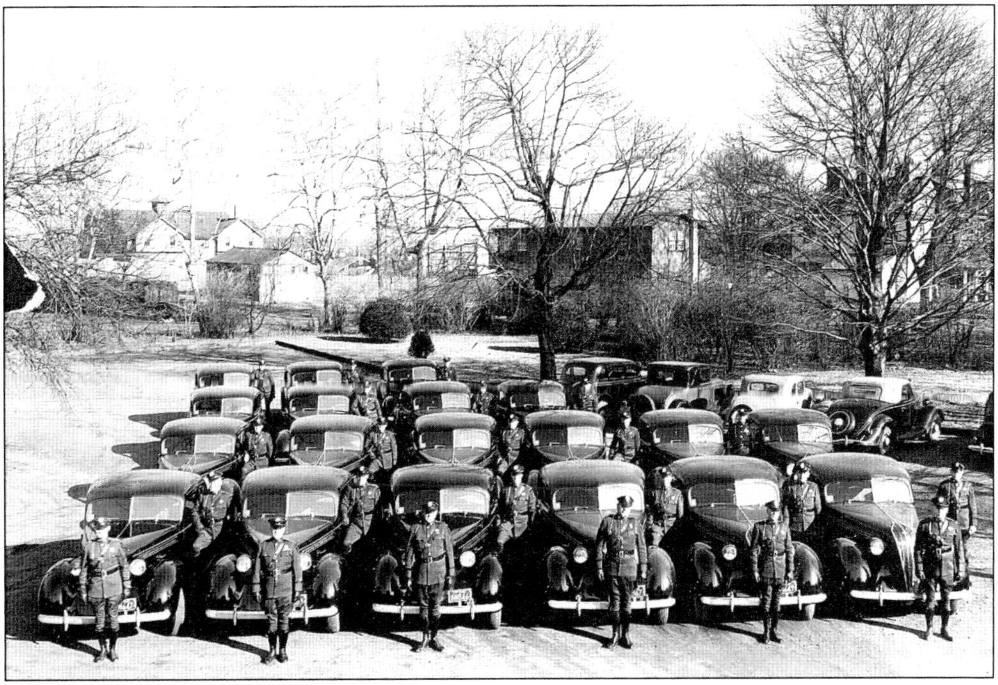

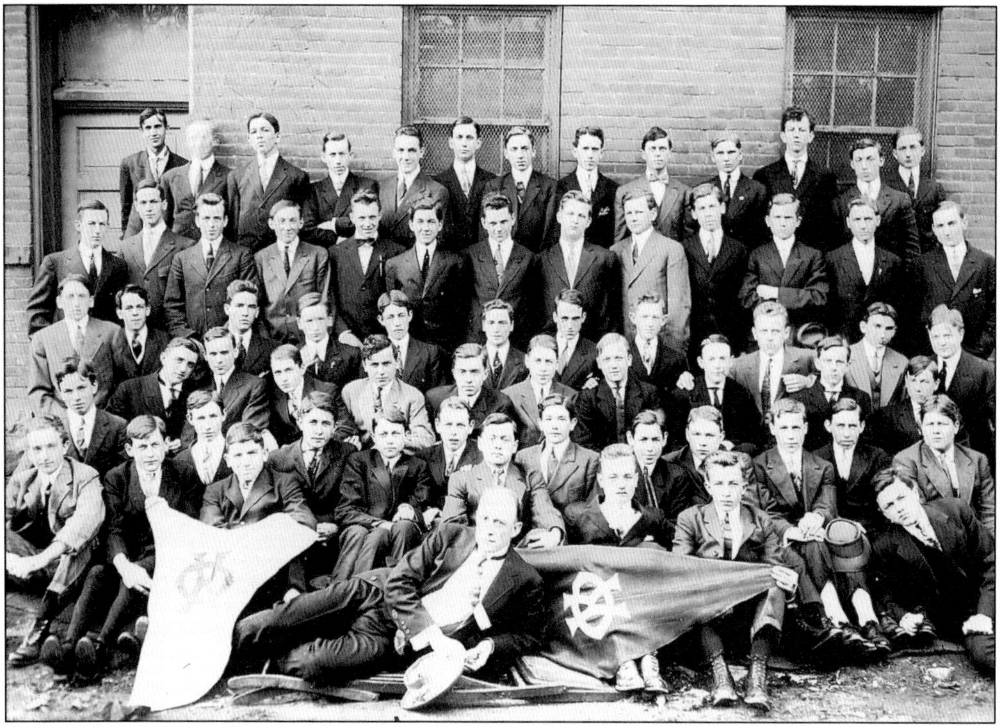

Group photographs were a staple of organizations throughout the country, including those in Coatesville, for many years. In the above photograph, the students all smile while some of them hold their banner. In the photograph below, a group of men poses near the post office during a cold and rainy day in Coatesville.

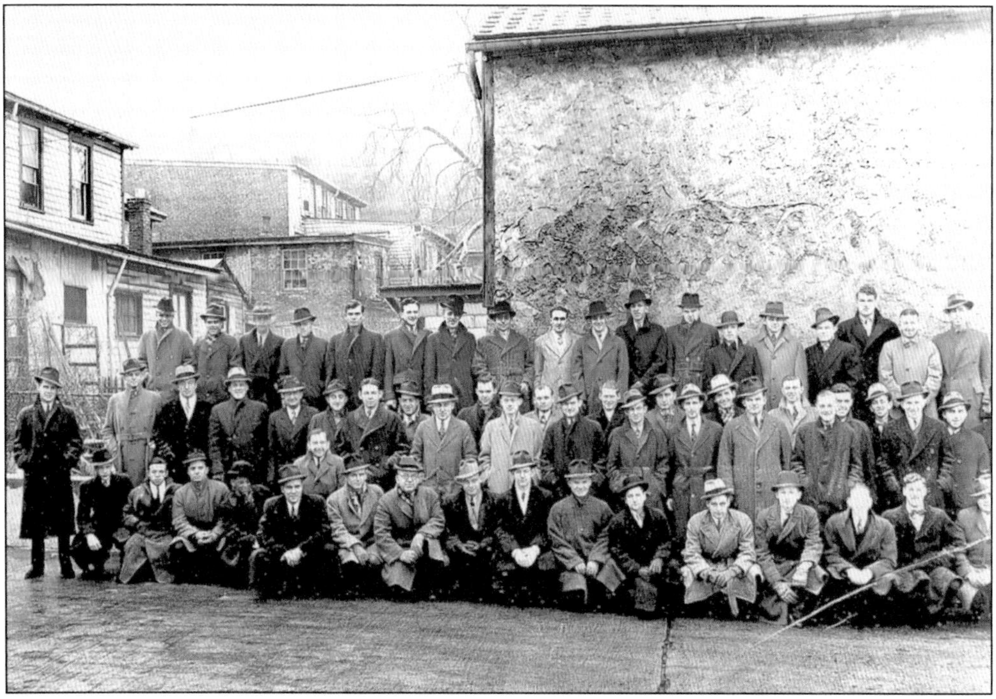

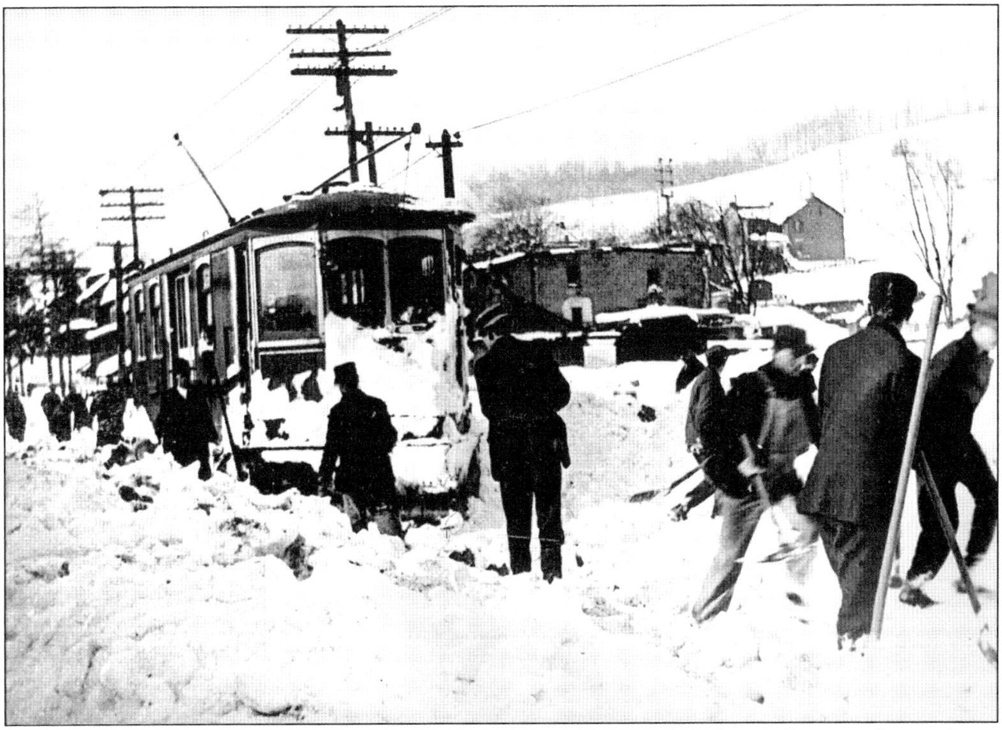

Living in Coatesville could be a lot of fun or a lot of work. In the above photograph, residents help dig out a trolley car during a heavy snowstorm. Below, young residents take a break from a hot summer's day to sit on a fence. One of them is enjoying an ice-cream cone.

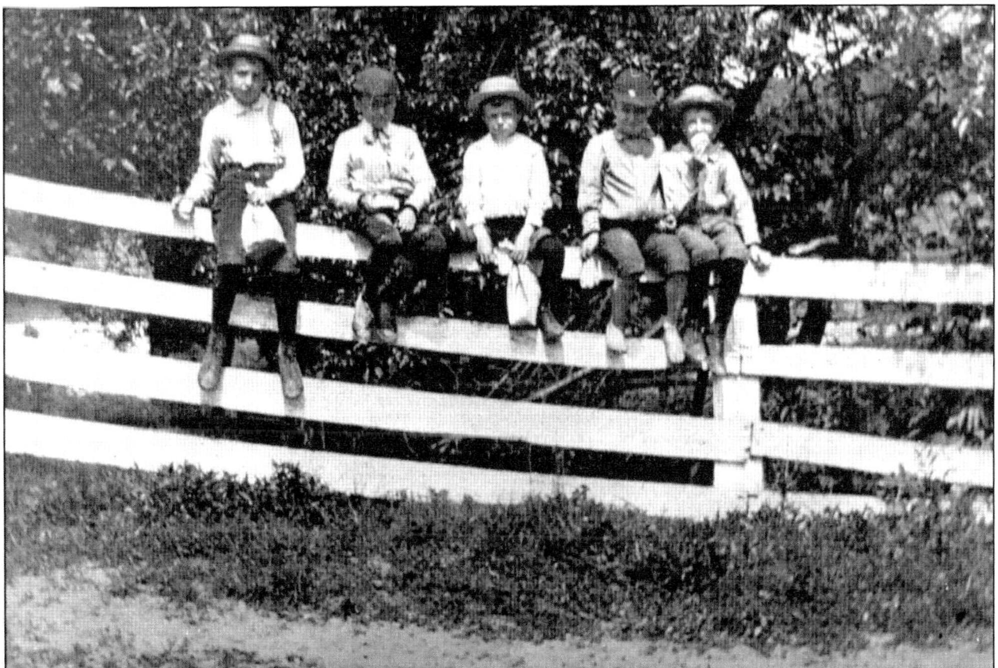

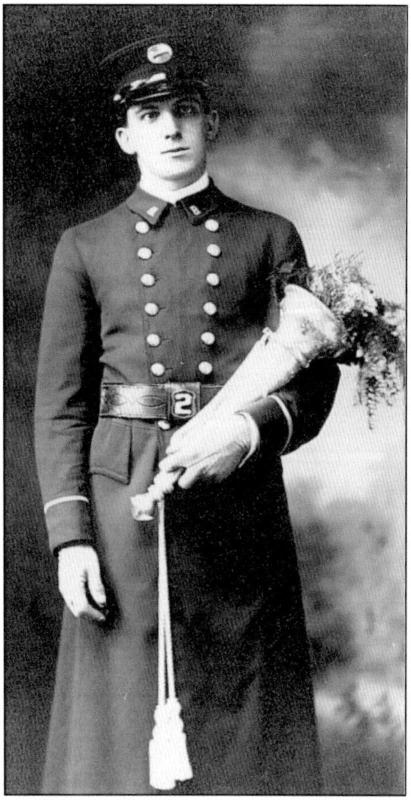

Brandywine Fire Company chief William H. Moore is shown to the left. Besides his duties with the fire company, Moore was Republican city chairman and a delegate to the Republican National Convention in 1952. He lived from 1888 to 1957. In the photograph below, Ray Currier (left, with his foot on a fire hose), Joe Hall (center), and Jim Greenwood pose during a fire truck demonstration.

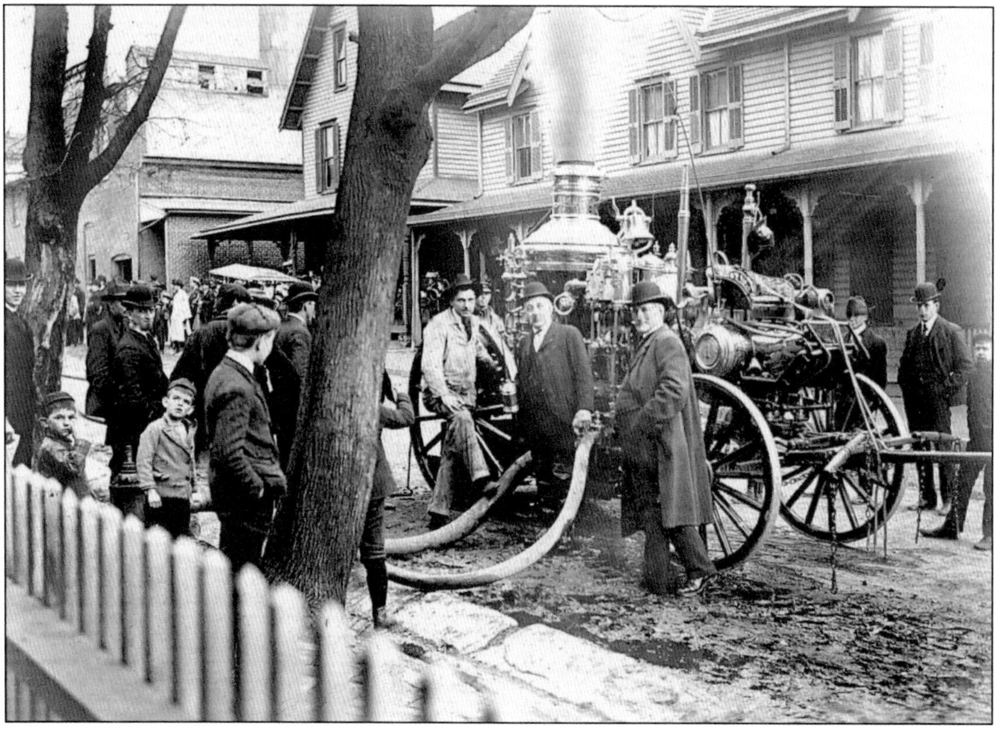

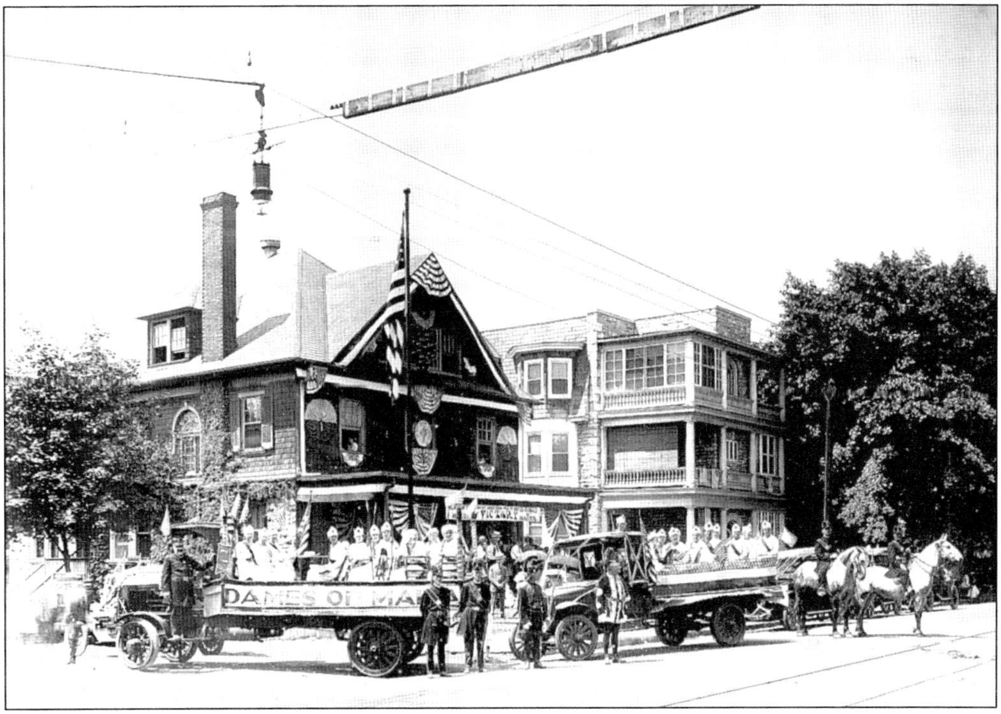

Parades and celebrations were plentiful over the years in Coatesville. In the 1860s, a group called the Wide Awakens held torchlight processions. In the above photograph, the Dames of Malta board a float in a victory parade. In the photograph below, a gathering takes place at the Knights of Malta home at Fifth Avenue and Main Street. Both photographs were taken at the same site.

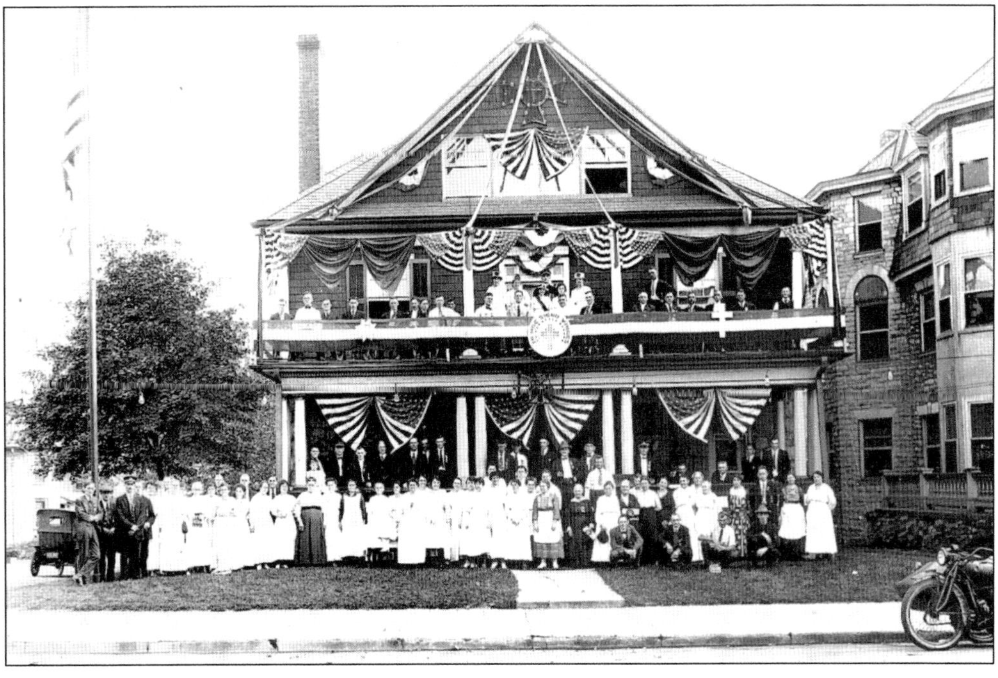

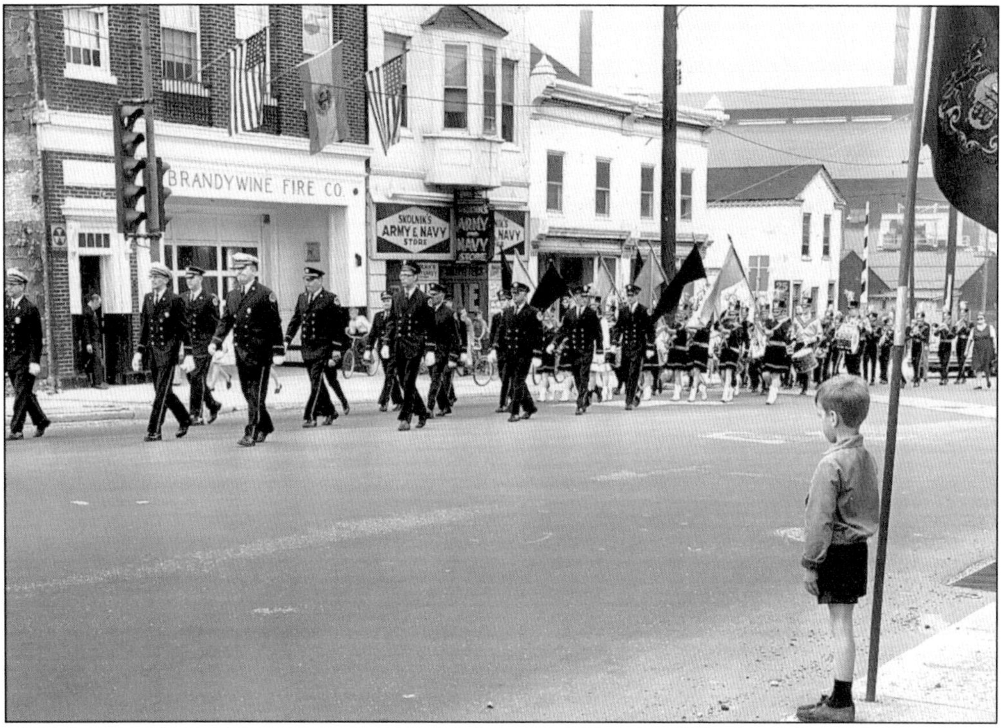

The photographs on this page are from the Frank P. Pennegar Collection. The above photograph shows a young boy underneath a Pennsylvania flag. He watches the parade as a group of firemen passes in front of the Brandywine Fire Company. The buildings have since been torn down. The photograph below shows the old Washington Hose Company and the Jesse Coates home.

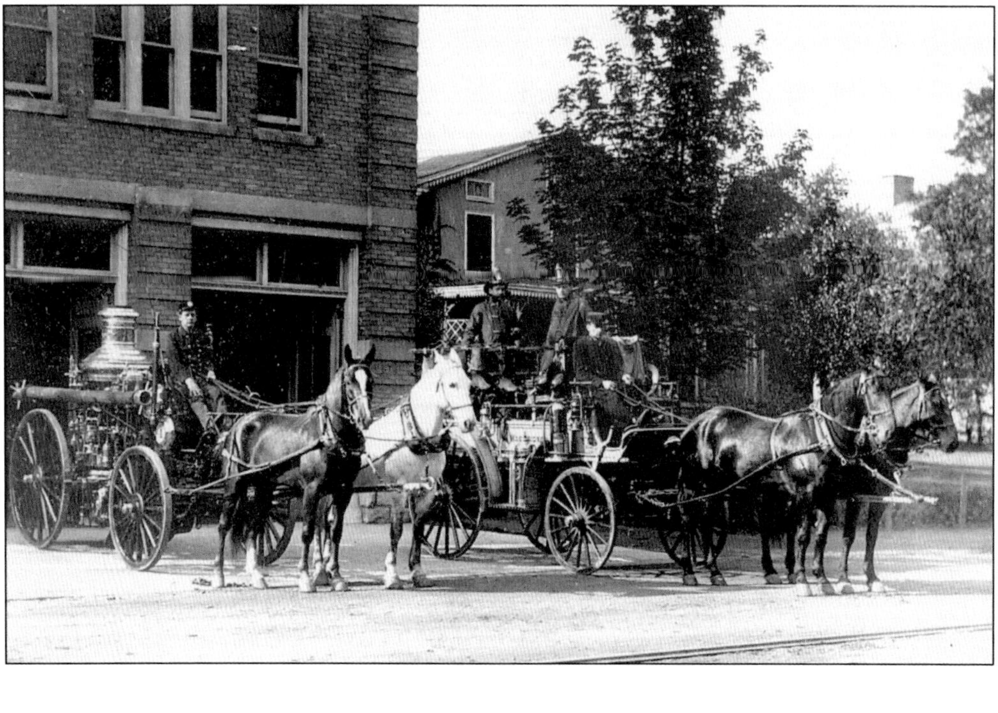

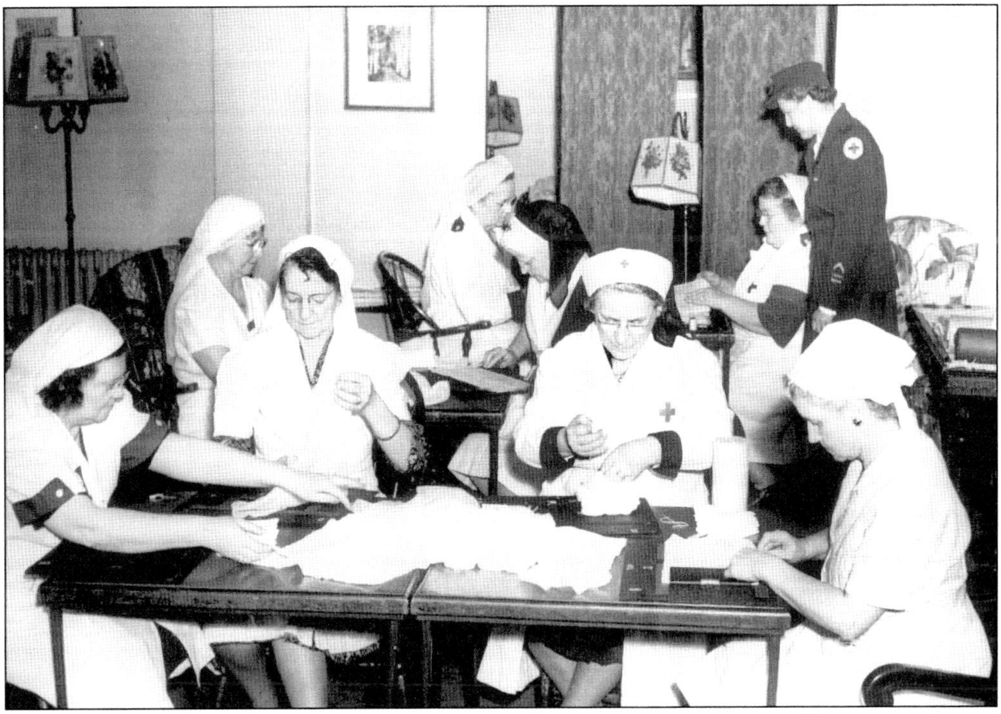

Red Cross workers from Coatesville made material in times of emergency. Above, members of the Red Cross are preparing supplies. Below, a view of Main Street in Coatesville looks west.

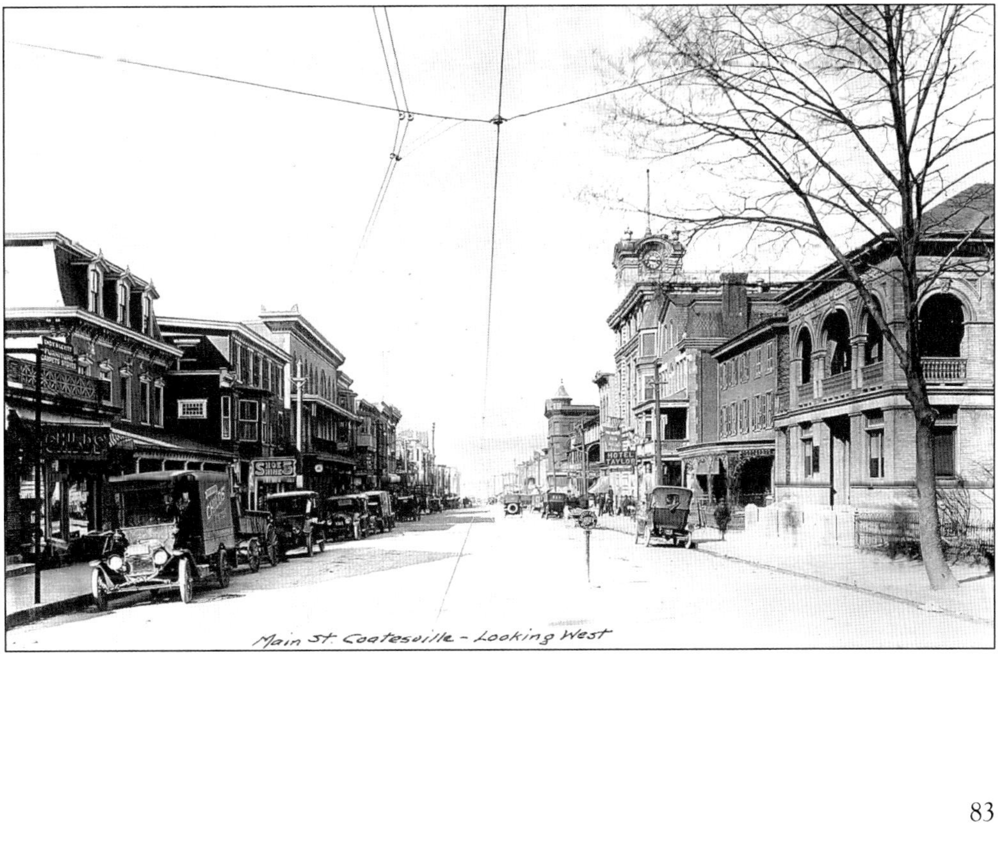

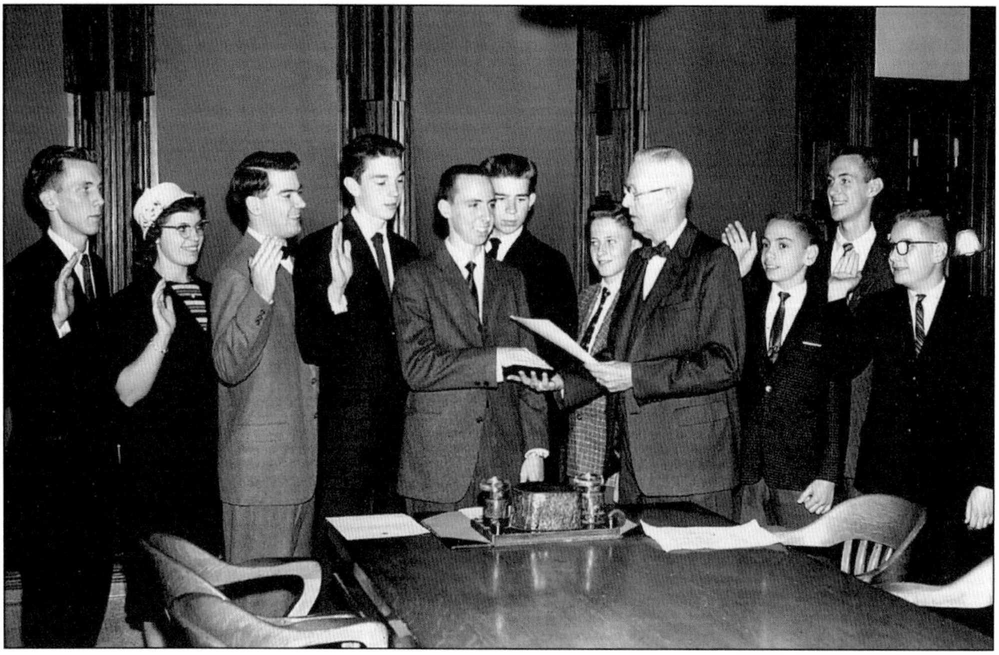

For years, the Coatesville city government and the Coatesville school system jointly administered a program that gave students a chance to see what it was like to be a city official for a day. In the above photograph, Frank Pennegar swears in students for a day. In the photograph below, the students have their day on October 21, 1949, along with some of the city officials.

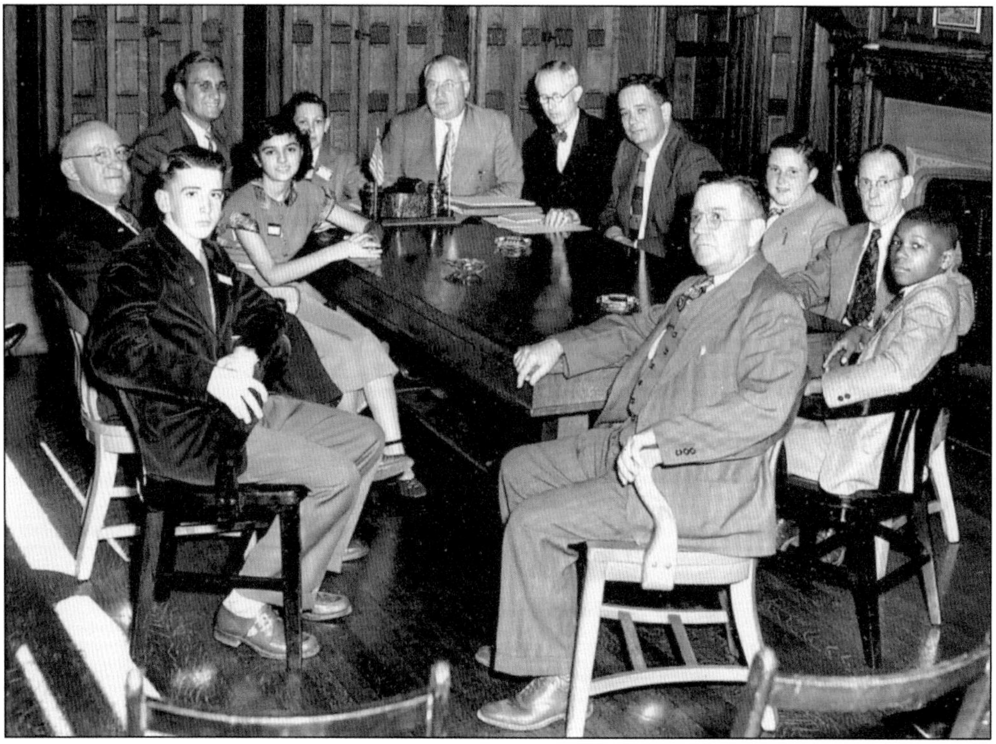

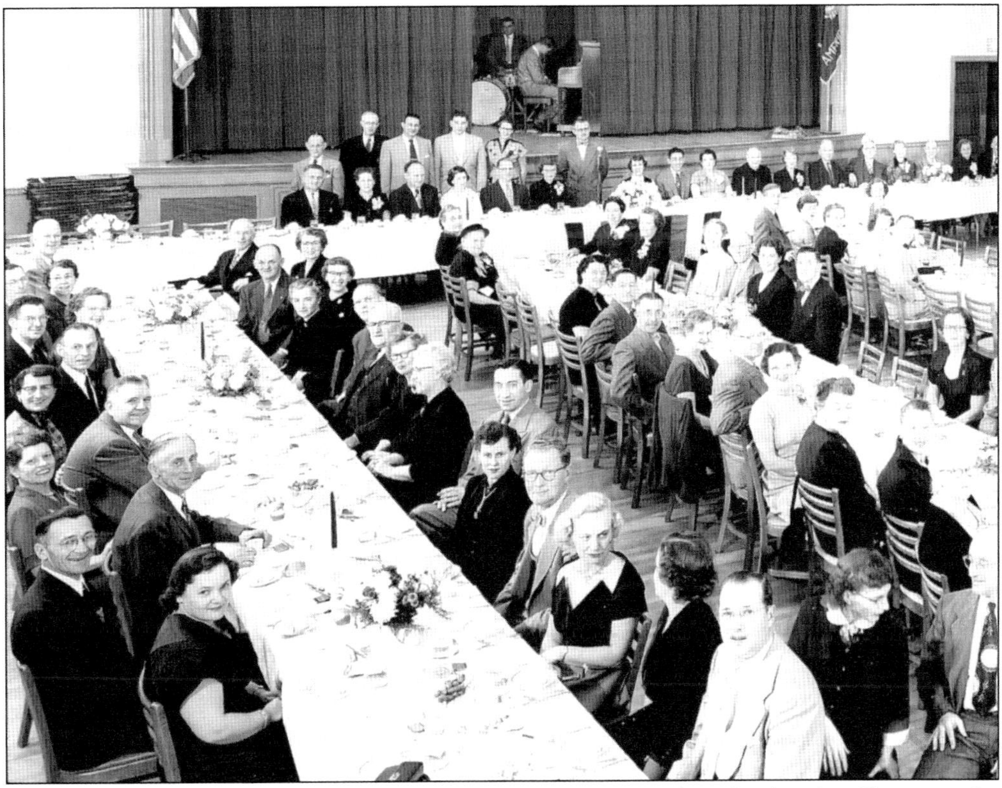

The LGM (Loggia Goffredo Mameli) hall has been a meeting place for decades. Shown in the above photograph is an American Legion dinner gathering. Members of a band wait on stage for their turn to play. Below, members of the Mennonite Mission Summer Bible School, on East Walnut Street near Pennsylvania Avenue, gather for a photograph in August 1938.

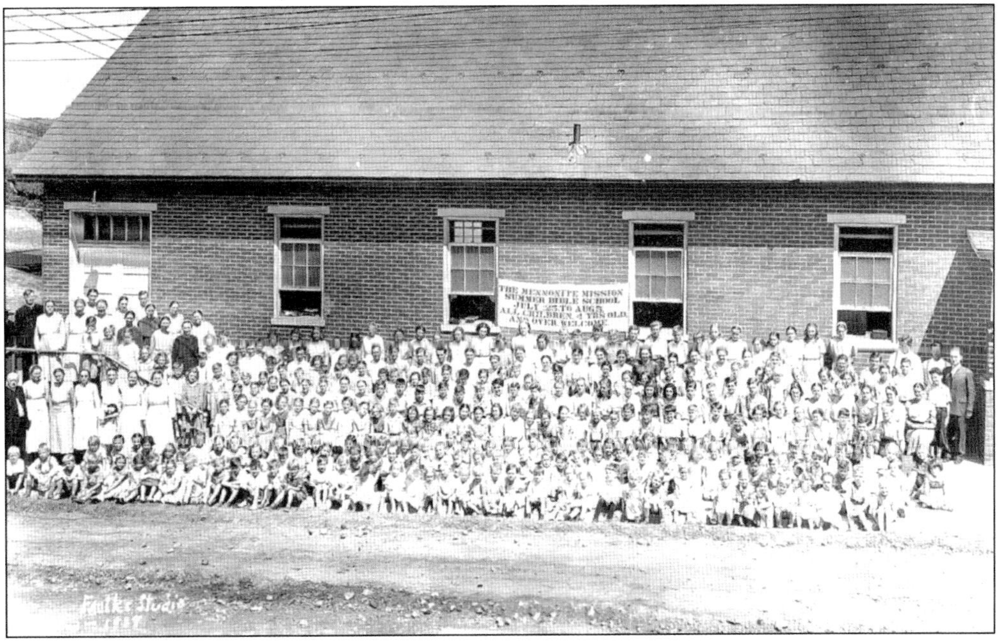

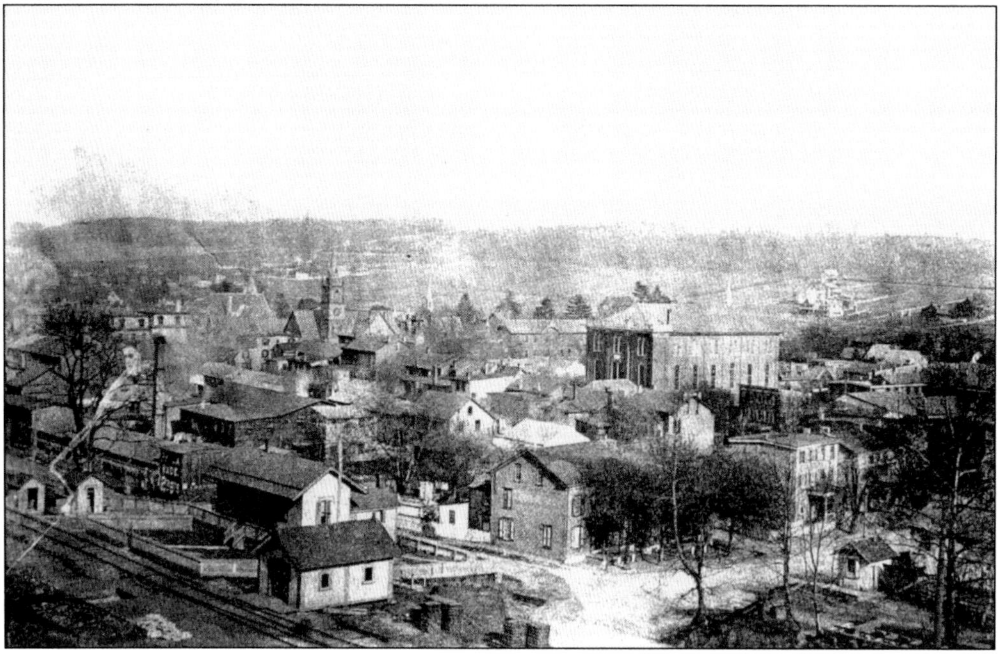

The community of Coatesville, along with the town, changed over the years. The above photograph gives a view from the Pennsylvania Railroad station at North Second Avenue, looking southeast. It shows the Opera House on Chestnut Street and the old railroad station. Below, Chestnut Street is shown in a view looking east toward St. Cecilia's Church.

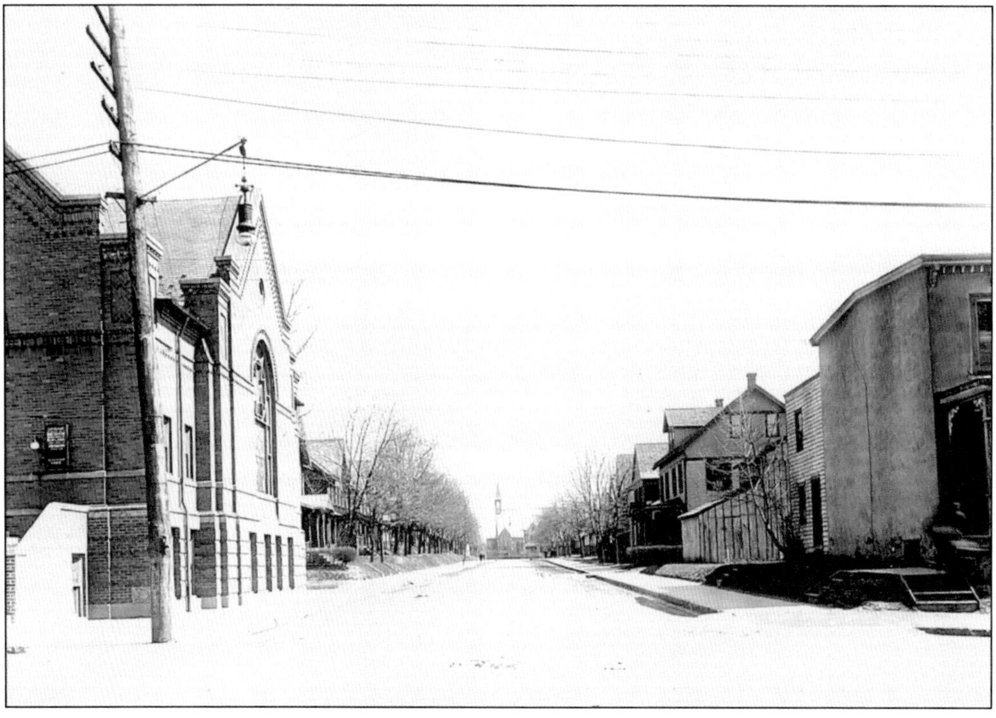

Five

PLACES

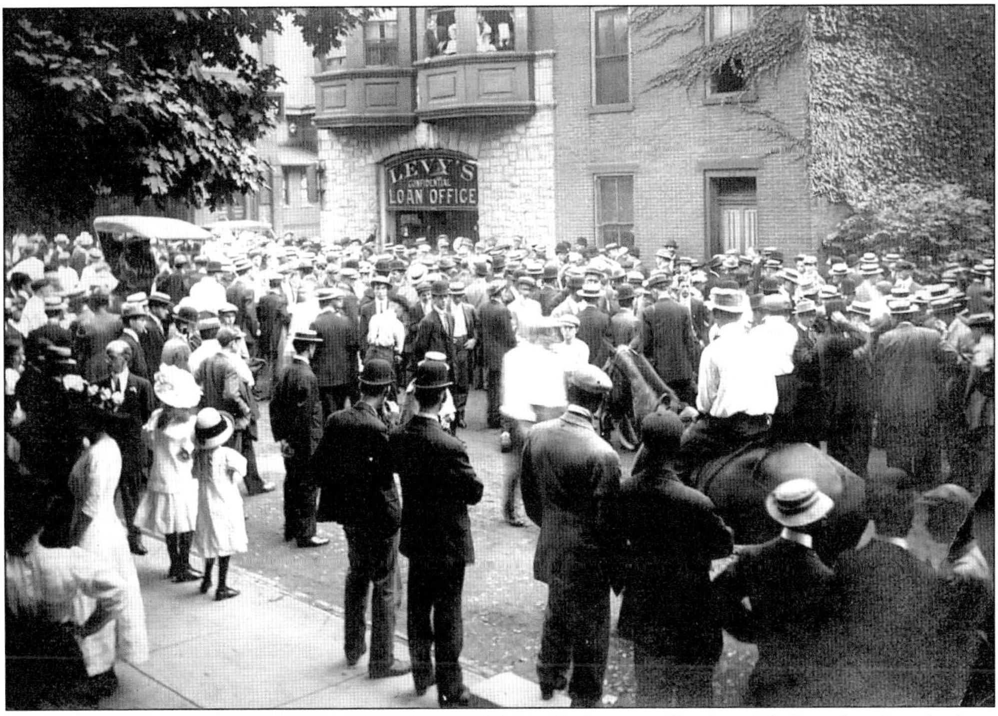

The crowd shown here is gathered in front of the old Coatesville City Hall and police lockup on August 13, 1911. They were there because Zackariah Walker, an African American, was charged with murdering a white police officer. Later, a crowd forcibly took Walker from his bed at Coatesville Hospital and burned him to death. It was the last lynching in Pennsylvania and caused great unrest among community members.

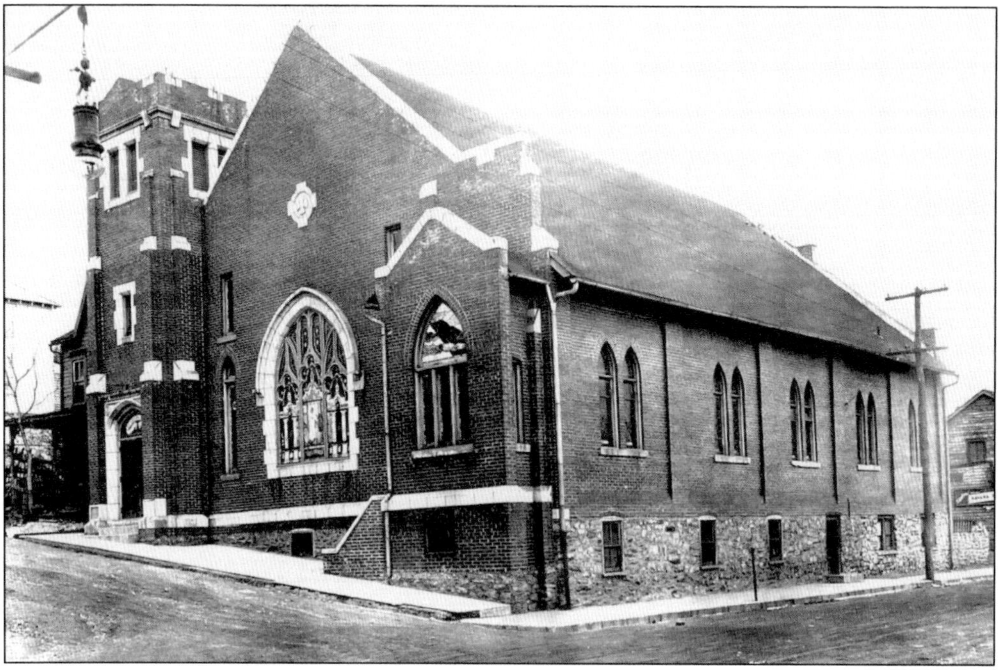

The Coatesville community has had a number of churches. There were 22 in 1932. Shown above is the Tabernacle Baptist Church, built in 1919 and 1920 at the northeast corner of Eighth Avenue and Coates Street. For the most part, members of the African American community made up its congregation. The photograph below shows the St. Nicholas Orthodox Catholic Church, built in 1917. It is located at the northeast corner of First Avenue and Oak Street.

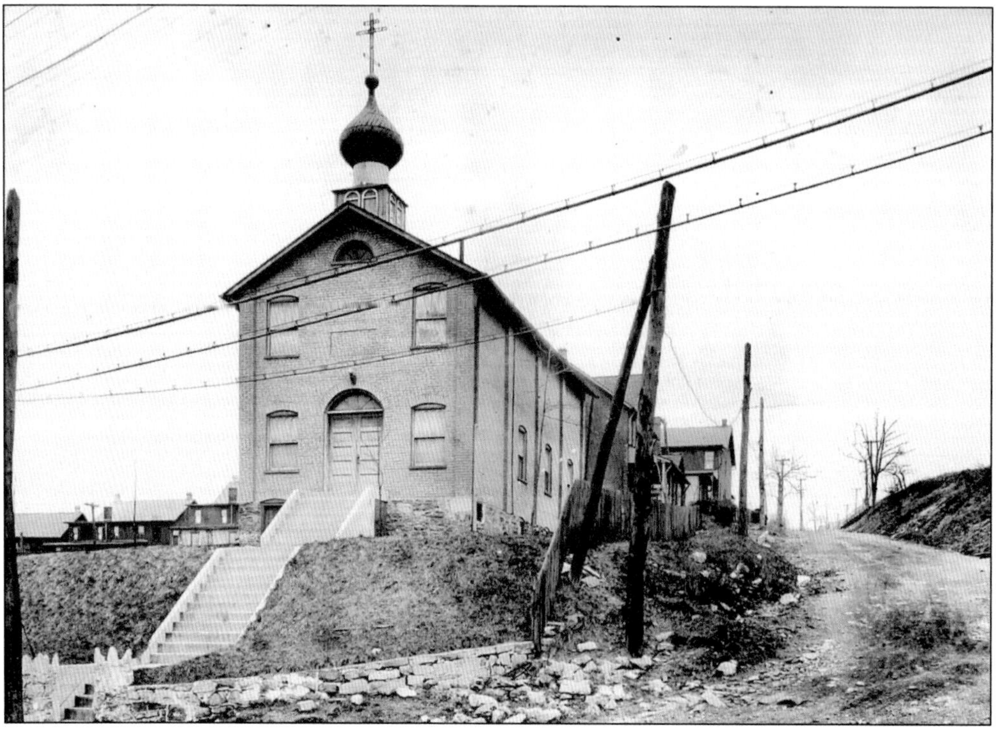

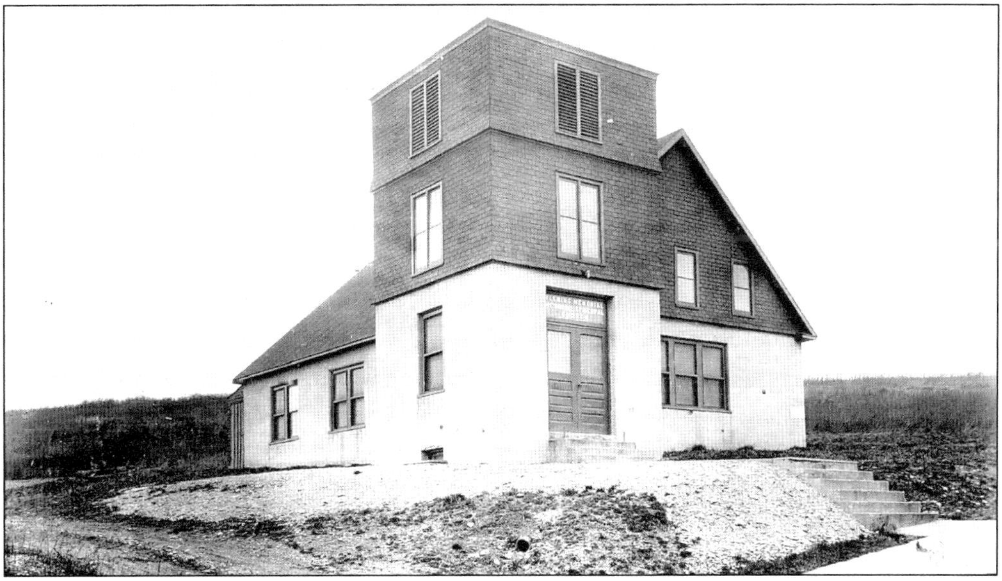

The above photograph shows the Fleming Memorial Methodist Episcopal Church, built in 1919. The building in the photograph below was another church frequented by members of the African American community, the St. Cyril's Protestant Episcopal Chapel. It was located on the south side of Chestnut Street between Eighth and Ninth Avenues. In 1870, Coatesville had a population of 2,025, but by the time these churches were constructed, the population was more than 5,000.

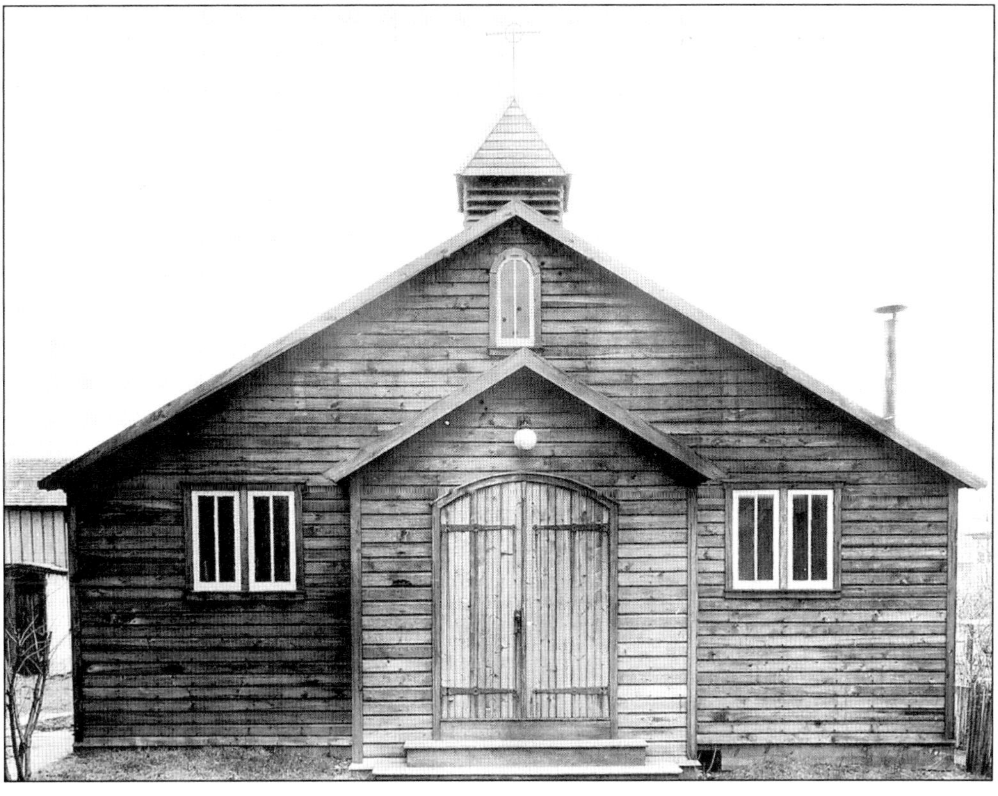

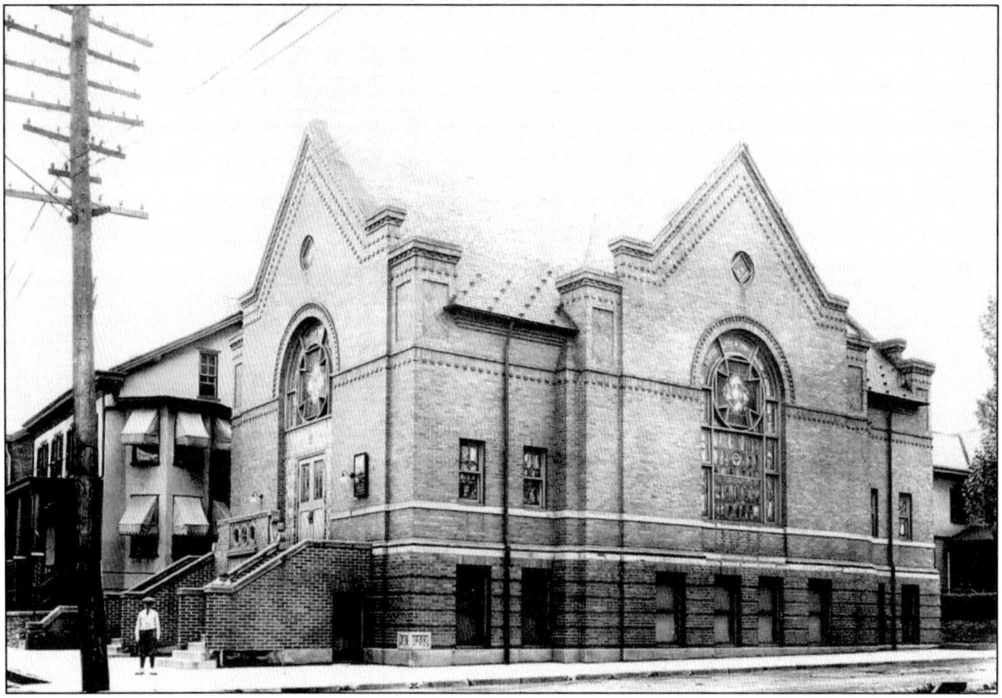

Many different religious denominations had churches in Coatesville. The above photograph is of the Lutheran Church of Our Savior, built in 1909 at the northeast corner of Fifth Avenue and Chestnut Street. The photograph below shows the Holy Ghost Reuthenian Catholic Church, built in 1917 at the south side of Charles Street, between Strode and Hope Avenues in the city's west end.

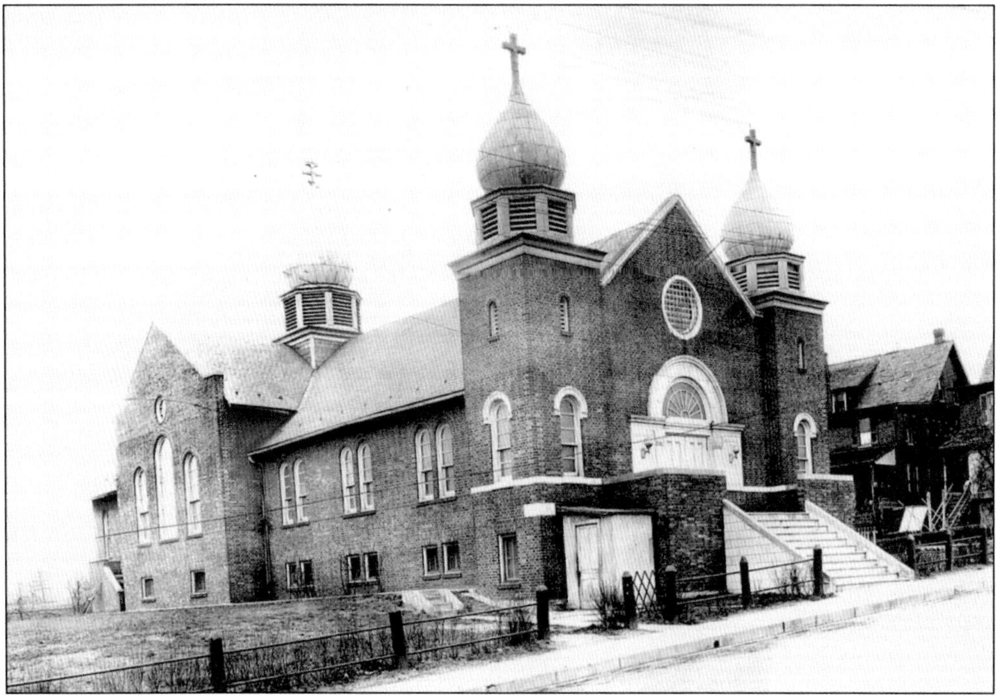

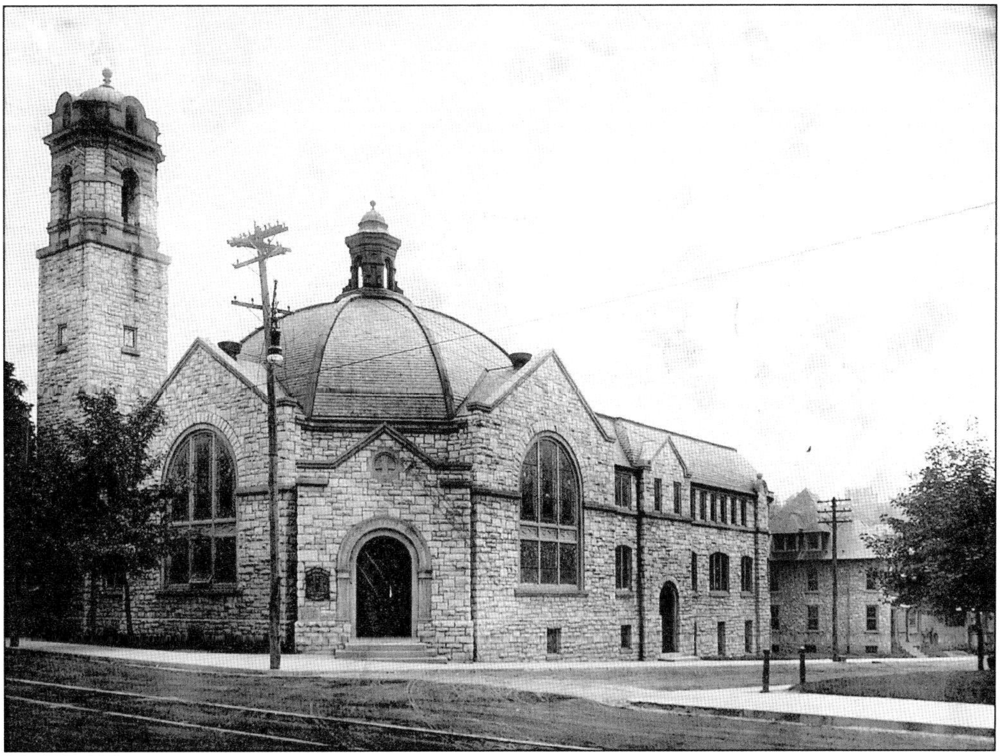

Many of the churches in Coatesville were constructed in the first part of the 20th century. Seen above, the First Baptist Church was built in 1906 and is located at the southeast corner of Fifth Avenue and Main Street. St. Mary's Greek Catholic Church, pictured in the photograph below, was constructed in 1918 and is located at the southeastern corner of Strode Avenue and Pine Street.

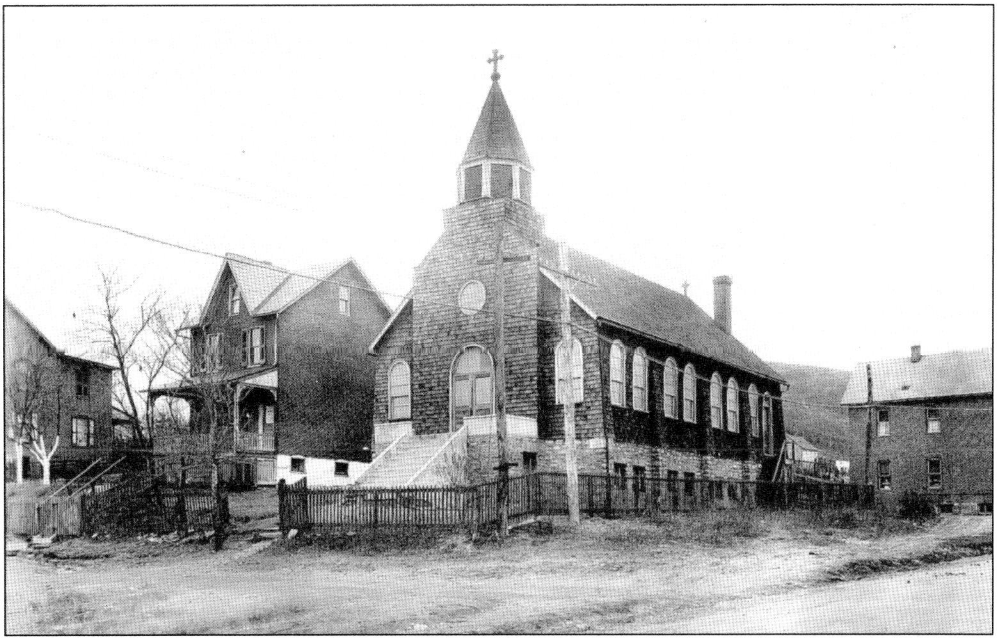

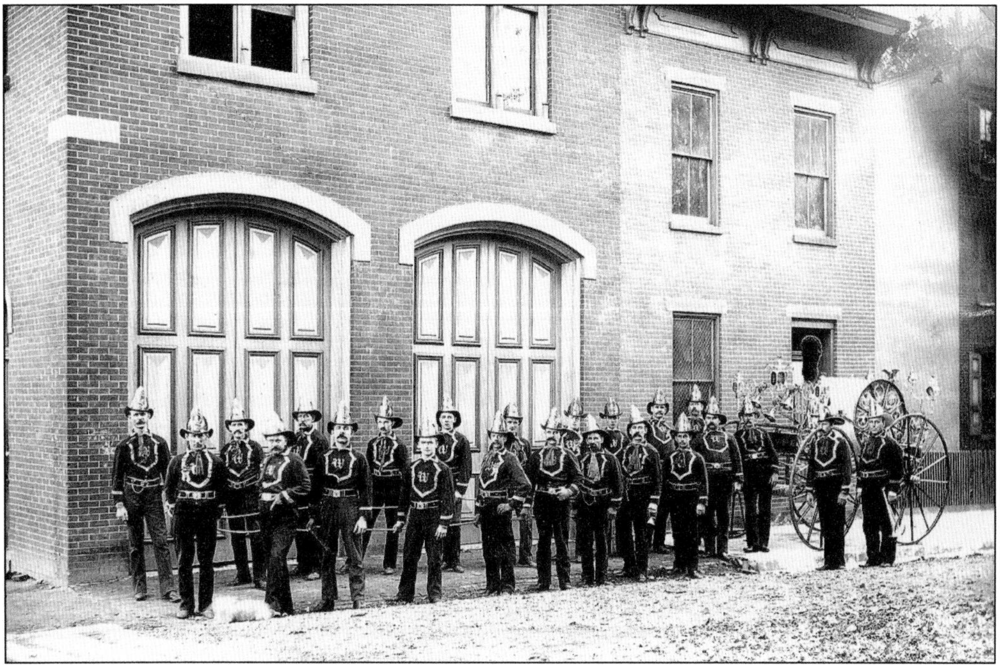

The Washington Hose Company was organized on June 12, 1871, and incorporated on August 17, 1871. In the above photograph, taken before the building was remodeled in 1890, members display their uniforms and equipment. The company received its first uniforms in 1873. They were issued long coats in 1898 and short coats in 1906. In the photograph below, members sport new uniforms. Their red shirts were discarded in 1898 for long blue coats and helmets.

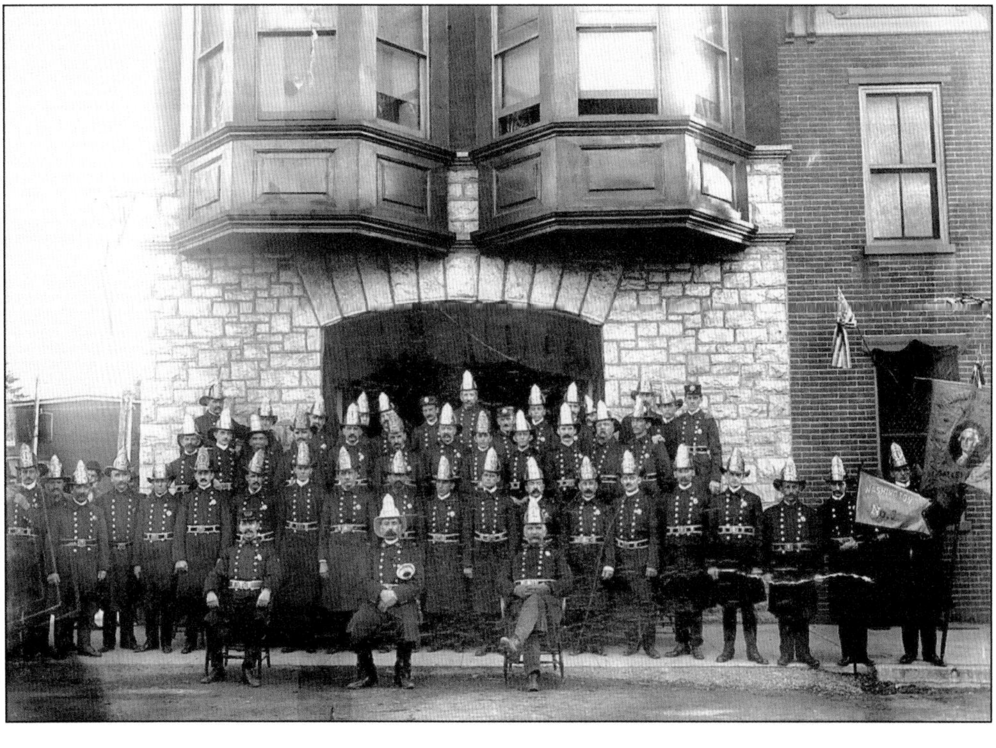

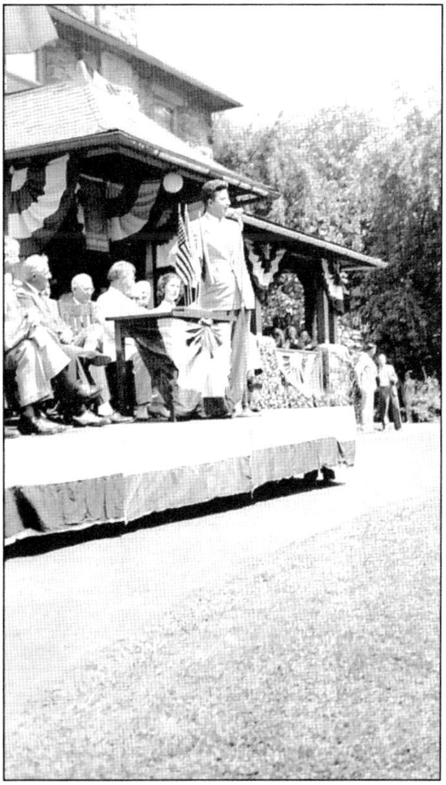

The Graystone mansion became Coatesville City Hall in 1939. The photograph to the right shows William S. Livegood speaking during the dedication of the building on July 19, 1939. The photograph below, from the Frank P. Pennegar Collection (housed at the Chester County Historical Society), shows the building while it was Coatesville City Hall.

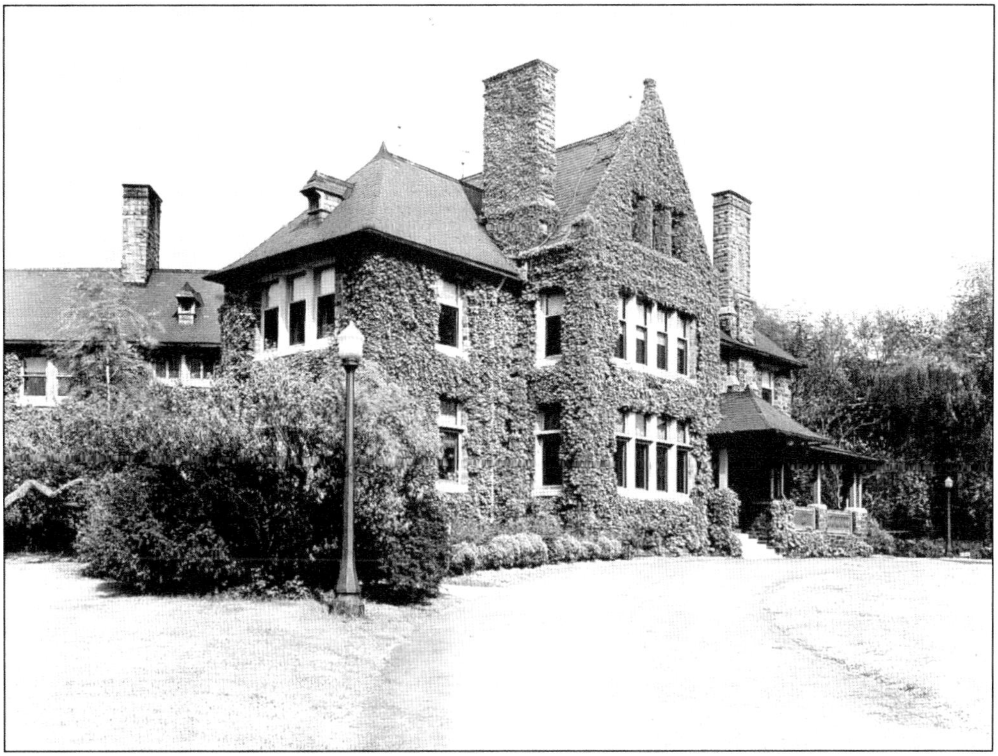

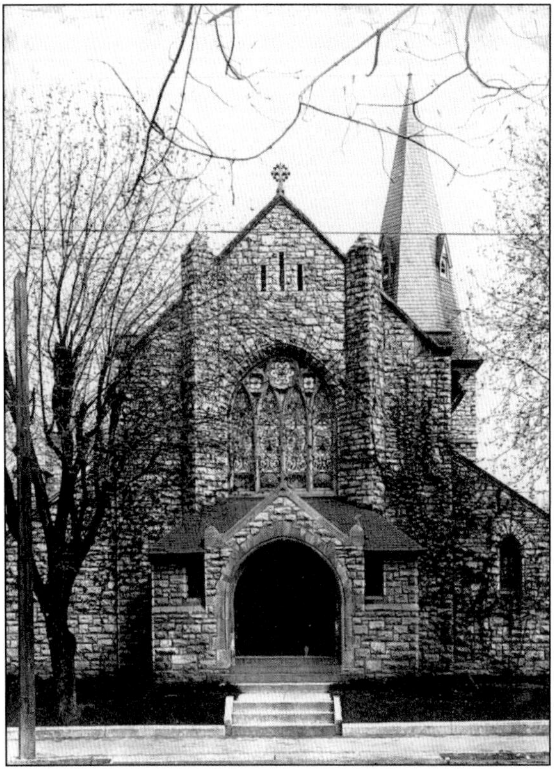

Seen to the left is one of the most recognized churches in the city—the Episcopal Church of the Trinity, on Main Street. The image below shows the National Bank of Coatesville building, on Main Street. The street was a busy place. The Hotel Taylor is shown on one side of the building, with the William J. Trunk Dry Goods store on the other side.

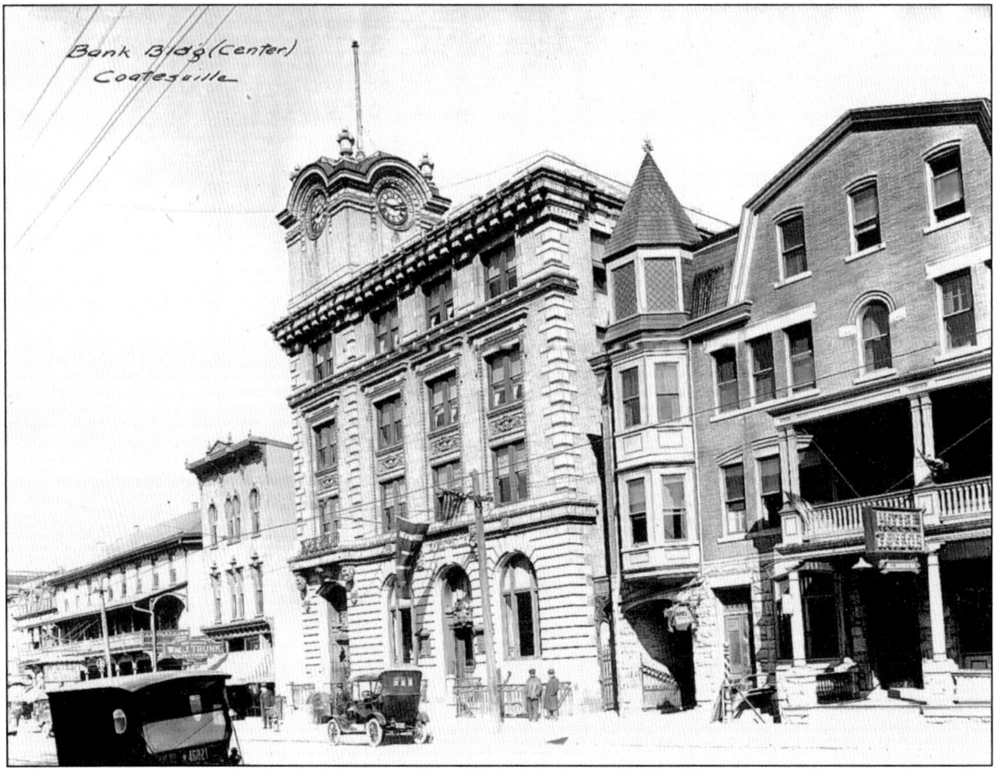

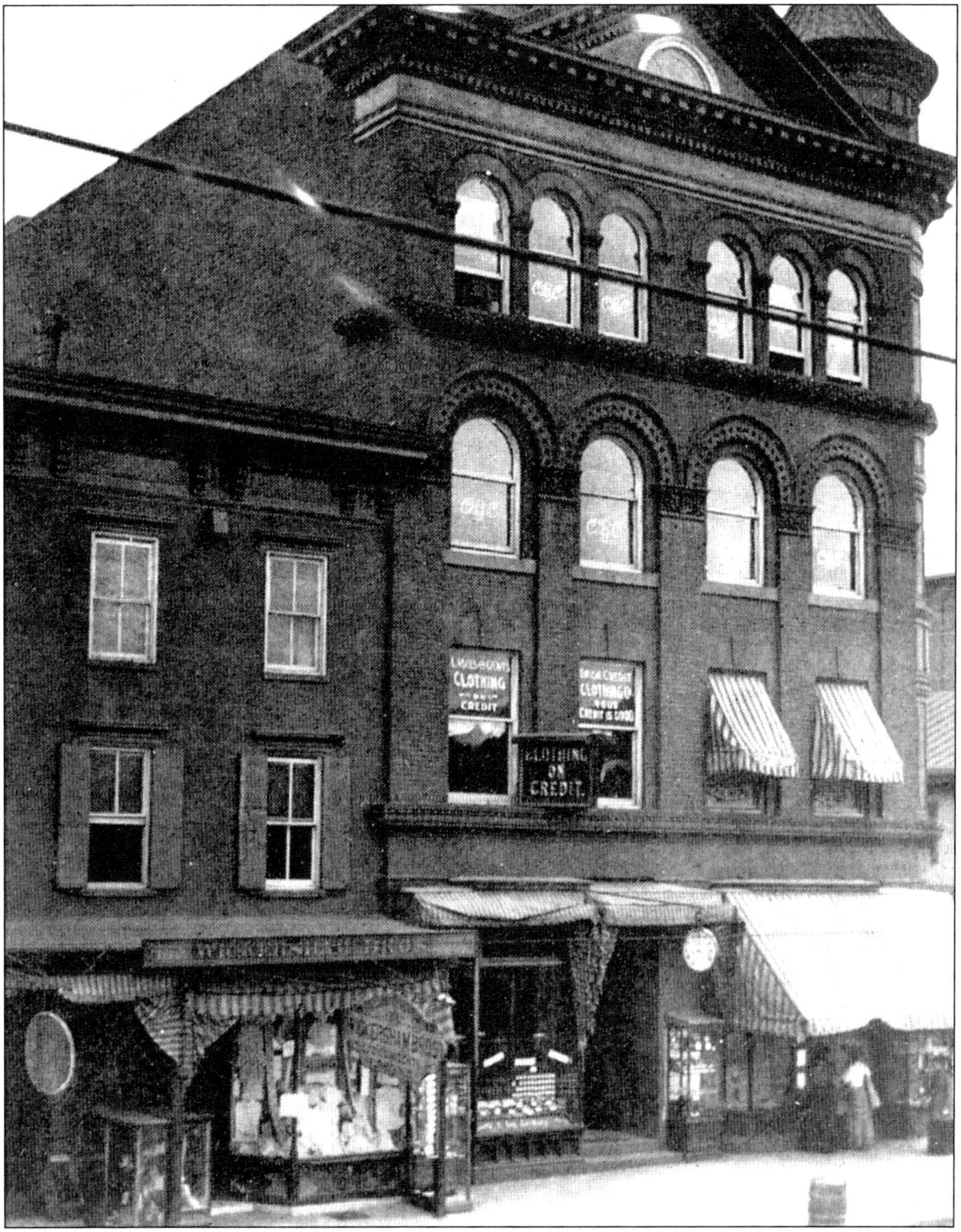

The Thompson Building was a landmark in the Coatesville business district for decades. It was constructed *c.* 1901 at the northwest corner of Second Avenue and Main Street, in the middle of the town's business district. One business in the Thompson Building offered citizens "clothing on credit." By the 1970s, some city leaders wanted to demolish the building, and it was taken down. A number of historic preservation groups tried to save the Thompson Building but were unsuccessful. Preservationists have managed to safeguard a number of historically significant buildings in the town, including many of the family buildings that are associated with the Lukens Steel Company. The town's business district is attempting to rebound by updating its image and restoring its turn-of-the-century ambiance.

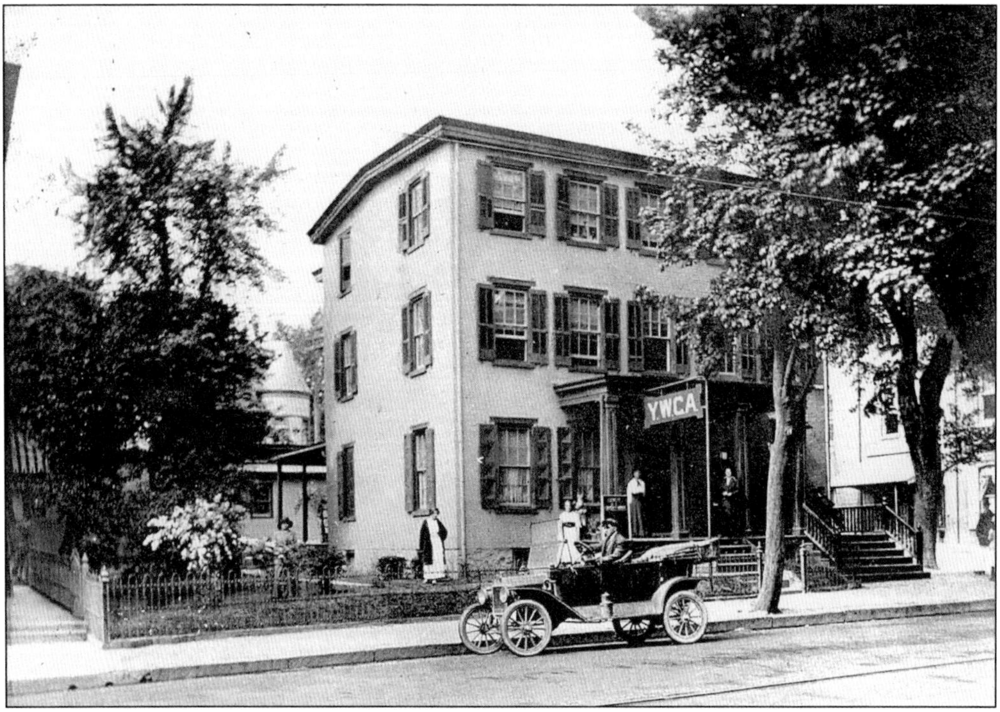

The YWCA was active in Coatesville for years. The organization's location was Main Street. The above photograph shows young women standing on the porch near the garden. In the 1900s, the Coatesville school system grew along with its population. Shown in the photograph below is the Columbia Avenue School.

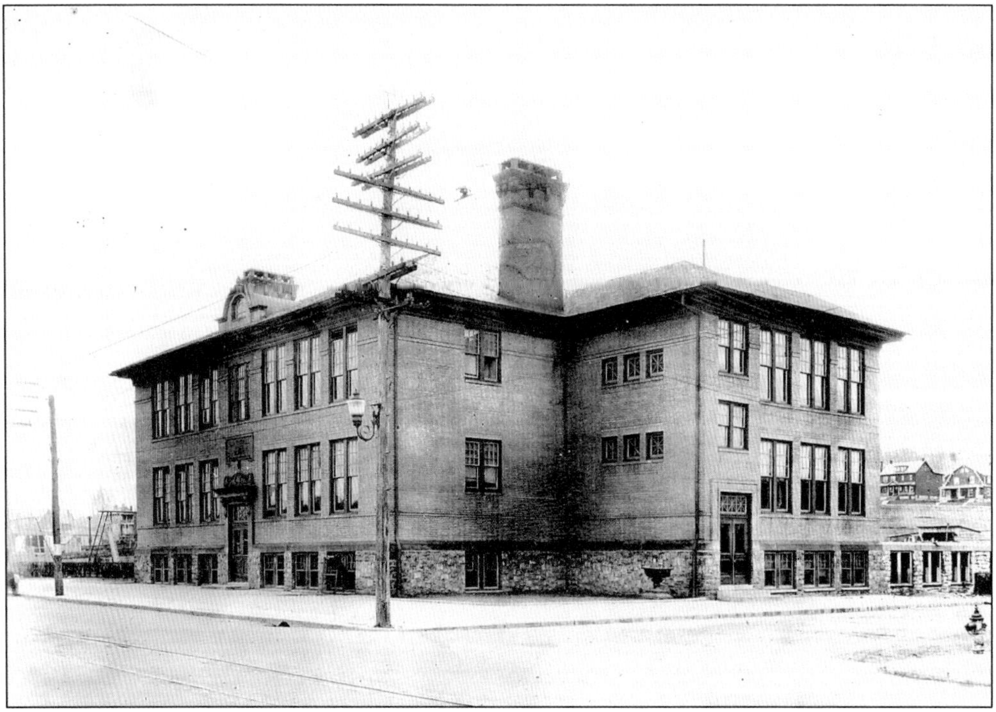

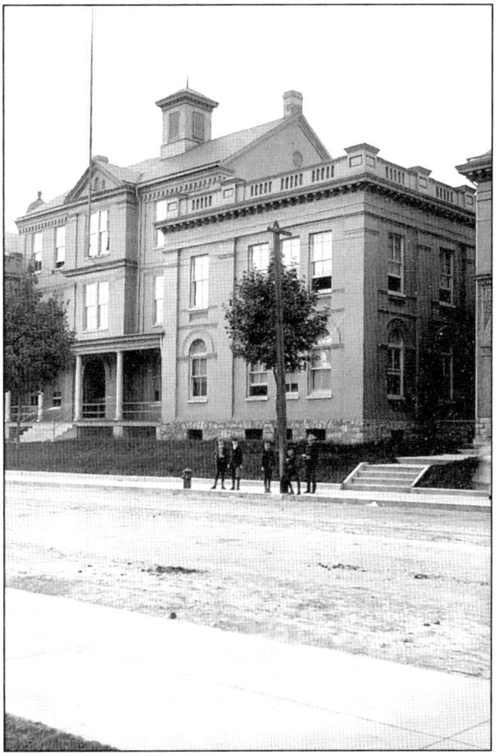

The old Coatesville High School building is shown to the right. The photograph below, taken in 1958, shows a late–Victorian Romanesque building erected in the late 1800s. It was home to the *Coatesville Record*, a daily newspaper. A sign for the Coatesville District United Charities Campaign is also visible in this image.

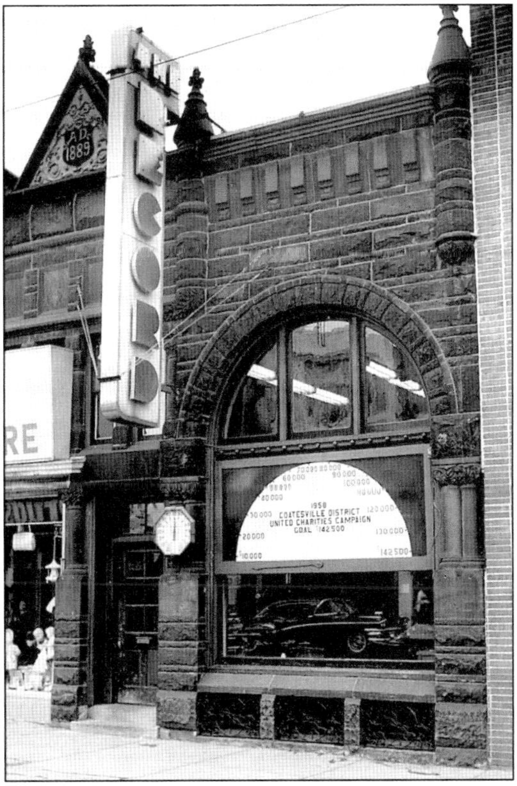

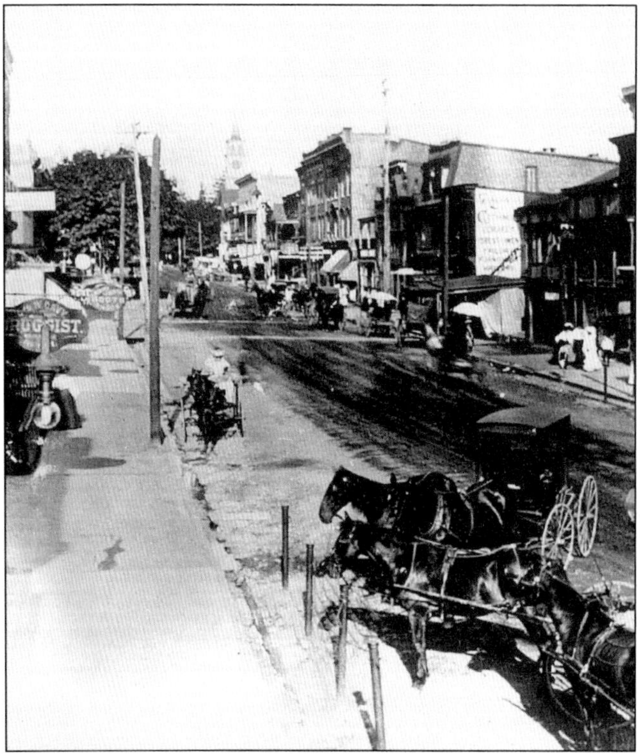

Main Street was the place to shop. At the beginning of the 20th century, customers hitched their horses to the posts in front of the many businesses in Coatesville. Main Street is shown to the left in a view looking east from the Davy Drug Store in 1906. The Baptist church and the town clock are visible in the distance. The *c.* 1911 view below also looks east, this time from Fifth Avenue.

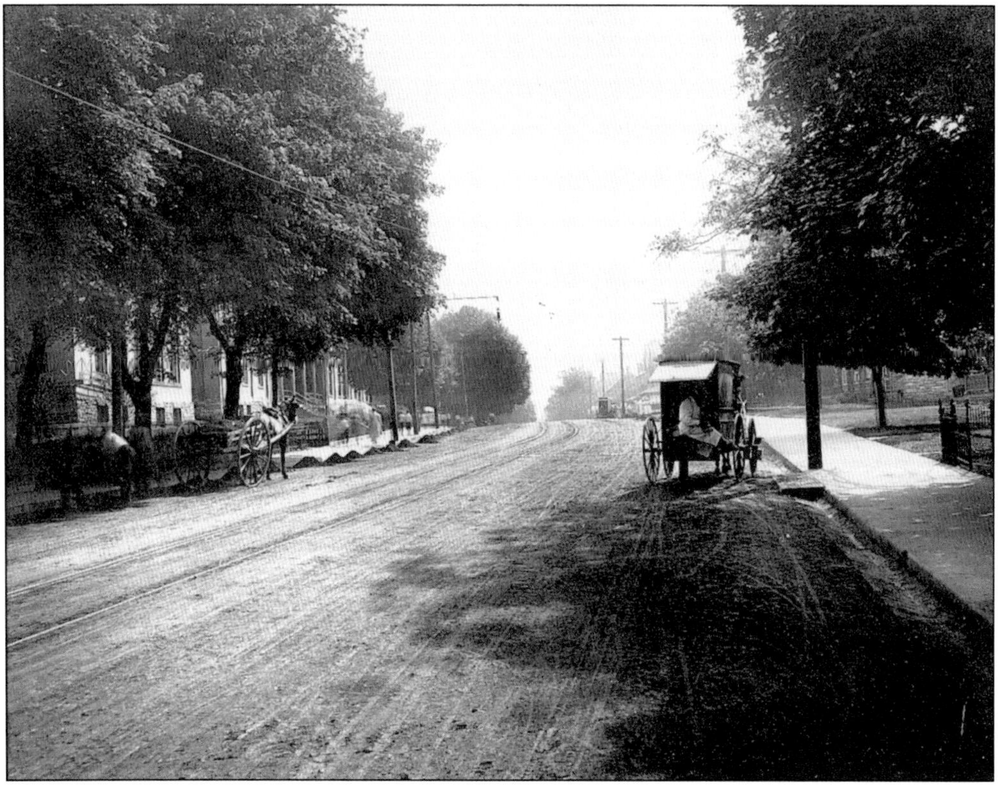

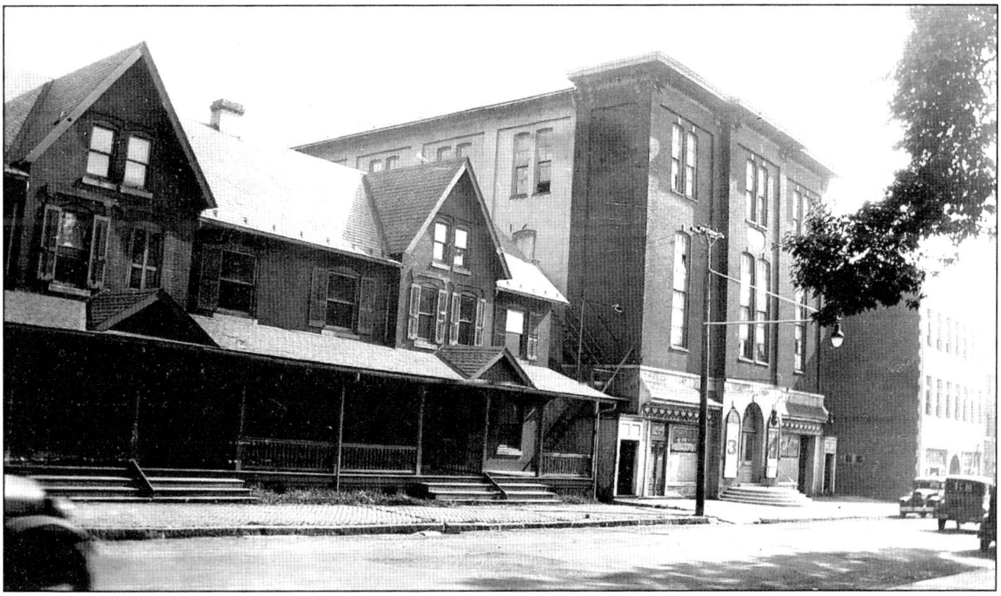

The Coatesville Opera House, shown in the above photograph, was used to entertain the citizens of Coatesville. It was razed to build the current post office on Chestnut Street. Shown to the right is Moose Hall. On top of the hill overlooking the city is the Coatesville Veterans Administration Hospital, shown in the photograph below.

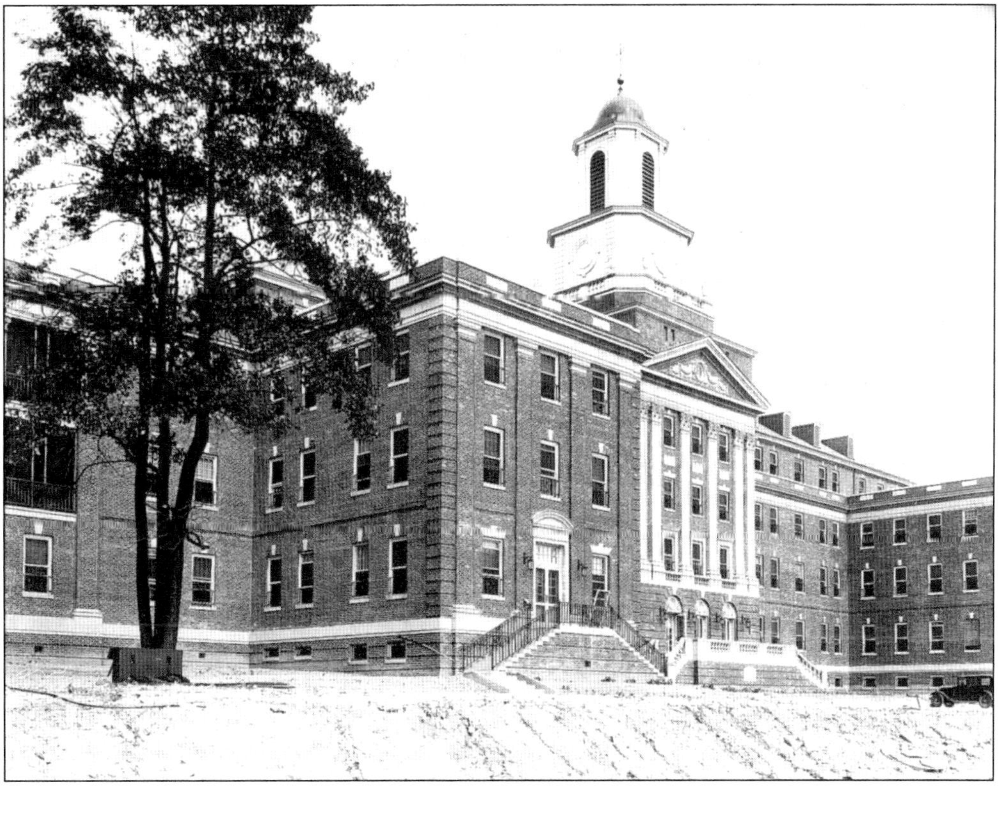

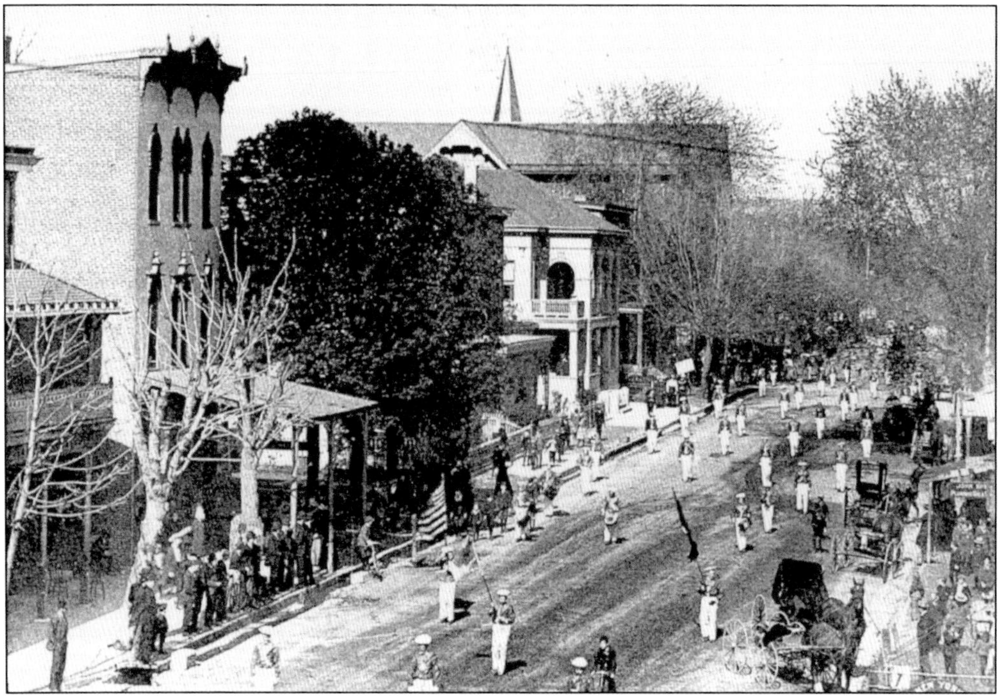

Main Street was the scene of a parade in 1889, as shown in the above photograph. It was also home to the Coatesville YMCA. The YMCA quarters featured a swimming pool and basketball court and offered other activities for the youth of the community as well. A piano store is shown in the photograph below.

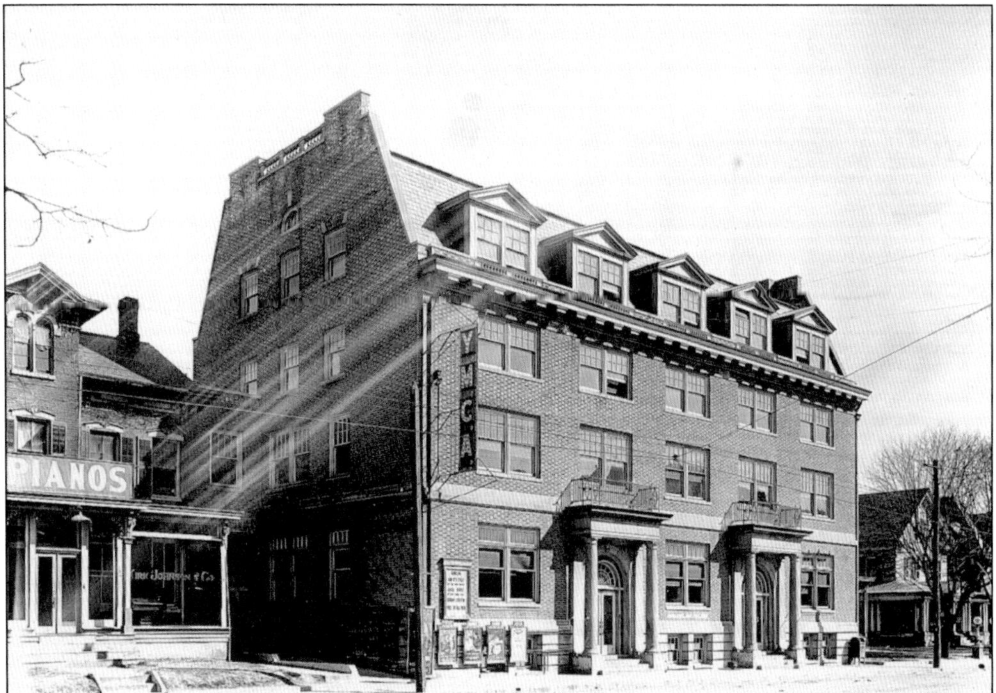

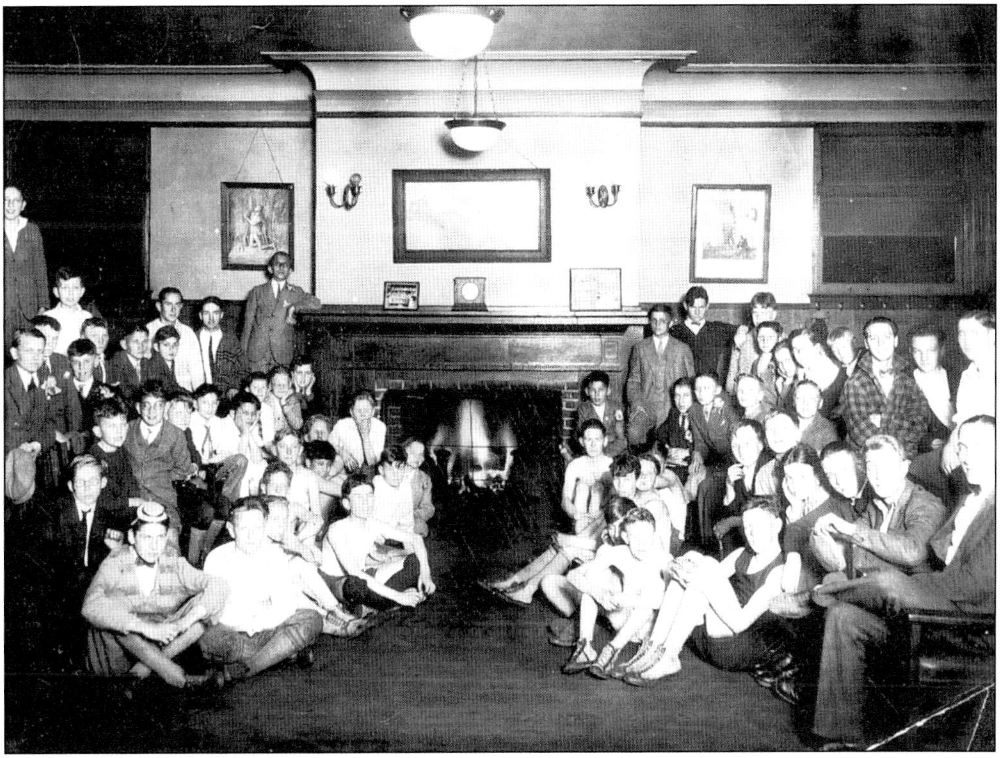

The Coatesville YMCA was the scene of many gatherings. Above, young men gather in the lobby lounge of the group's quarters on Main Street. A picture depicting the Roman Forum is displayed over the mantle in the lounge. Groups of Lukens Steel Company employees also gathered in various areas, and the photograph below shows a group in front of a mill building.

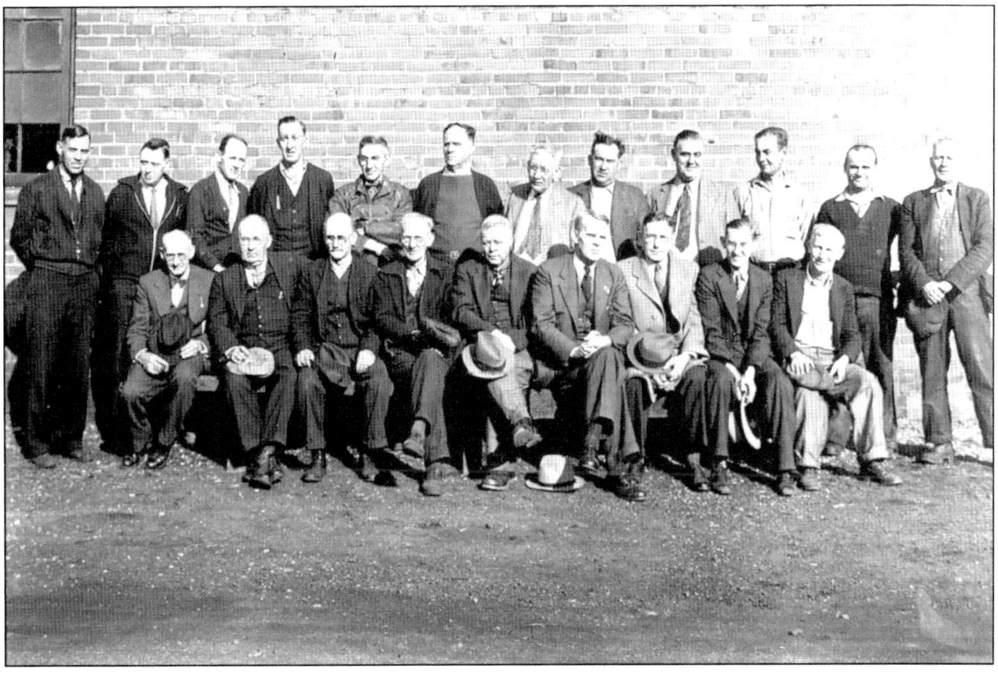

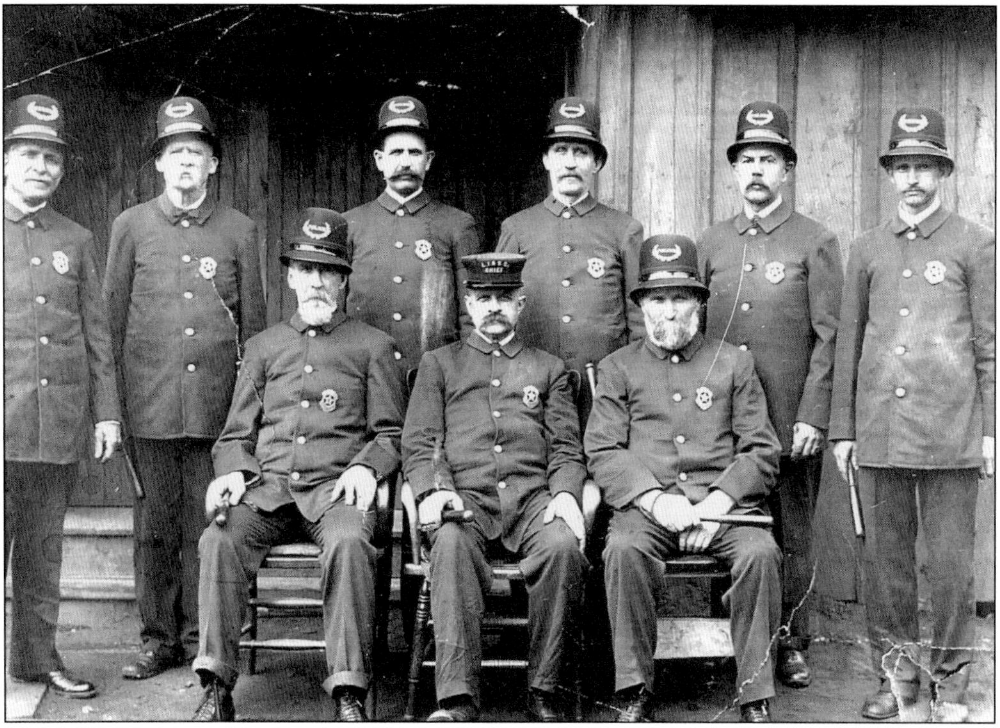

Lukens had its own police department. Above, its members gather for a photograph in the plant. In the photograph below, taken sometime before 1917, Lukens officials pose in front of the main office on First Avenue. Executives A.F. Huston, on the left, and C.L. Huston are in the front row.

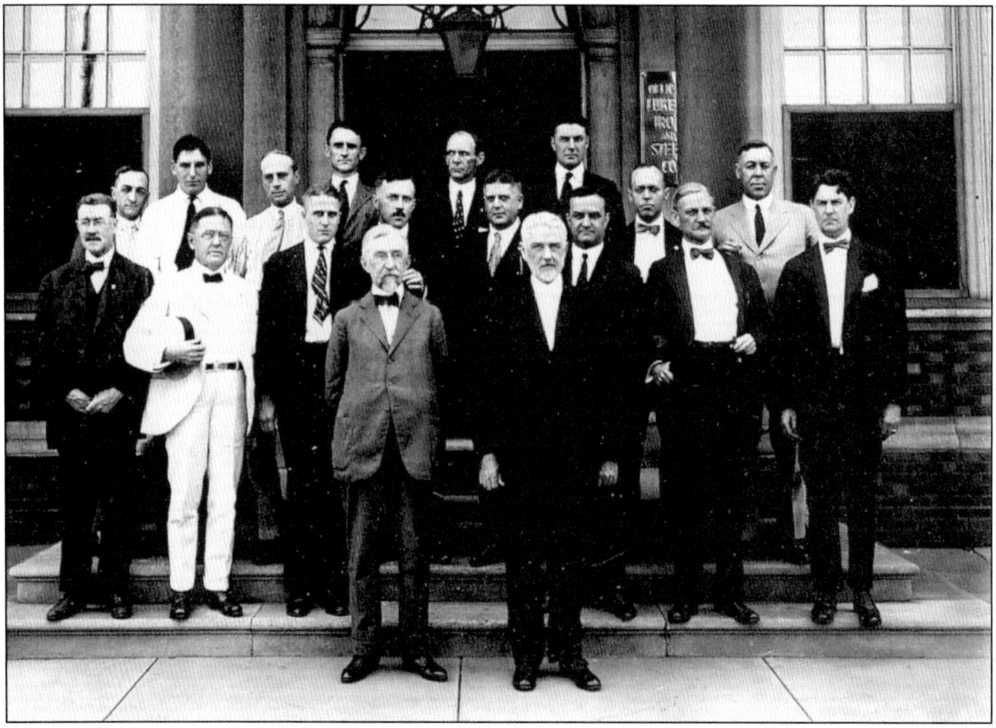

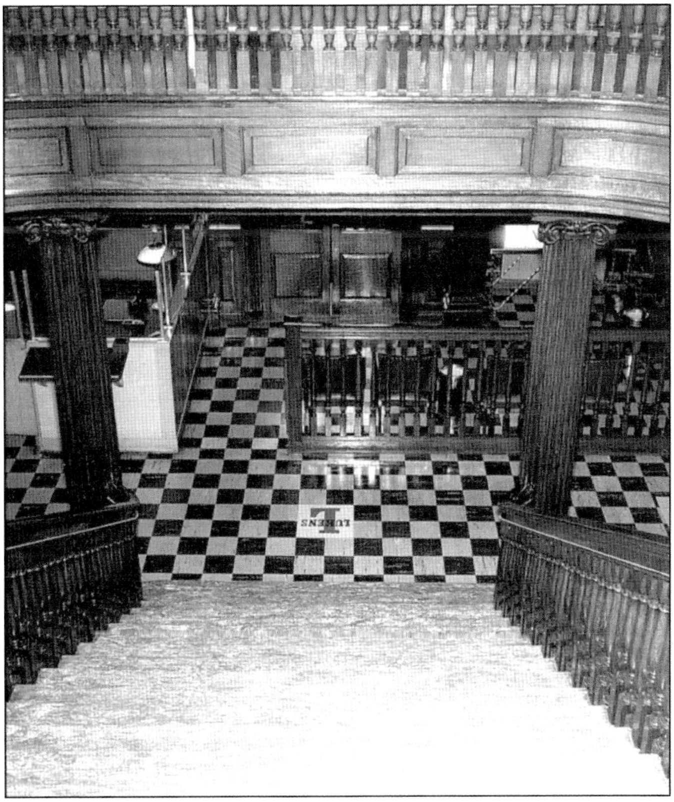

The place where decisions were made at the Lukens Steel Company was the main office building on First Avenue. The photograph to the right was taken from the second floor, looking down the stairwell to the "Lukens" tile mosaic set in the center of the floor. The lobby, as shown in the photograph below, features fine golden oak woodworking, as designed by architects Cope and Stedwardson.

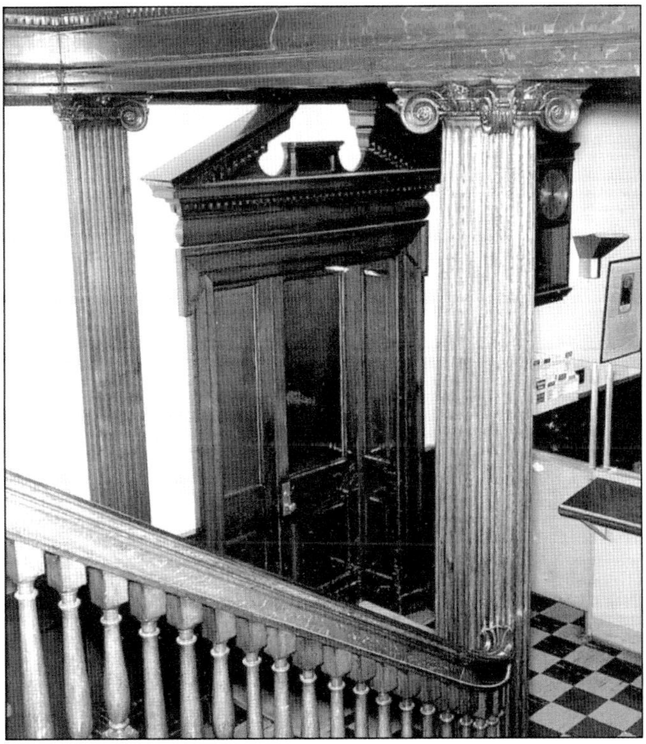

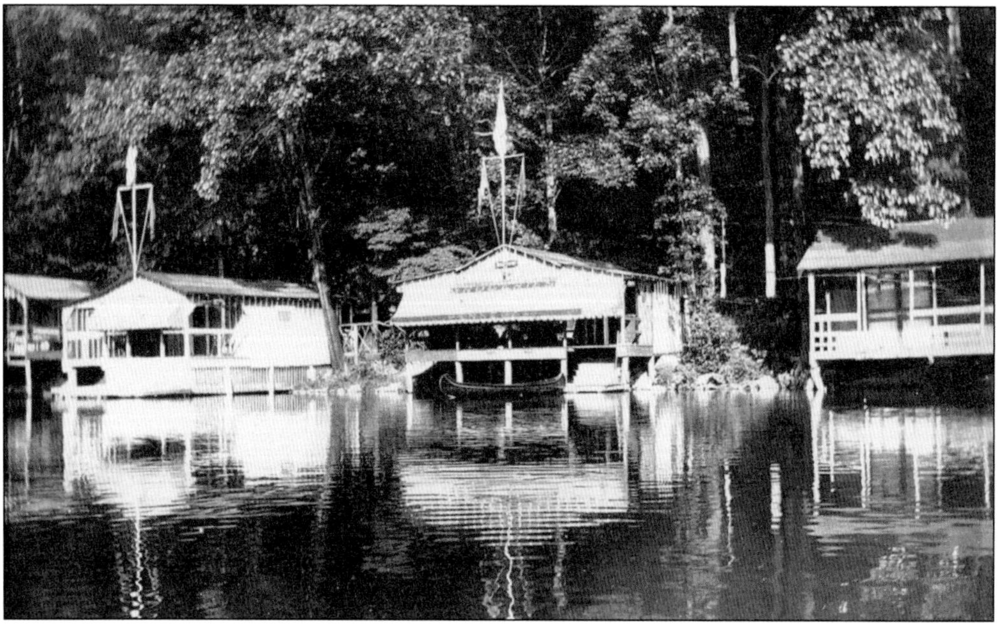

Coatesville also had places to relax, such as Kurtz's Dam on the outskirts of the city. The area had summer cabins for residents, as shown in the photographs on this page, and was used for many different activities, including canoeing. A summer camp was also operated. The cabins were known as Boat House Row.

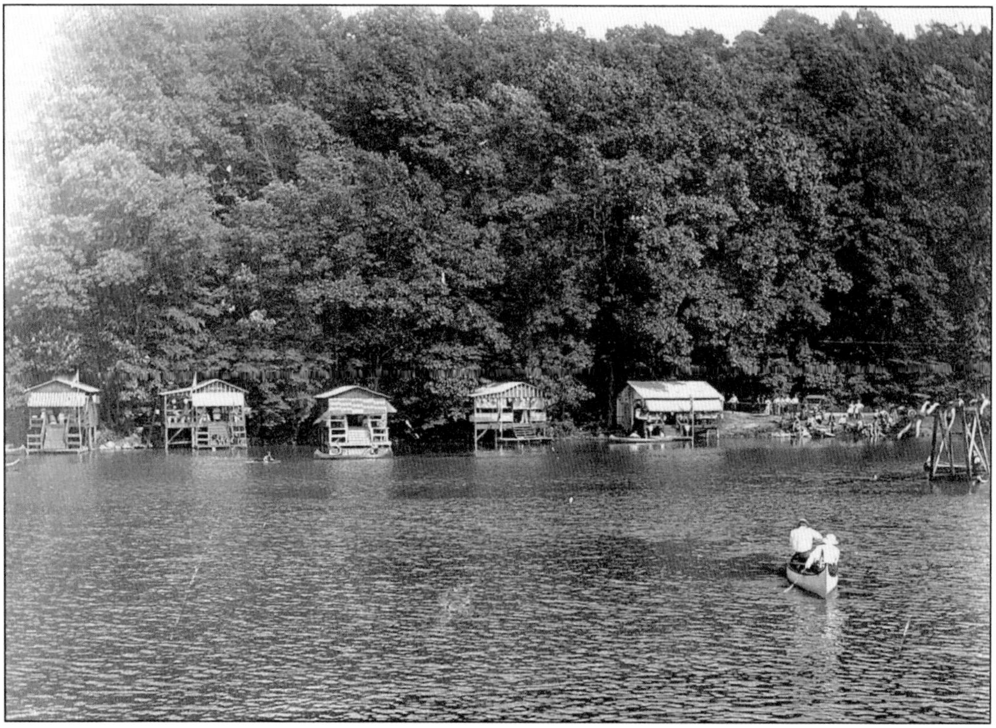

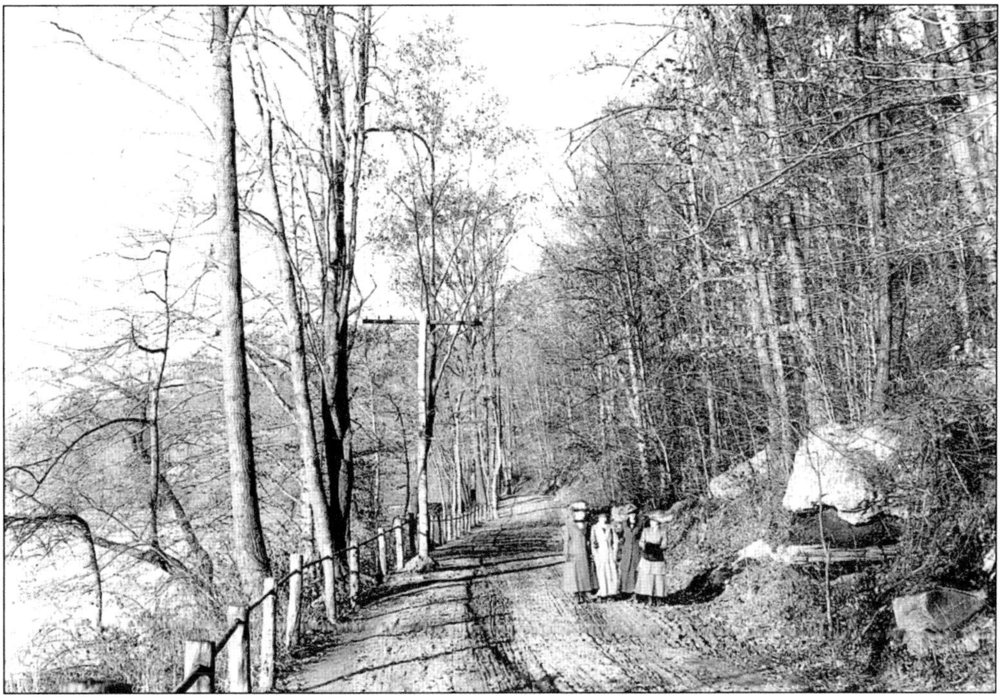

The Kurtz's Dam area was a favorite place for a stroll. The women above are walking on the Rock Run dirt road. Below, a YMCA costume party is held in the organization's main building on Main Street. The YMCA was one of the most used buildings in the town.

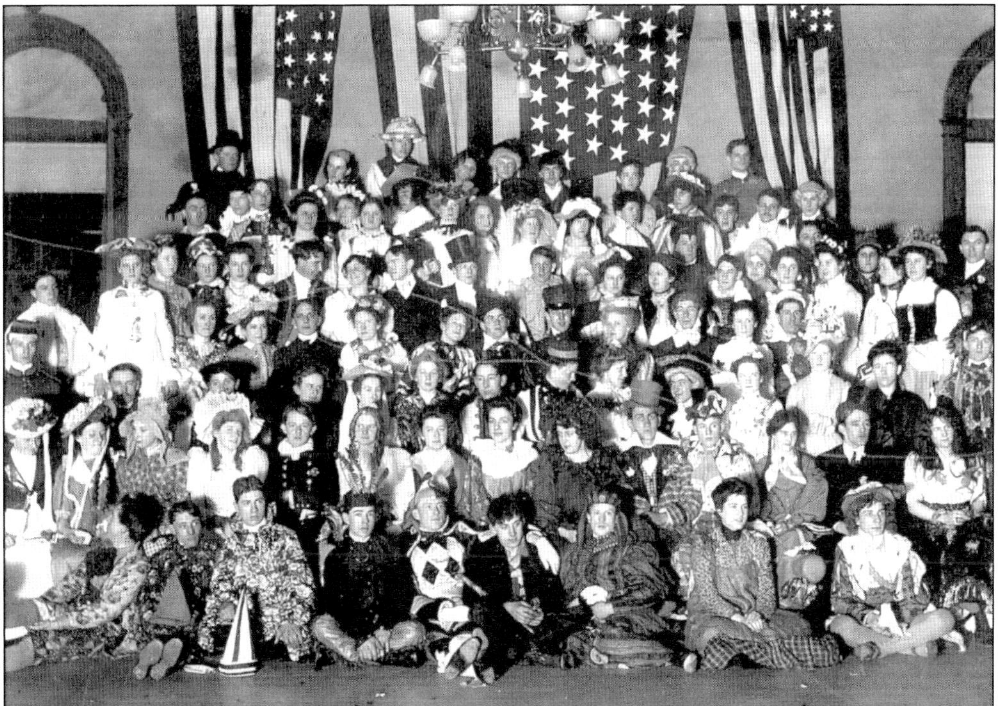

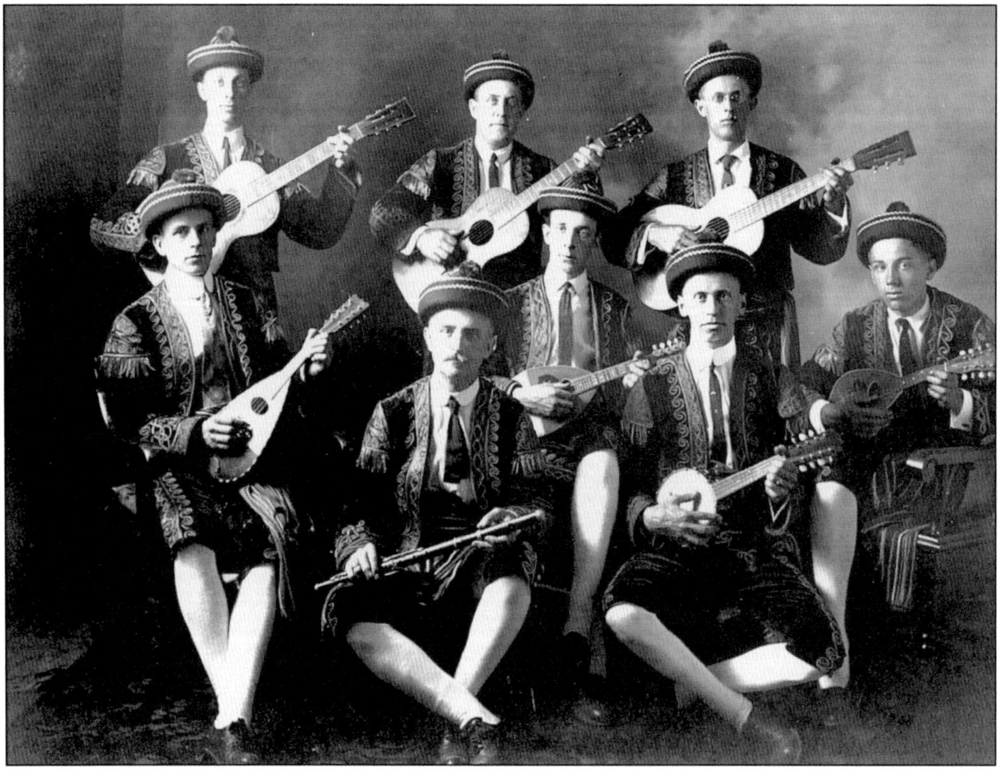

The mandolin group shown above played at a number of events in Coatesville in the early part of the 20th century. Below, the Lukens Band plays during Coatesville's centennial in 1910. The Lukens Band continues to play at community events today, not only in Coatesville but across Chester County as well.

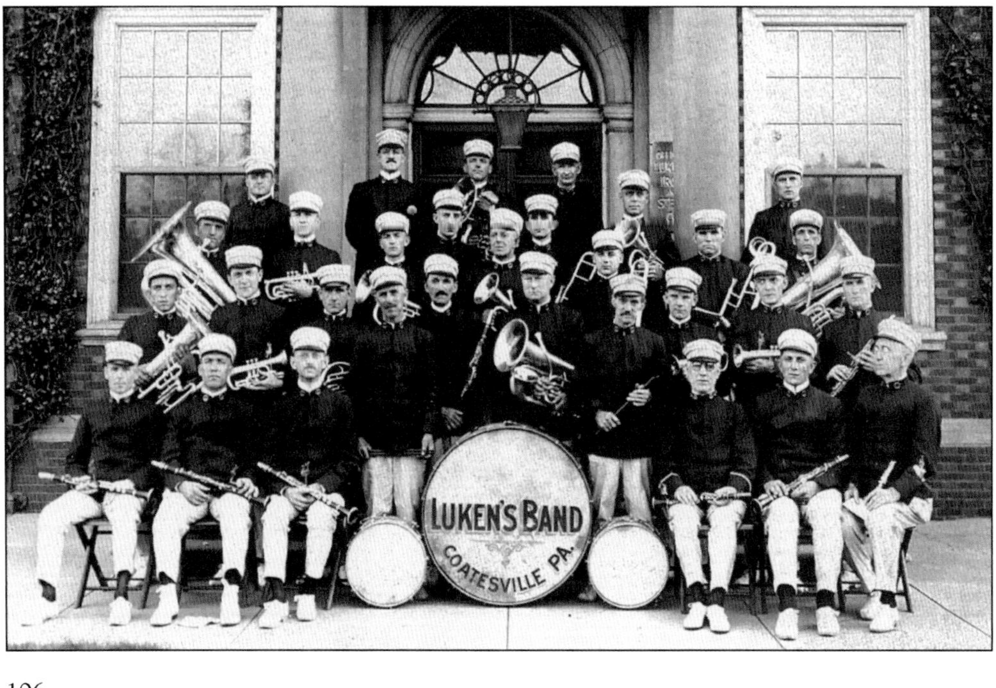

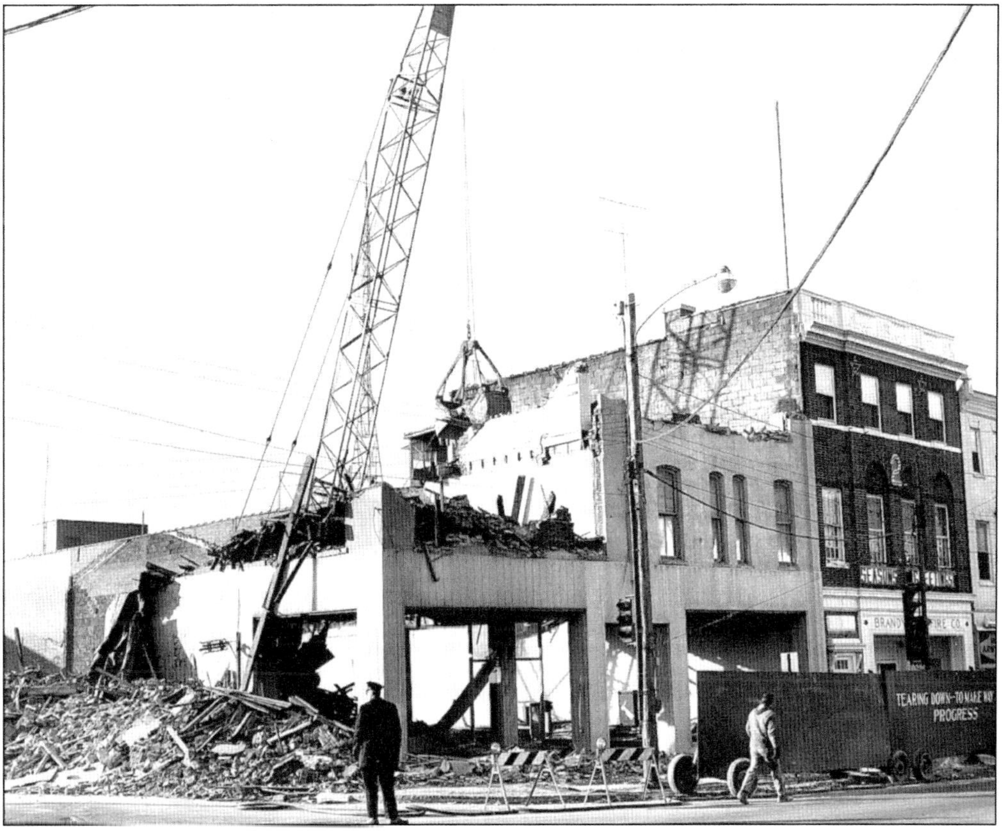

Not all of the places that were landmarks to generations of Coatesville residents remain. Seen above, the buildings along Main Street at First Avenue, including the Brandywine Fire Company, no longer exist, and a park has replaced them. The photograph below shows the former William P. Worth mansion, at the southeast corner of Third Avenue and Main Street. The mansion was demolished in the late 1940s.

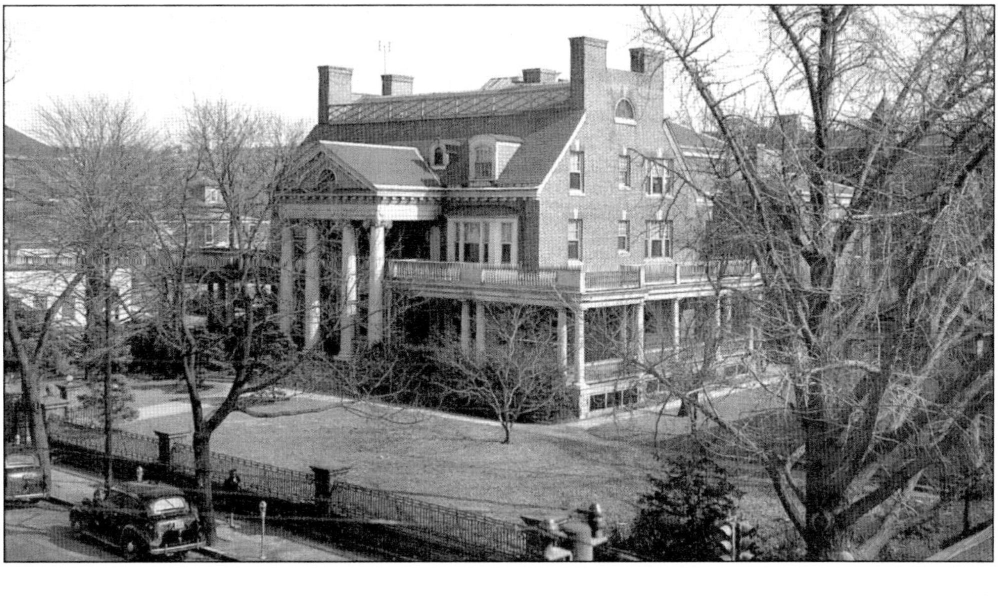

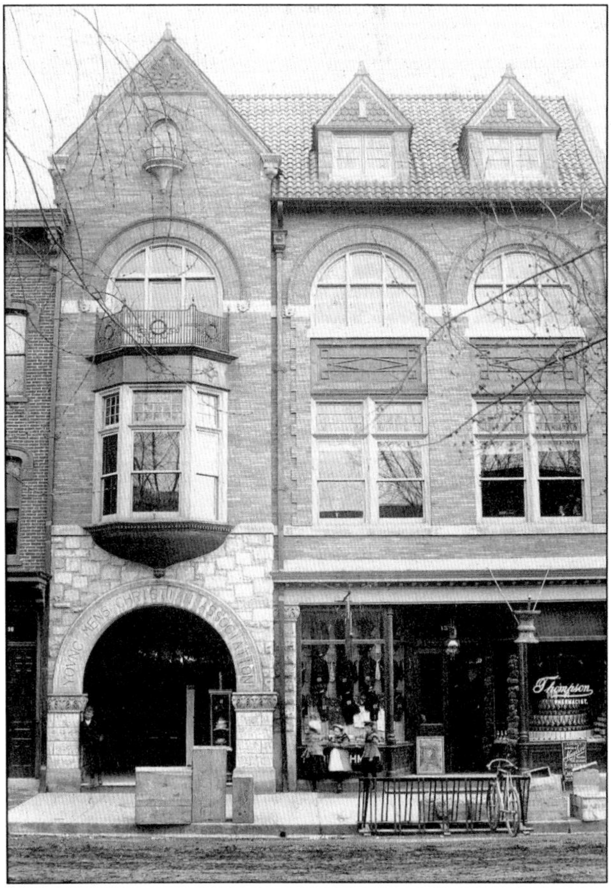

The original YMCA building is shown to the left. A bicycle rack stands in front of the Thompson establishment. The YMCA building survives today but is now used for other purposes. Shown in the photograph below, the school building on Main Street between Fifth and Sixth Avenues used to be the high school. It burned in the early 1900s.

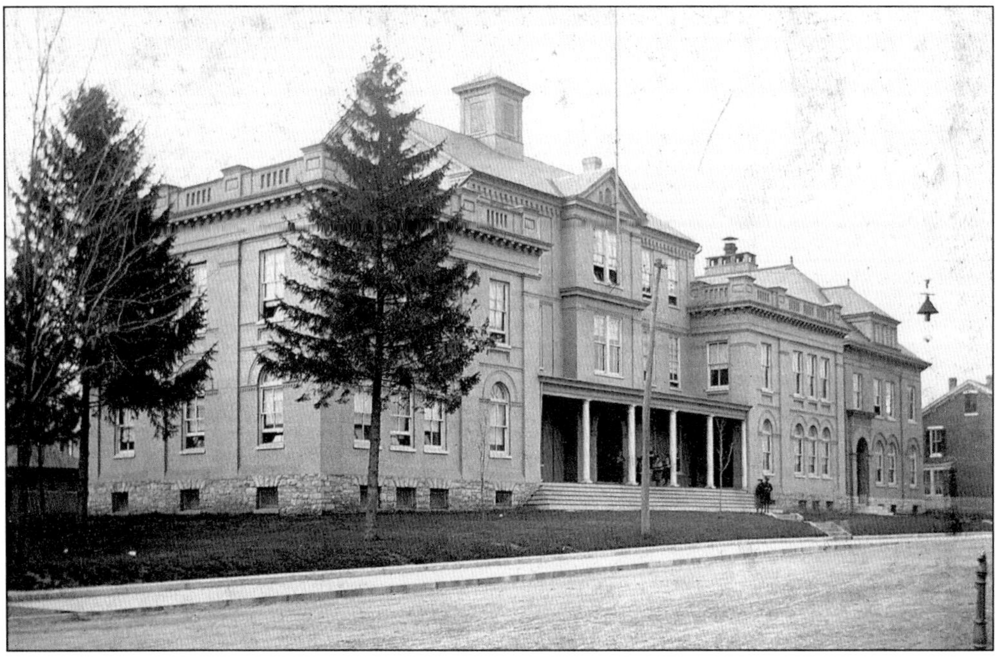

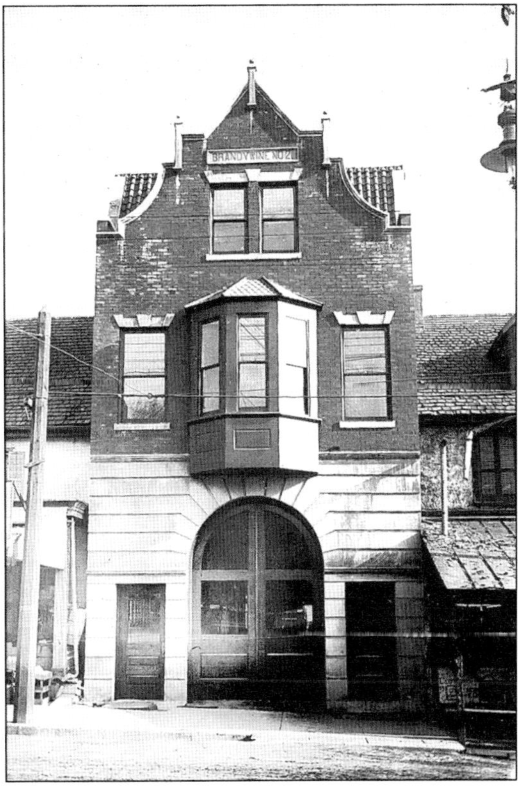

At one time, the city had three fire companies. The original building of the Brandywine Fire Company No. 2 is shown to the right. Below, the main business district of Coatesville shows a number of shops that served the community for years (including the St. Regis Restaurant) but that no longer exist.

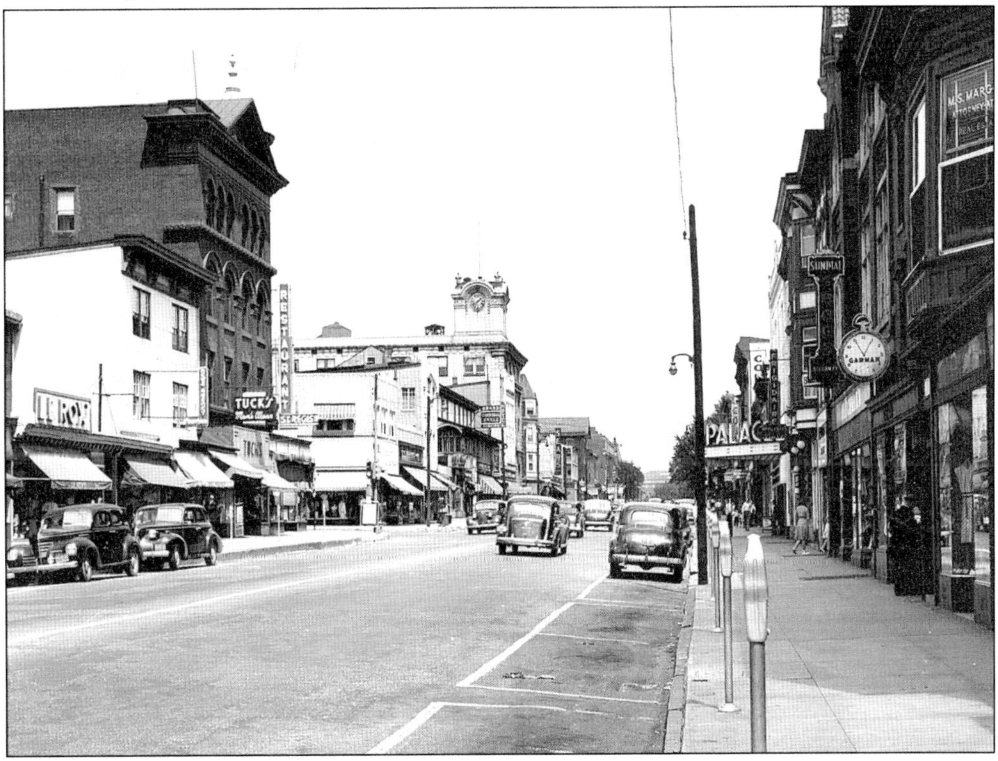

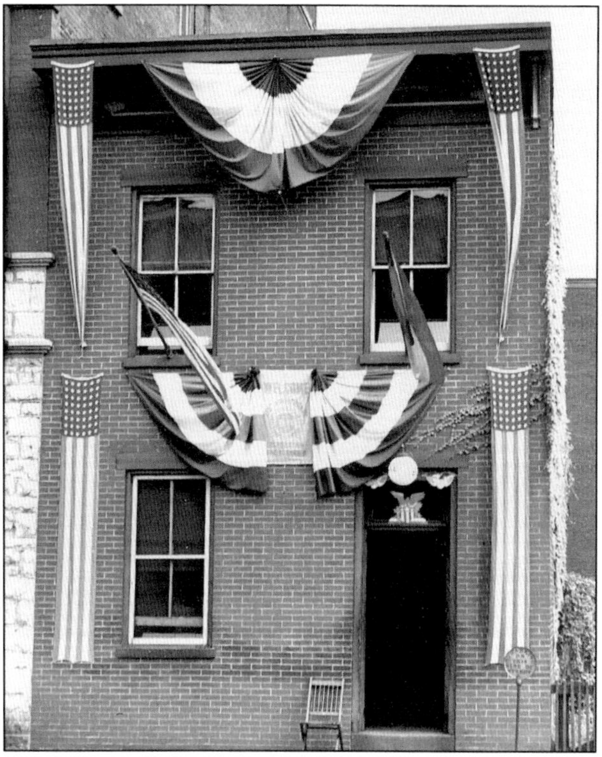

To the left, the former Coatesville City Hall is all decked out for a celebration. The lighted glass ball indicating the police station is shown here, just below one of the banners and on top of the Eagle emblem. The Coatesville Presbyterian Church, shown below, has served the city's population for years. It stands at the corner of Fourth Avenue and Main Street.

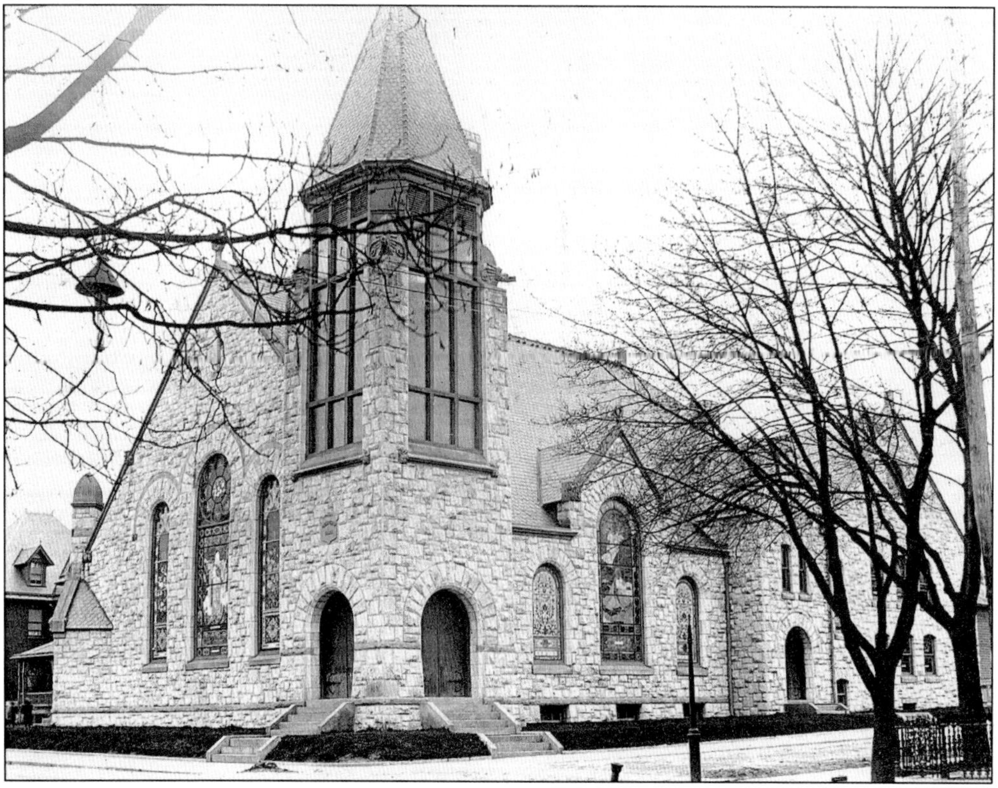

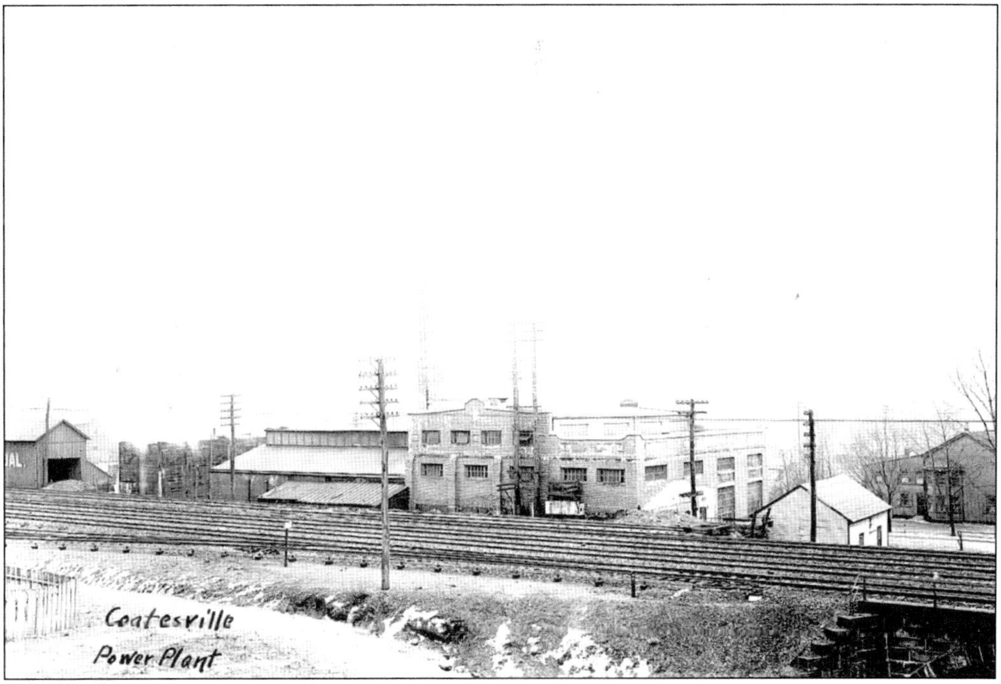

Shown above is a photograph of the old Coatesville power plant, situated along the railroad tracks in the northern section of the town. The bottom photograph was taken in 1911 by George Kacy and shows the old Pennsylvania Railroad passenger station to the left. In the center is Moses Coates's home, constructed in 1809.

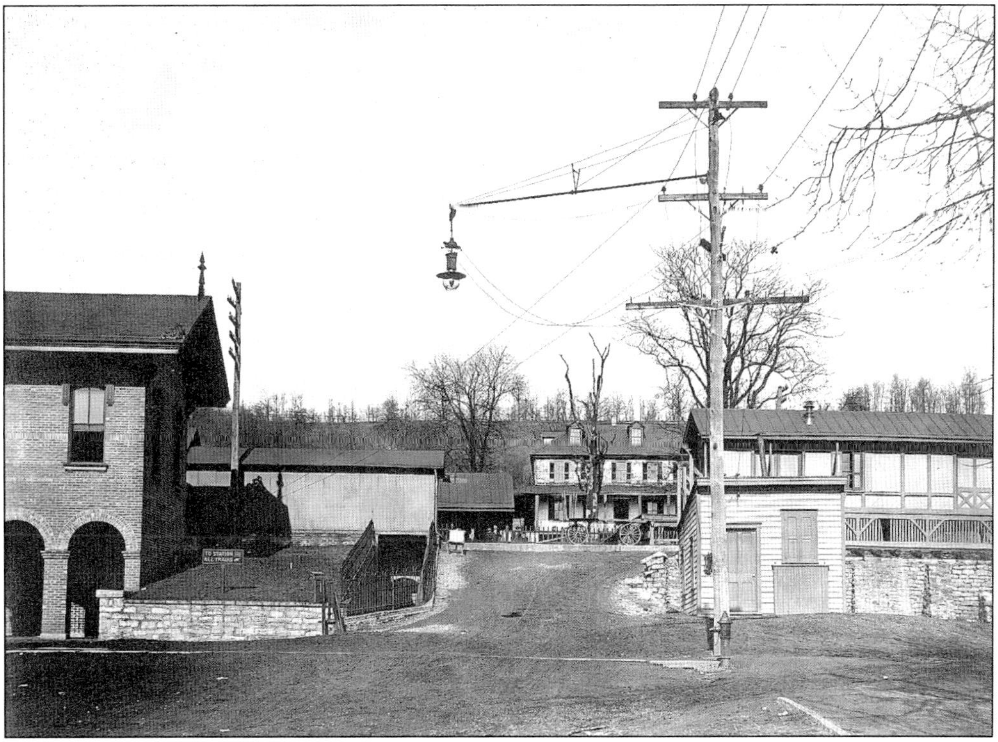

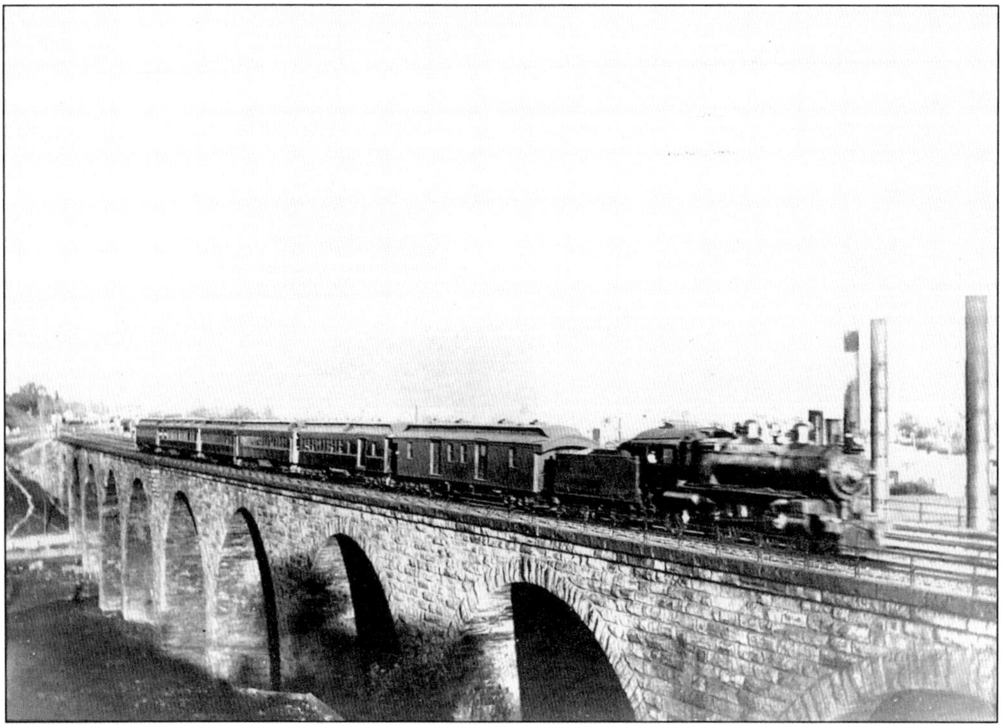

Over the years, Coatesville has been known for its railroads. The above photograph shows a train going over the Pennsylvania Railroad Bridge, the fourth one to be built that spanned the Brandywine River. The photograph below gives a view of Coatesville from the third high bridge.

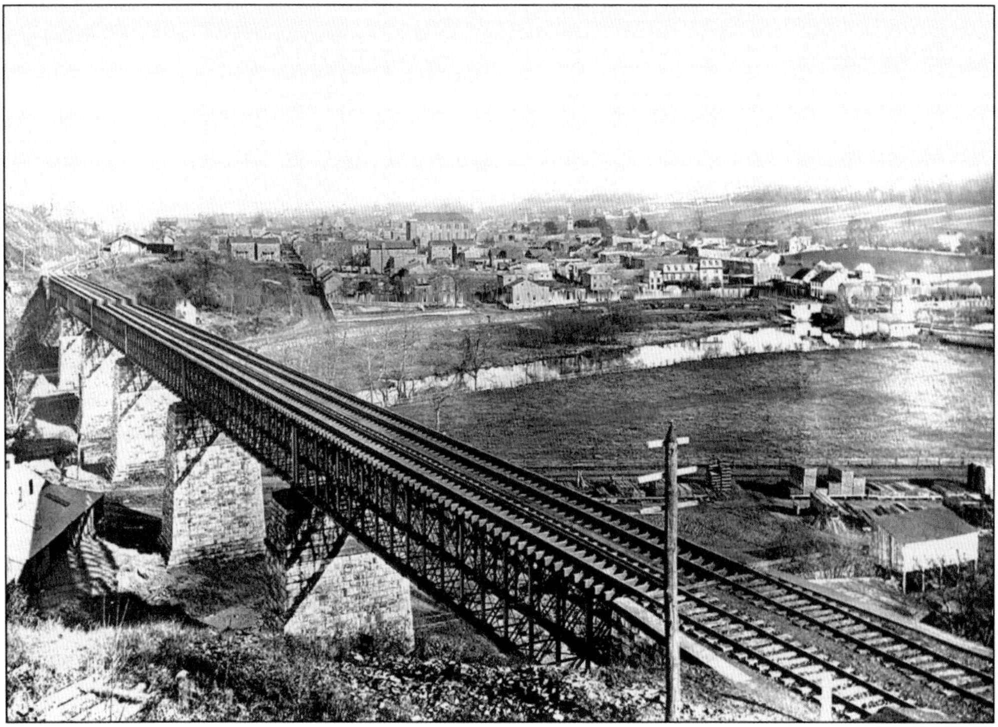

Six

LATER INDUSTRY

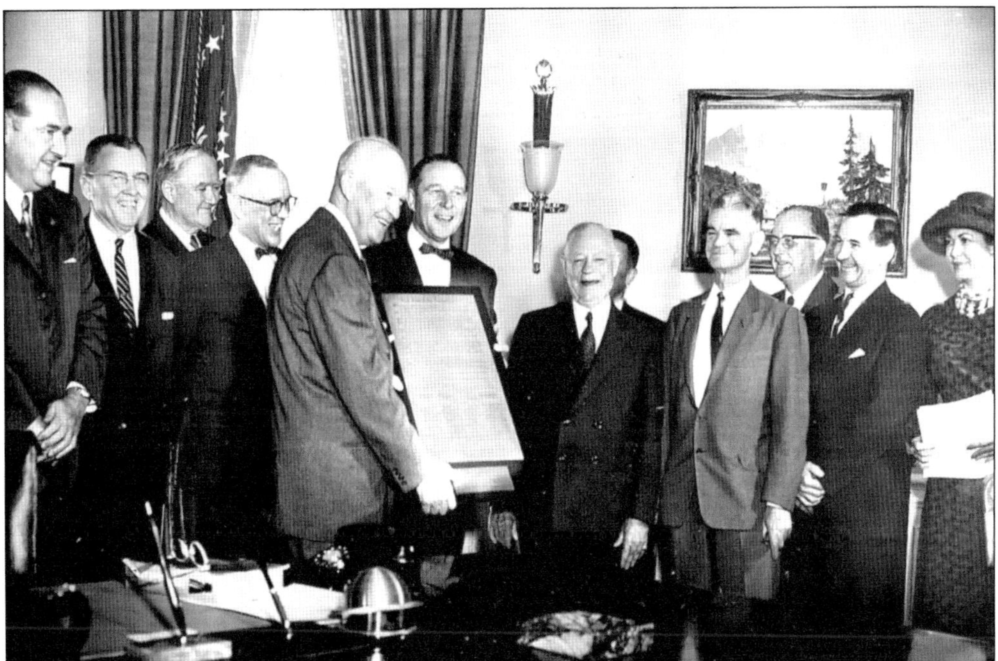

The Lukens Steel Company provided not only jobs for the Coatesville community but also needed material for America's war efforts during World War II and for many of the major structures in the world. In this view, Pres. Dwight E. Eisenhower accepts a Declaration of Economic Freedom from Lukens president Charles Lukens Huston Jr. (in the bow tie) in 1960 at the White House.

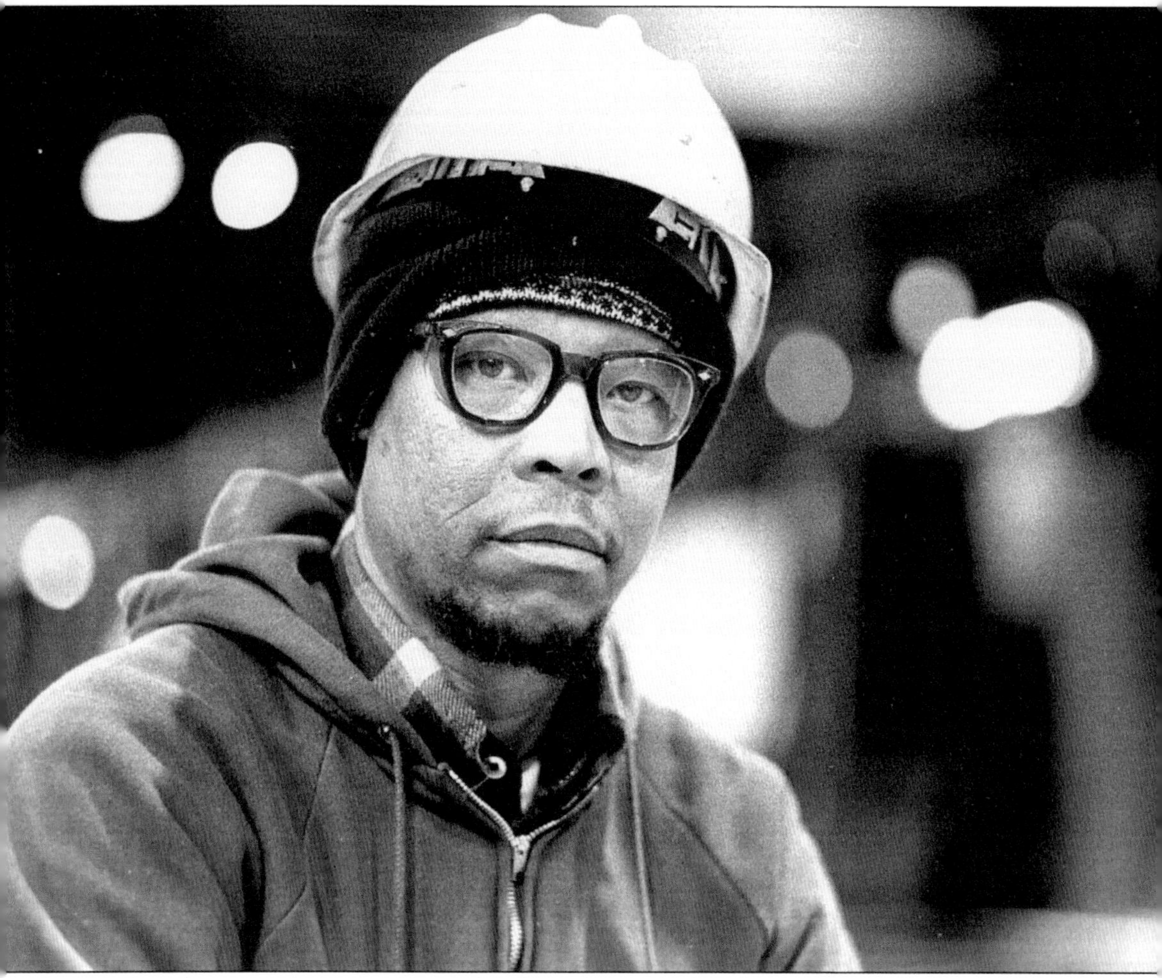

Lukens became a leader in the steel industry because of its dedicated workforce. Shown here is one of the workers in the plant. At one time, more than 5,000 workers were employed at Lukens, and a number of other residents had jobs in businesses and shops that supplied material to Lukens, as well as providing necessities to workers and their families. Lukens also operated a company store on South First Avenue, just south of its main office building. The store was especially known for its meat products and offered credit to members of the Lukens workforce. Lukens executives were encouraged to take active roles in community organizations. They were instrumental in founding many of them, including the Coatesville Hospital.

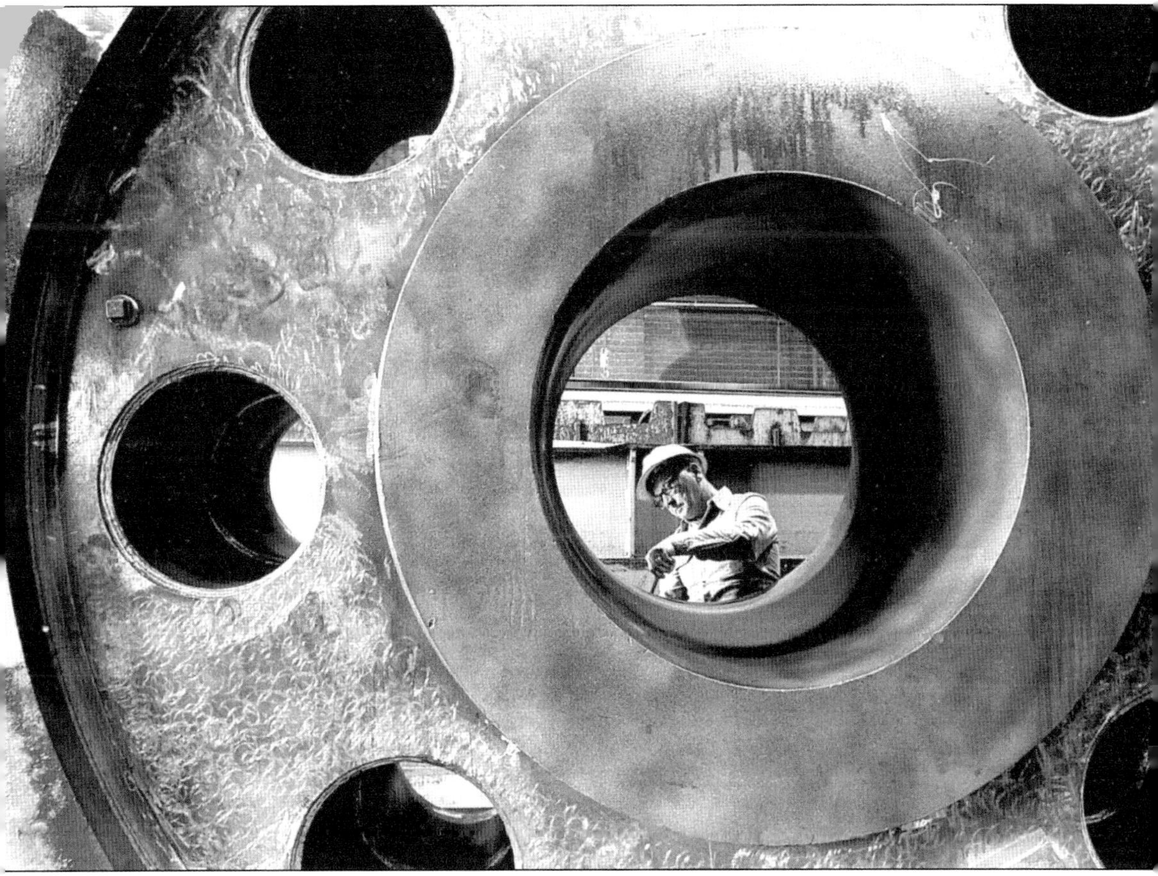

Lukens was known as the leader in specialty steel products. Shown in this photograph is a gear manufactured in Coatesville for the Philadelphia Gear Company, one of the many customers of the steel company in the 20th century. The gears were used in equipment such as large generators and would be shipped by railroad flatcars to where they were needed. Lukens was called upon to cut and form especially complex manufacturing equipment. As the steel industry declined in the United States, the Bethlehem Steel Company purchased the company and operated it for a number of years.

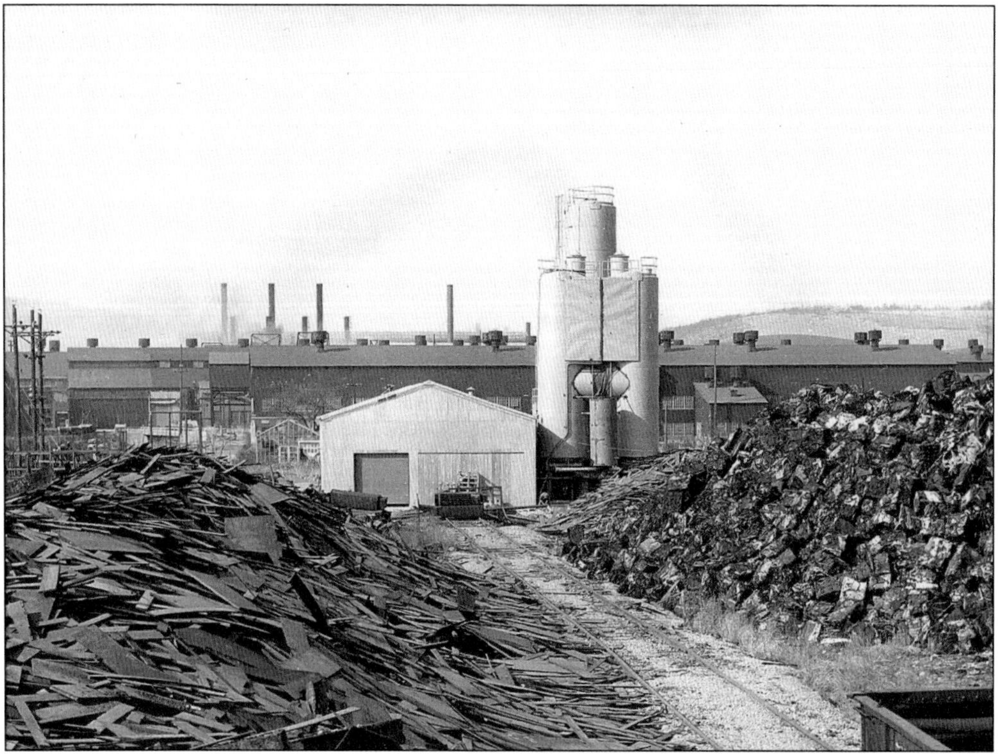

For Lukens to produce its products, tons of raw materials were needed each day. Shown above is a Lukens scrap yard. Two ingots are waiting in front of the shed for transportation on the company's railroad system. Below, an employee is using a crane to properly position a plate.

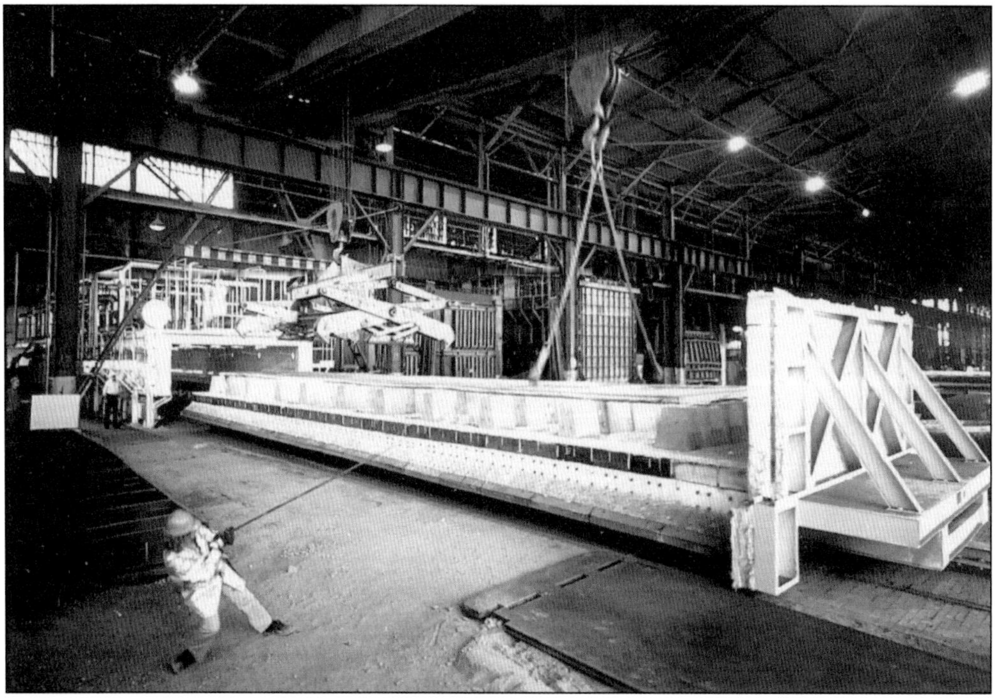

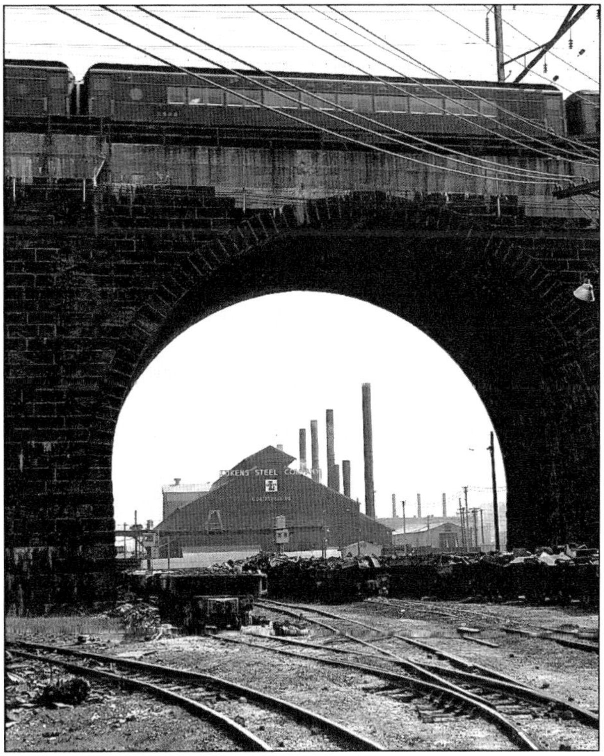

The signature Lukens sign and smokestacks are seen along Lincoln Highway in the photograph to the right. The view is from underneath the high bridge on the town's northern side as a passenger train passes above the yard where scrap iron fills rail cars. In the photograph below, Lukens transportation executives check out the rail system, including C.L. Lukens Jr., on the train at the left.

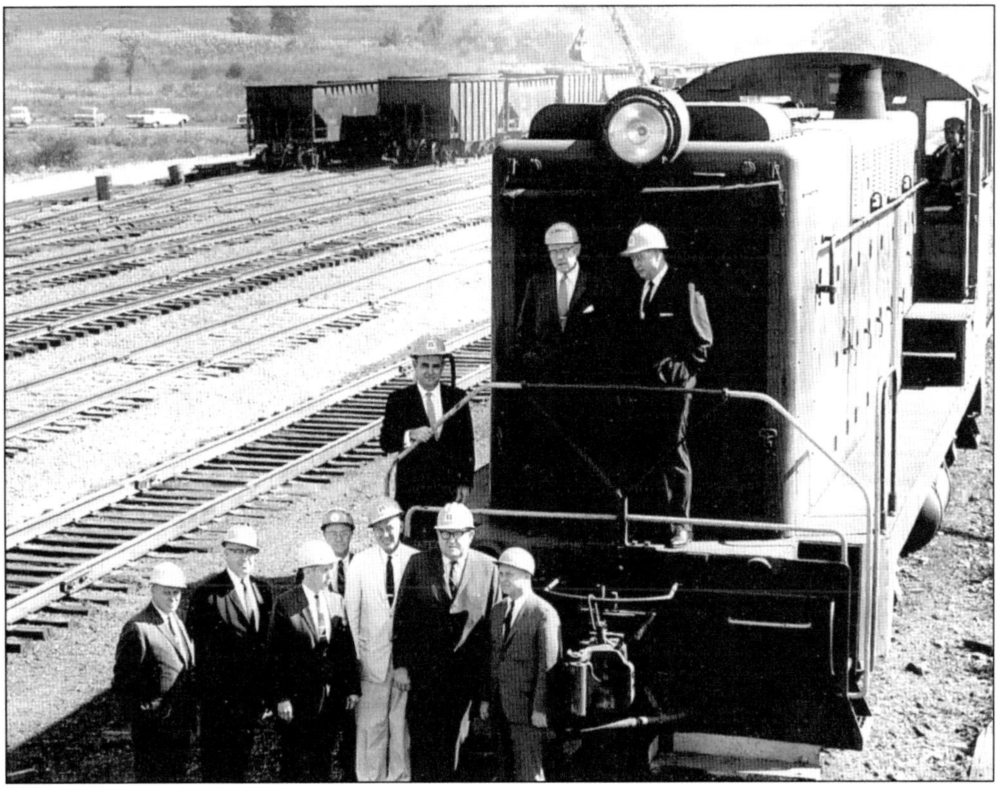

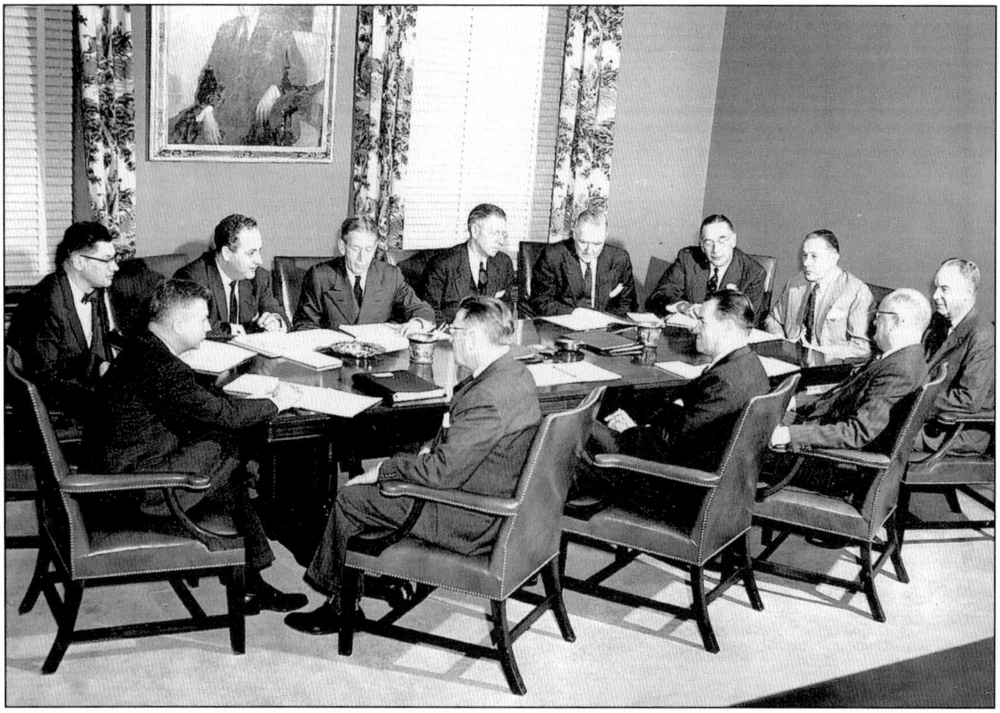

The executive decisions for Lukens were made in the executive boardroom of the main office building, on First Avenue, as shown above. Below, executives from Lukens and the G.O. Carlson Steel Company of Coatesville gather around the table to sign a cooperation agreement. Both companies had plants along the Lincoln Highway.

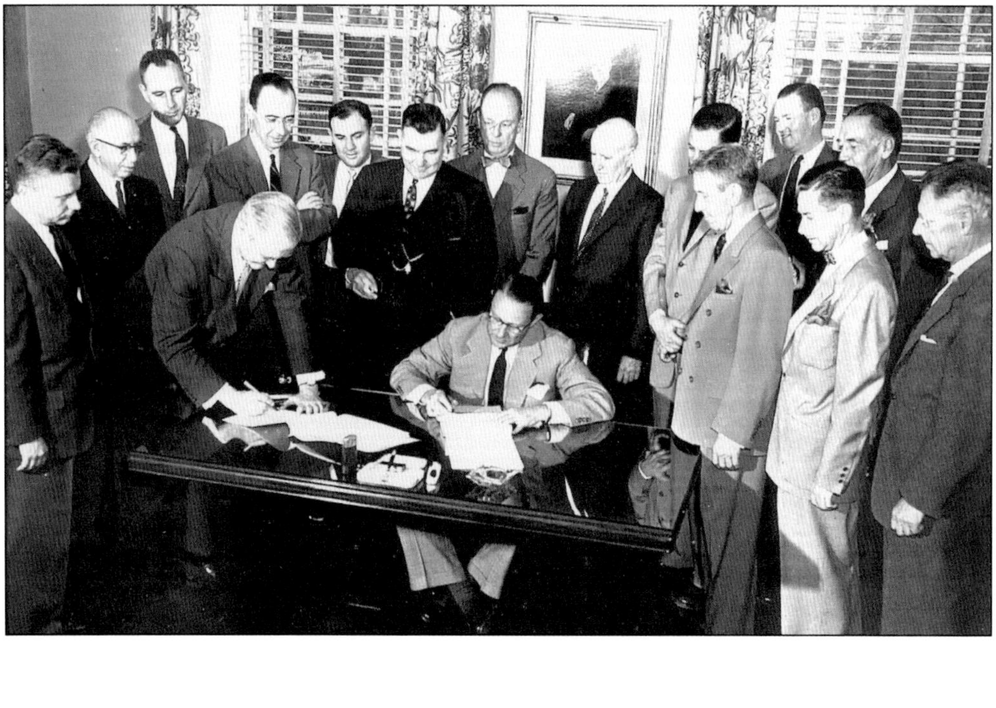

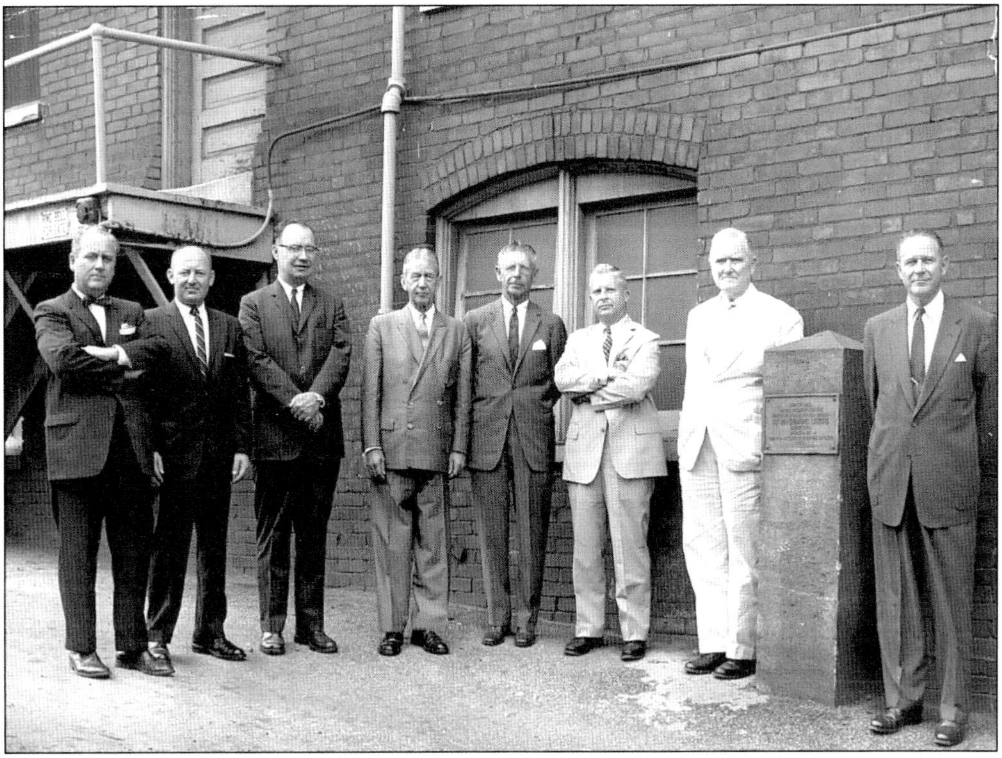

Above, a celebration takes place to commemorate 150 years of operations by Lukens. The photograph of the monument was taken outside of a mill building. From left to right are Robert Bowman, Ed Myers, Dan Igoe, James Herman, Fred Weisse, William Mullestein, Stewart Huston, and C.L. Huston. In the photograph below, mill workers gather around for an announcement and a photo opportunity.

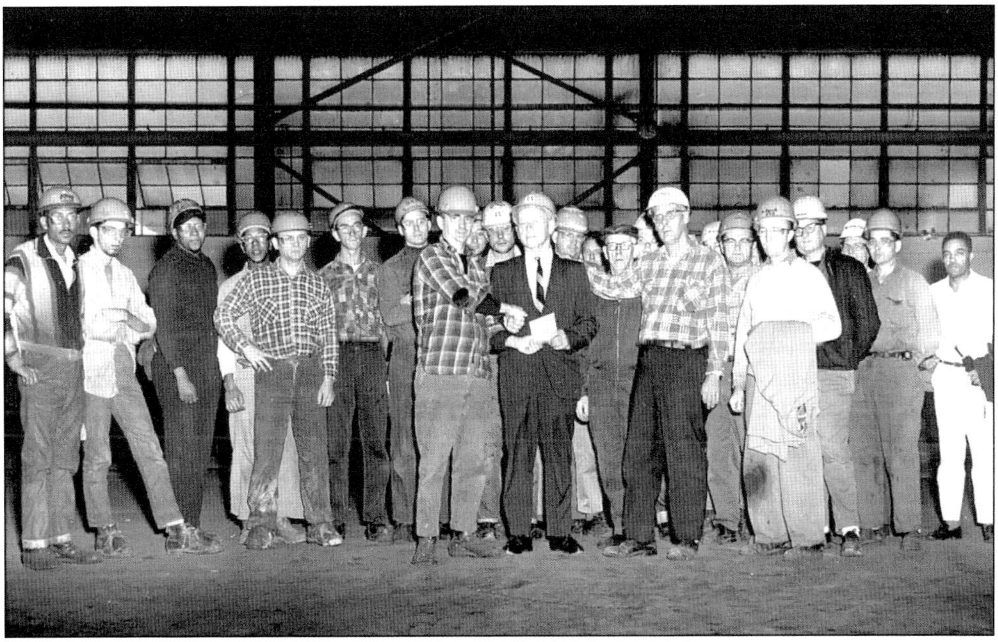

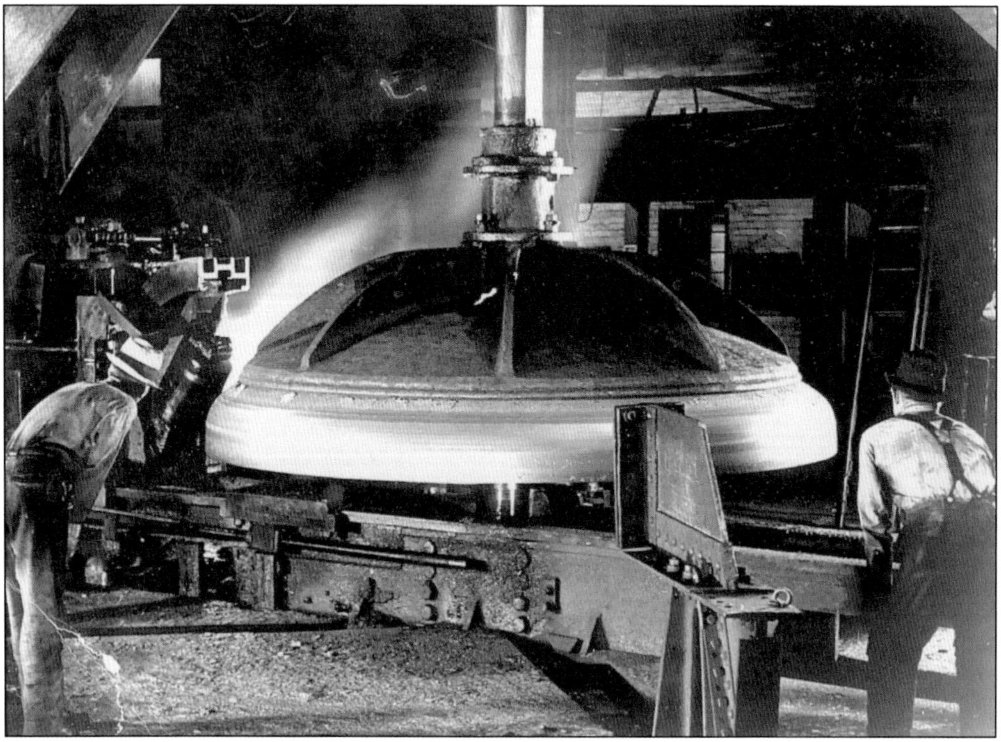

One of the specialty products of Lukens was spun heads. Shown in the above photograph are two workers turning a spun head. In the photograph below, a flame cutter is used to cut a pattern on a steel slab. As new and improved manufacturing tools were produced, Lukens modernized its plants.

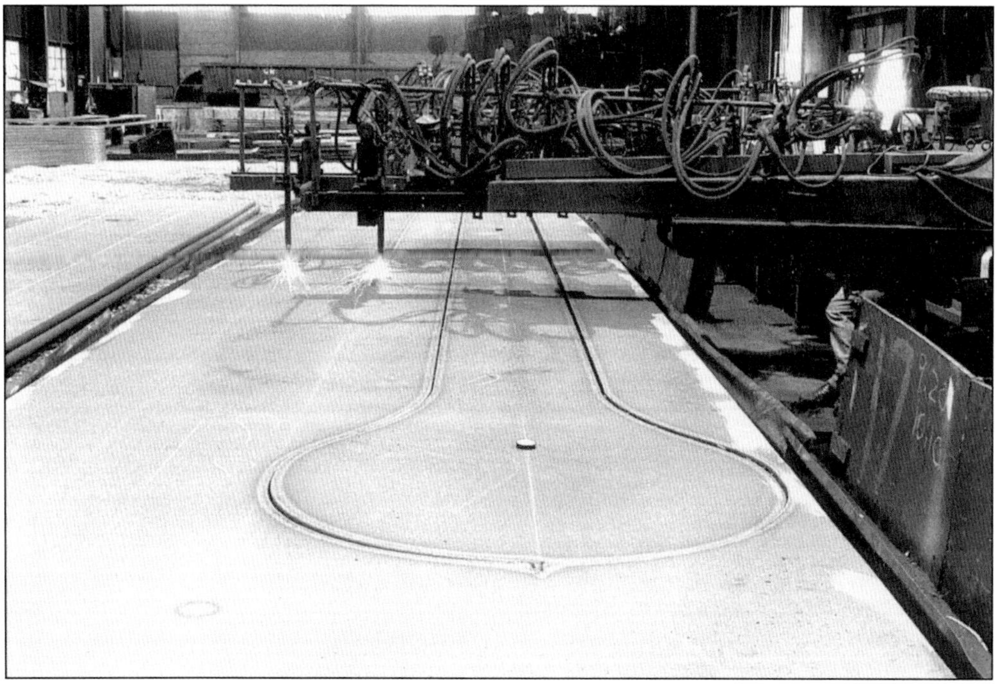

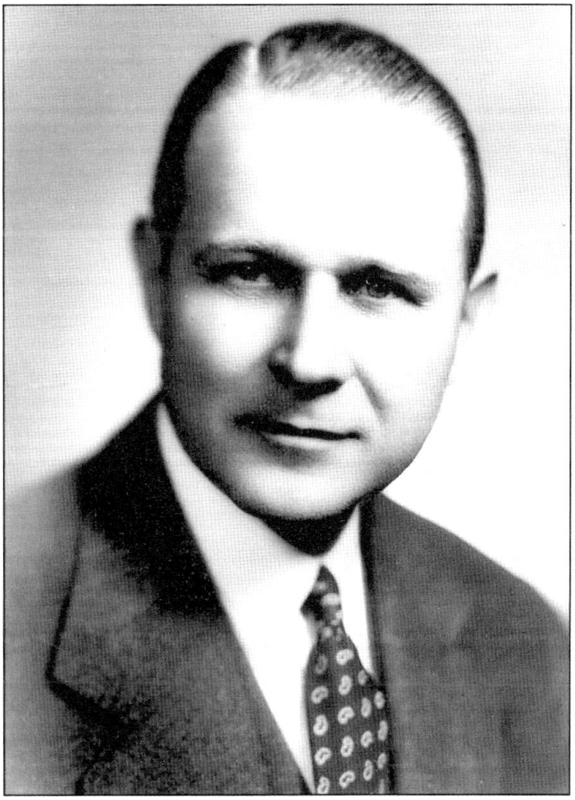

Charles Lukens Huston Jr., shown to the right, headed the Lukens Steel Company for 25 years. He continued the Huston tradition of offering community leadership. In the photograph below, members of the Lukens executive team absorb a presentation on company sales. Lukens was a sales leader for decades.

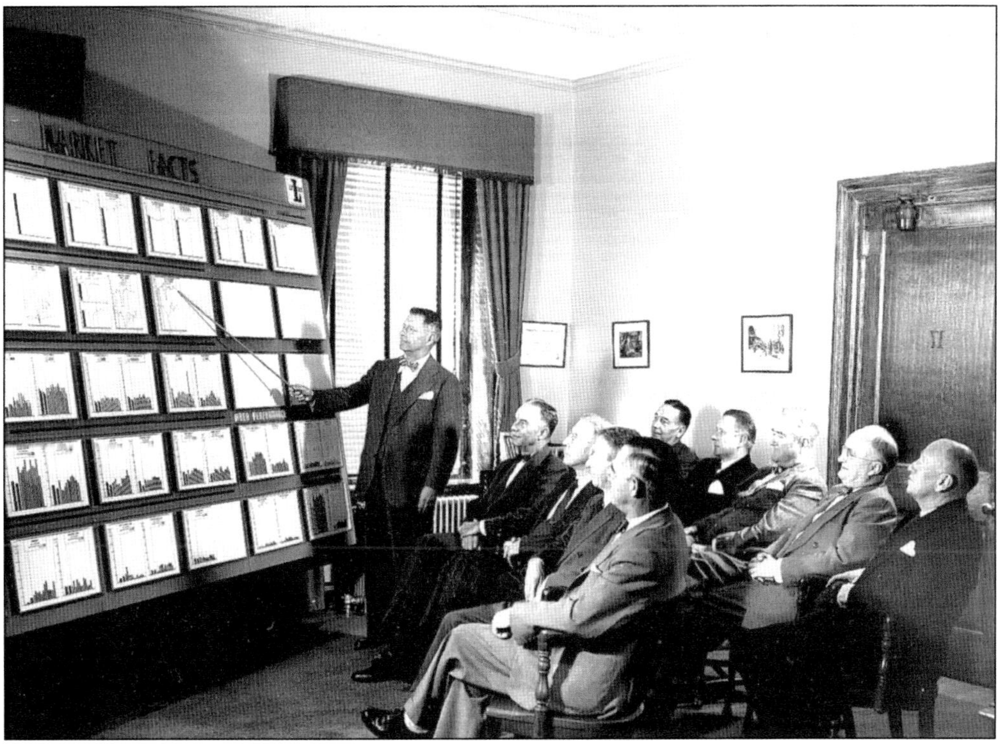

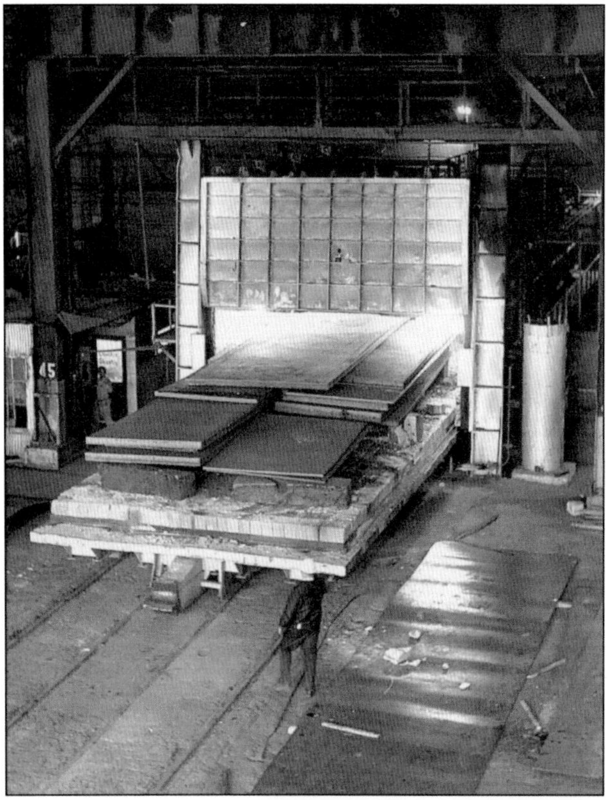

Shown to the left is a batch of plates being readied for treatment. Below, a Lukens employee is grinding one of the plates. For many years, Lukens employed three shifts a day during its busy seasons. Manpower was needed to keep the plants operating.

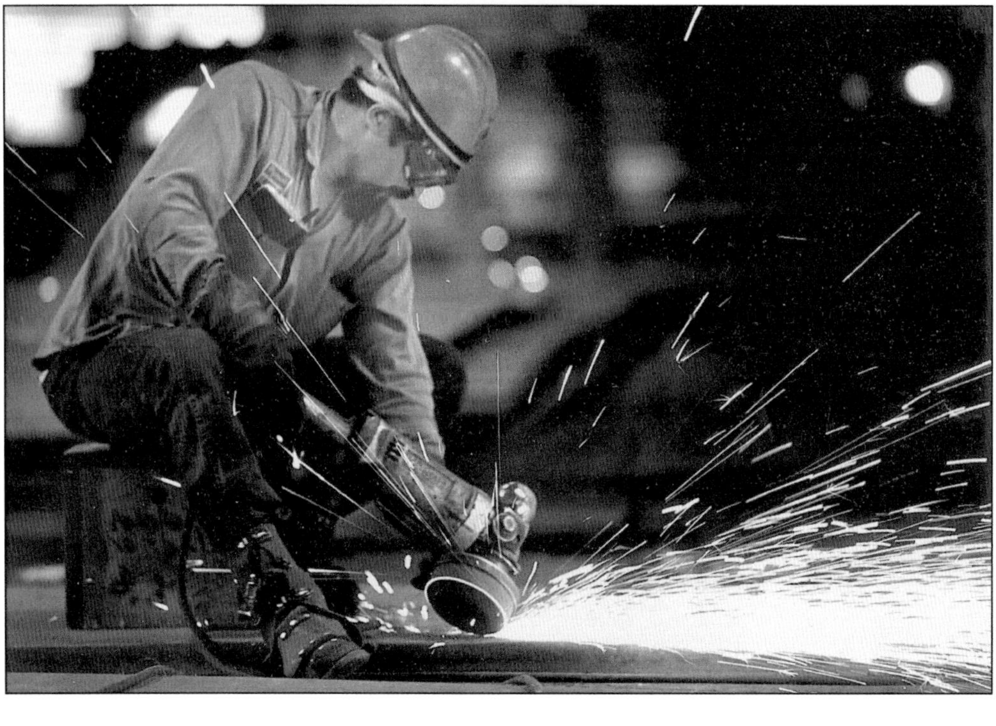

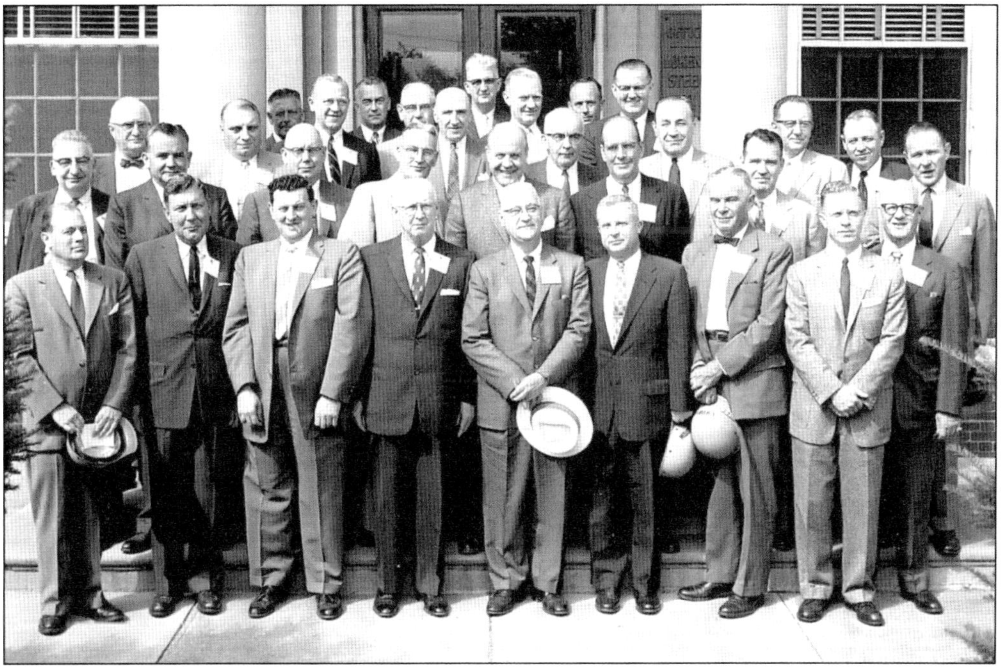

Lukens Steel Company executives are gathered above in front of the main office building in the 1950s. For years, executives held business retreats at Mount Pocono at the Skytop Lodge, where they discussed and planned the direction of the Lukens Steel Company. The photograph below was taken during one such meeting.

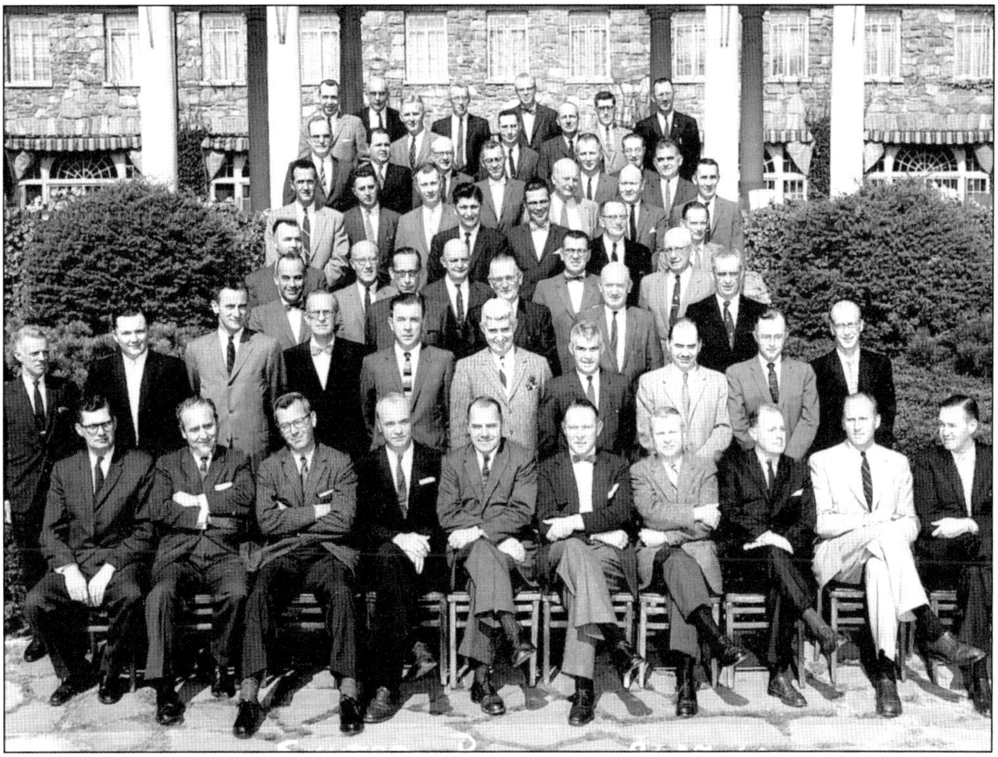

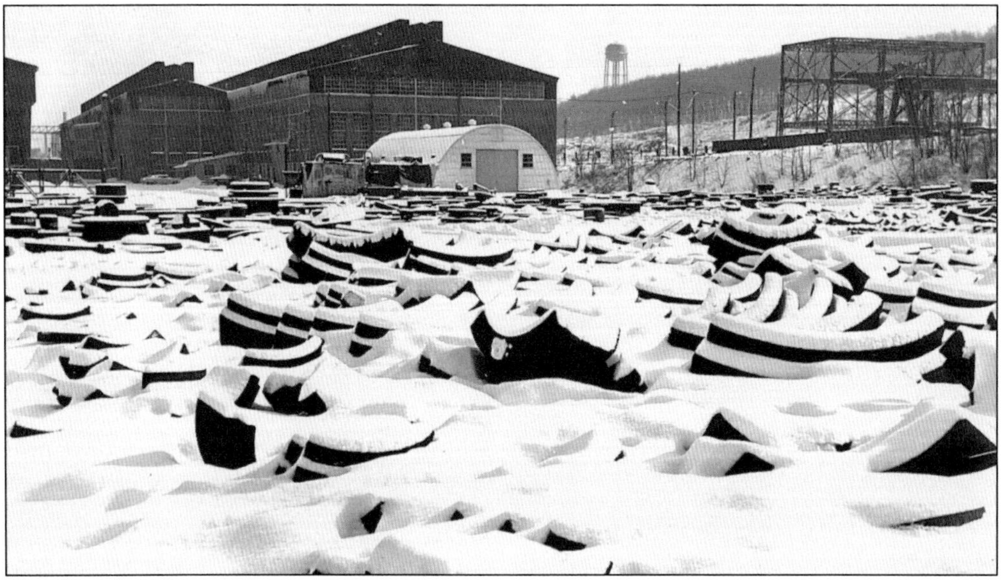

Snowy days turned the iron-filled yards of the Lukens Steel Company in the town's west side into a work of art, as seen in the above view. Most days, those yards were filled with workers turning out products, as a letter from Pres. Lyndon Johnson to Lukens president Charles L. Huston Jr. attested.

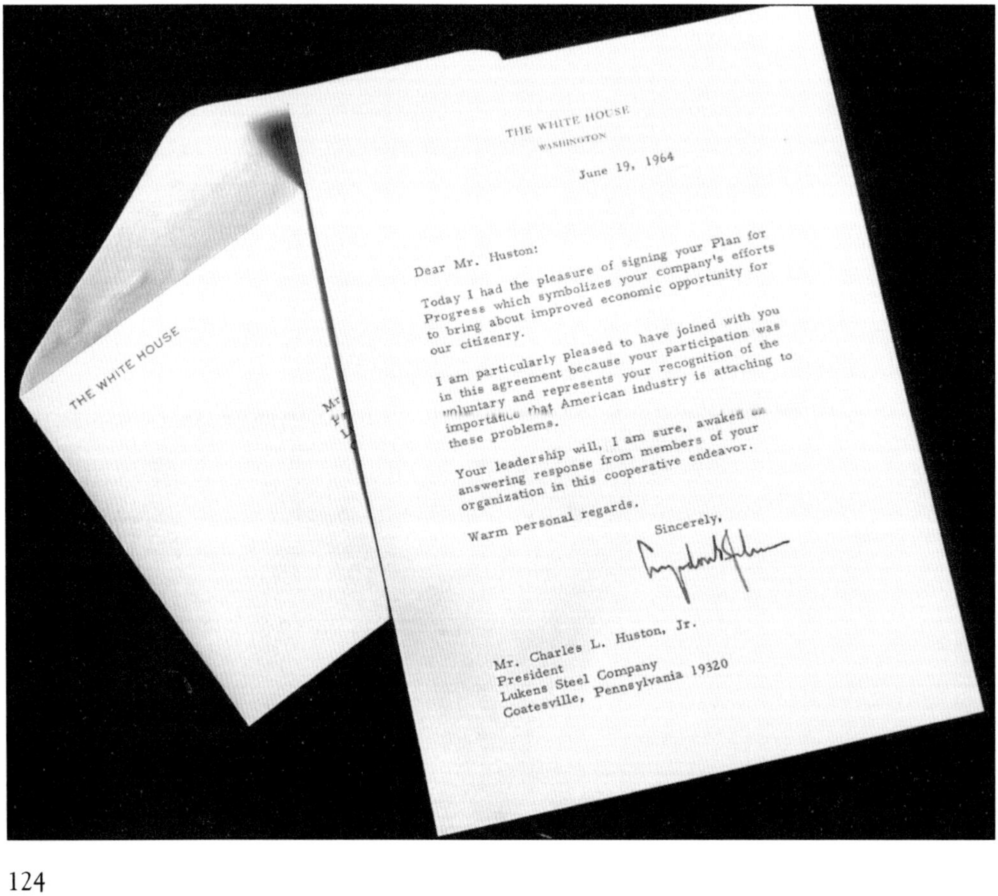

THE WHITE HOUSE

THE WHITE HOUSE
WASHINGTON

June 19, 1964

Dear Mr. Huston:

Today I had the pleasure of signing your Plan for Progress which symbolizes your company's efforts to bring about improved economic opportunity for our citizenry.

I am particularly pleased to have joined with you in this agreement because your participation was voluntary and represents your recognition of the importance that American industry is attaching to these problems.

Your leadership will, I am sure, awaken an answering response from members of your organization in this cooperative endeavor.

Warm personal regards.

Sincerely,

Mr. Charles L. Huston, Jr.
President
Lukens Steel Company
Coatesville, Pennsylvania 19320

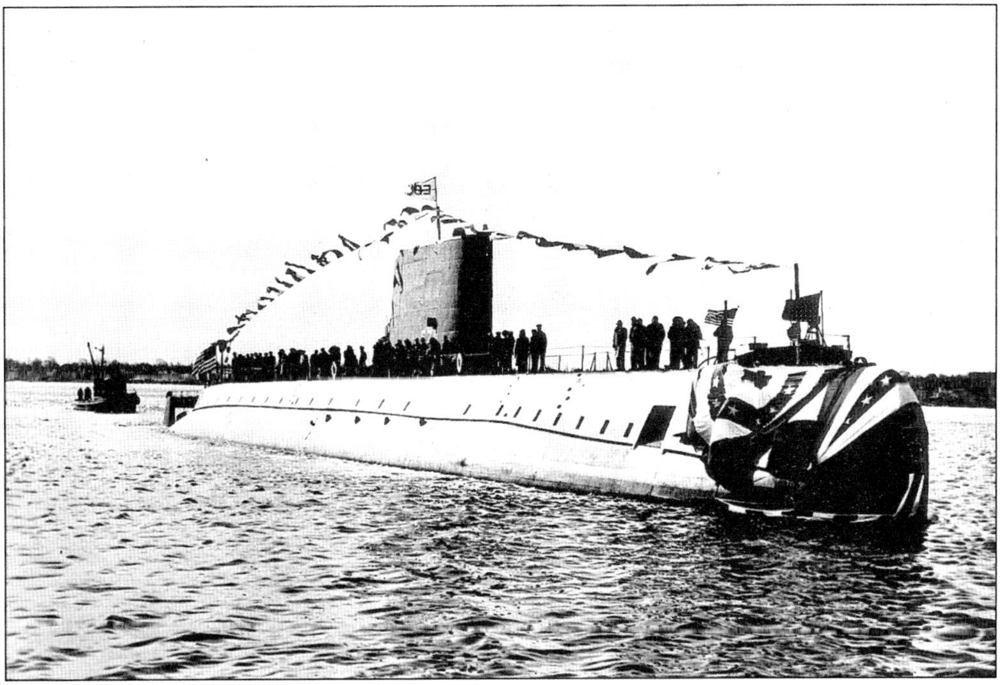

Material from the many mills of Coatesville, especially the Lukens Steel Company, and the surrounding area fed by the Brandywine River have been used in many U.S. military projects, including the two submarines shown here. Above is the USS *Nautilus*, the first atomic submarine. The USS *Ohio* is pictured below.

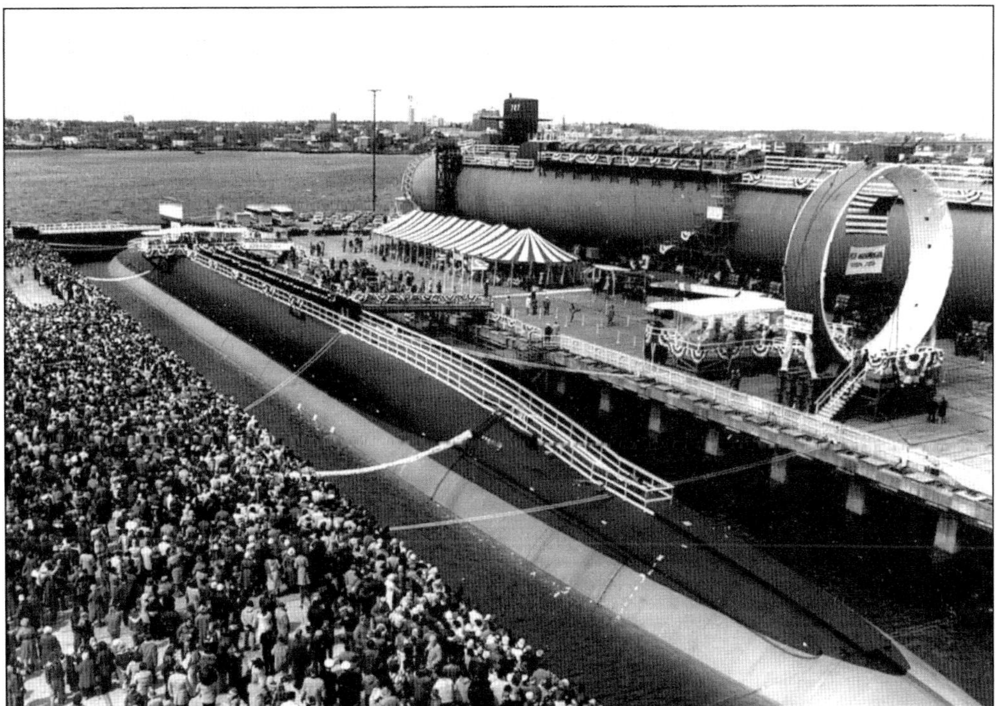

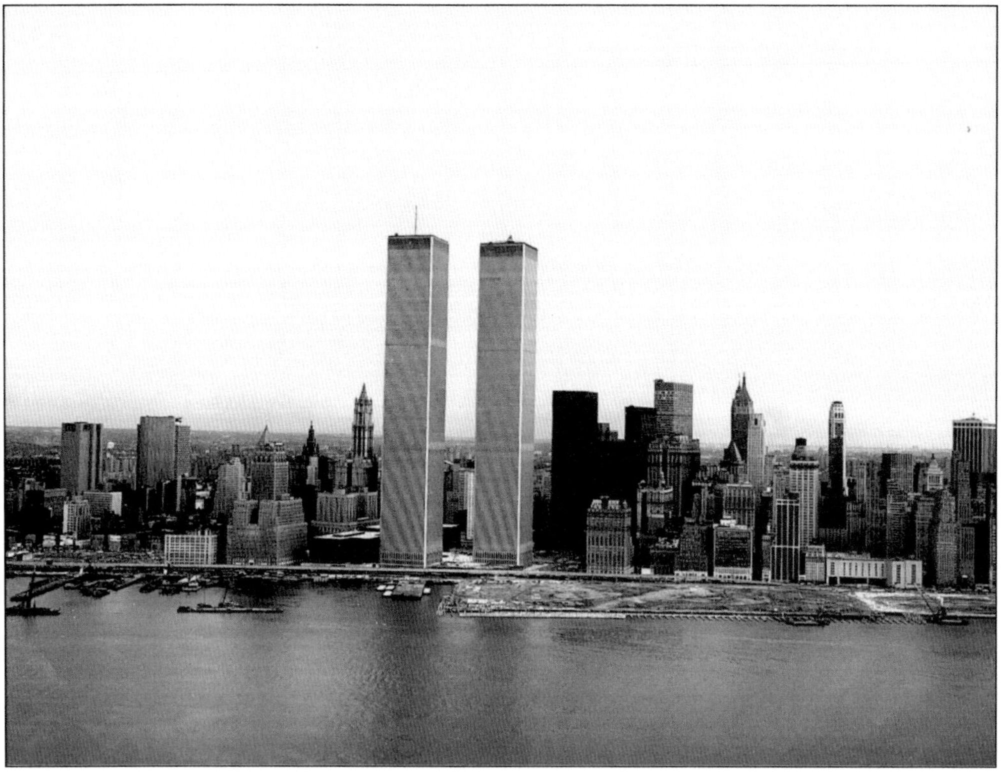

Besides military material, products from the Lukens Steel Company have been used in many well-known structures throughout the United States in the last century, as shown here. The World Trade Center, in New York, used material from Lukens. Terrorists destroyed the buildings on September 11, 2001. Below is the St. Louis Arch.

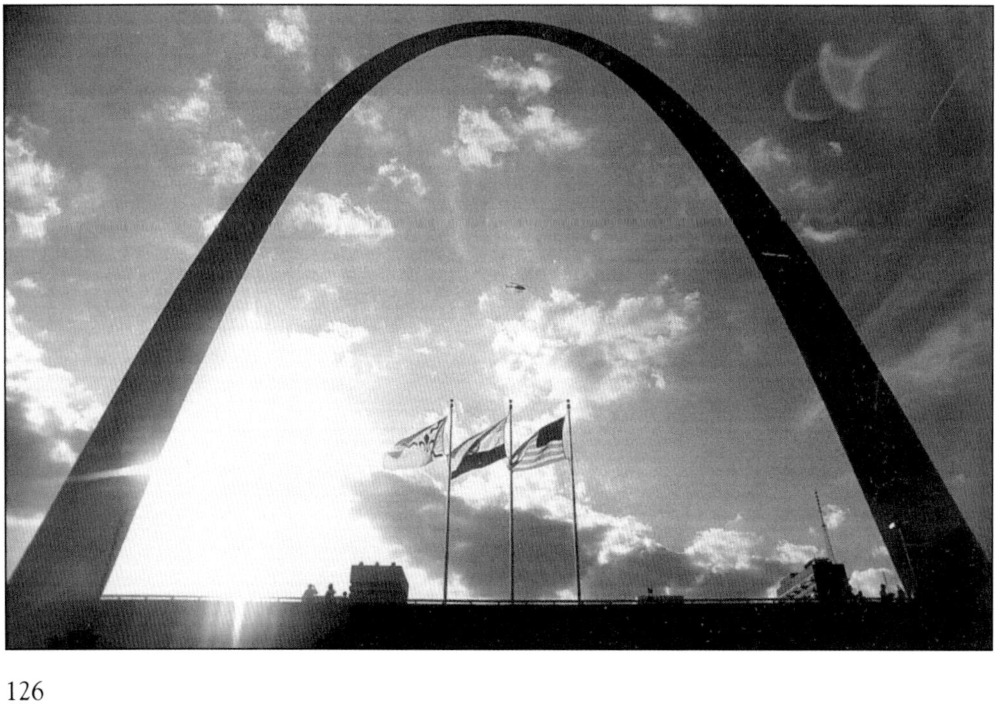

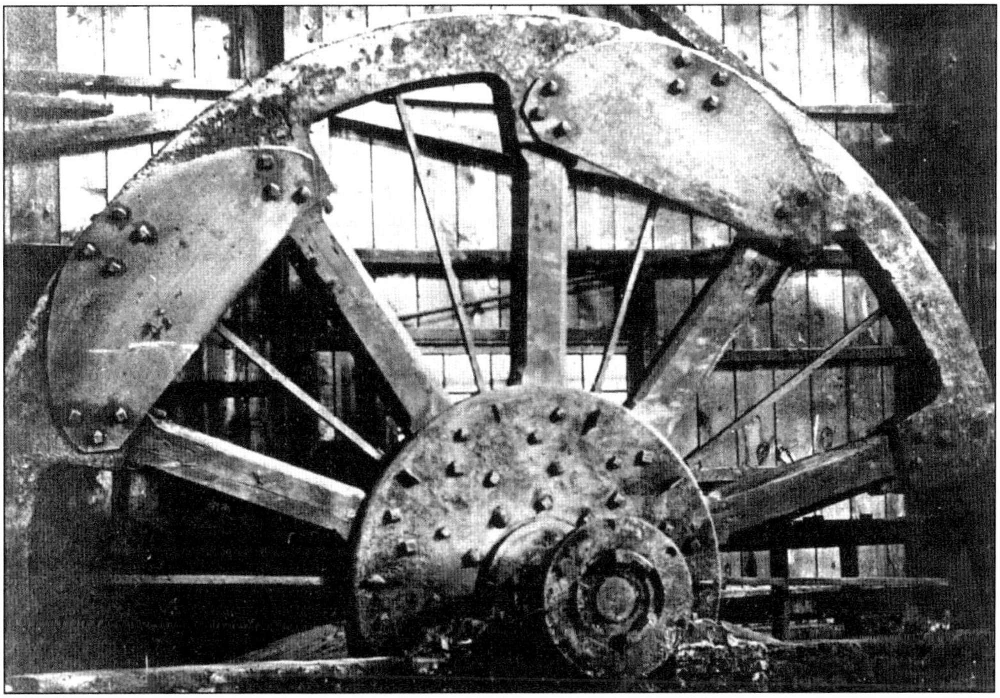

Coatesville and the Lukens Steel Company have progressed and prospered at times in the past century. The above photograph shows an old flywheel that was used when the Brandywine River supplied power to the mills. Lukens went on to produce many quality products, as shown in the photograph below, for many customers.

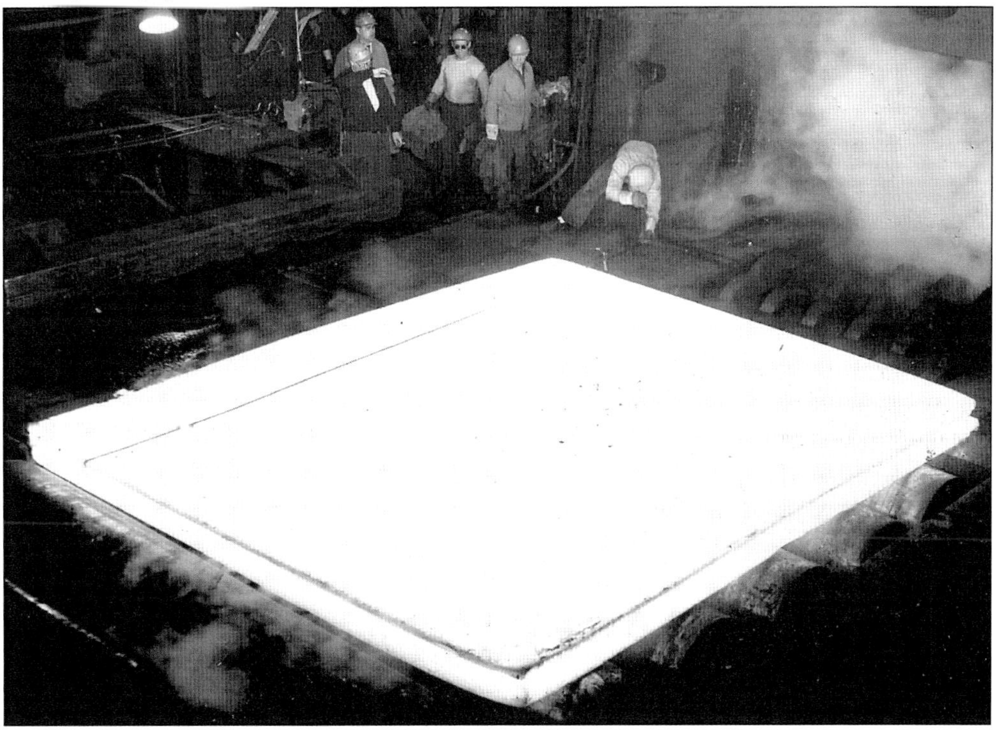

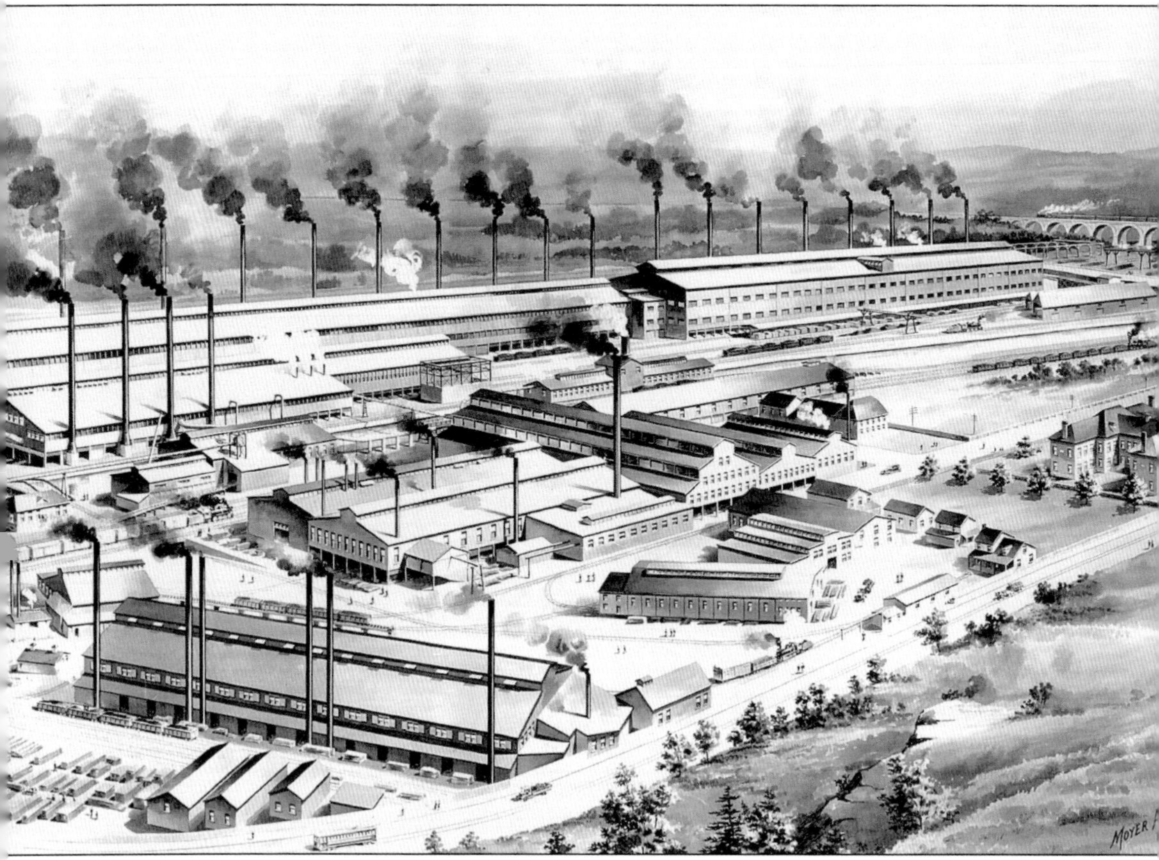

The growth of Coatesville as a city and a community is forever tied to the Lukens Steel Company, the town's major corporation and a great corporate citizen for more than a century. A painting of the company still hangs in the old main office building on First Avenue, home today to the Stewart Huston Charitable Trust.